DEVIL'S
COIN

Jennifer McAdam

WITH DOUGLAS THOMPSON

DEVIL'S COIN

MY BATTLE
TO TAKE
DOWN THE
NOTORIOUS ONECOIN
CRYPTOQUEEN

WM

WILLIAM MORROW
An Imprint of HarperCollins*Publishers*

FIRST EDITION

Designed by Elina Cohen
Title art courtesy of Shutterstock/chekart
Chapter Opener art courtesy of Shutterstock/mydegage

Library of Congress Cataloging-in-Publication Data has been applied for.

ISBN 978-0-06-321918-2 (hardcover)
ISBN 978-0-06-327098-5 (international edition)

23 24 25 26 27 LBC 5 4 3 2 1

To my dad, my hero. I miss and love you so much. I'm sorry.

To my dear family, loved ones, and friends, thank you so very much for your immense love, care, and support, and for always being by my side. You never failed to bring me strength when I was feeling weak thanks to your many kind and comforting words of encouragement. And the endless cups of tea and coffee. Every one of you knows who you are. I love you with all my heart. I am truly blessed.

To the victims and those who helped to support the victims worldwide, thank you for being brave and inspiring me to keep fighting for justice. Your strength of courage is as admirable as your bravery.

When things go wrong, as they sometimes will,
When the road you're trudging seems all uphill,
When the funds are low and the debts are high
And you want to smile, but you have to sigh,
When care is pressing you down a bit,
Rest, if you must, but don't you quit.

—*Edgar A. Guest (1881–1959)*

SOME OF THE NAMES IN MY STORY HAVE BEEN
CHANGED AND SOME DIALOGUE HAS BEEN RE-CREATED.
I TALK ABOUT A NUMBER OF PEOPLE WHO WERE
INVOLVED IN ONECOIN, INCLUDING AS RECRUITERS.
WHILE THOSE AT THE TOP ARE FACING JUSTICE, MANY,
MANY OF THOSE WHO APPEAR IN THE BOOK WILL
BE INNOCENT VICTIMS WHO COULDN'T KNOW WHAT
THEY GOT INTO—JUST LIKE ME. AS EVENTS ARE STILL
EVOLVING, THE STATUS OF LEGAL ACTIONS AND LAW
ENFORCEMENT INVESTIGATIONS ARE AS THEY WERE IN
SEPTEMBER 2022.

THE ONLY THING REAL WERE THE DEATH THREATS.

—*Jennifer McAdam, Glasgow, October 2022*

THE BEST-LAID SCHEMES O' MICE AN' MEN
GANG AFT AGLEY,
AN' LEA'E US NOUGHT BUT GRIEF AN' PAIN,
FOR PROMIS'D JOY!

—*Robert Burns, "To a Mouse, on Turning Her Up*
in Her Nest with the Plough," November 1785

CONTENTS

CONTENTS

The Promise

The startling image of a bagpiper walking in front of my dad's hearse is freeze-framed in my mind. His body was cremated, and I felt his soul went into the sky all the faster. He loved life, he had so much spirit, and I promised to keep that alive with the help of the money he left me. In moments of distress that memory of him being piped along on his final journey is my talisman, part of my inheritance.

He was an old-school Scottish gentleman who never had a lot but would give you the jacket off his back on a cold day. I never had to worry about him because he lived in a cul-de-sac three doors away from my sister, Adele. She was opposite, and every morning she'd watch for him to pull his blinds to know he was up and about. He'd been diagnosed with leukemia in 2000, but that hadn't changed his lifestyle. He was an early riser who liked to get out into the day, enjoy the world. He loved the open countryside and air, birds singing and the freedom and wonders of nature. When Dad came to visit me, normally every other day, he'd arrive on his bicycle, come in the door, and bellow, "Hello, lass, are you in?"

He slowed up a little and wasn't so hearty in his voice a few years before he died, but his cheerful attitude never changed. He always entered whistling, something he did all the time in his final years; it drove my sister nuts, the constant whistling, but I liked it and always smiled to myself. He was at peace in his own wee world and showed it. Dad would tinker about in my front and back gardens and at the small hut at the very back of my garden, his favorite spot, where I would hear him whistling away with the birds. It was his happy place at my home.

A couple of weeks before Christmas in 2014, I was in bed when my son ran into the house. "Papa has been rushed into the hospital, he's away in the ambulance. Aunt Adele is at Papa's house." I got out of bed, threw on leggings, and took off down to his house and ran upstairs. Adele was still in shock and in tears. Dad had been late opening his blinds and she'd gone over. When she got in the door she heard groaning, and upstairs she found him covered in blood. It was like something from a horror film as he stood there trying to clean it up.

He'd suffered massive internal bleeding, a hemorrhage; at first Adele thought that mess was overflow from the toilet, because the blood was so dark. He fell into her arms, and she managed to get him into the bedroom, where he was in and out of consciousness. She kept saying, "Dad, don't leave me, don't leave me." She managed to phone an ambulance, and when I showed up we went straight to the hospital, about ten minutes behind the ambulance.

When we arrived, there he was sitting in the emergency room, and it was so sad, with blood still dripping down his face. He was quiet but the lights were bright, like spotlights in your eyes, and he said, "Jesus Christ, can't somebody dim these lights." He was aware. It took some time, but then they took him up to intensive care. We stayed the night, and the next morning we saw him in a single room. He was starting to hallucinate and there were intravenous drips coming out of him, as if they were growing out of him, and I'd never seen my dad like that. It was the drugs they'd given him, and he looked so helpless. It was a horrible day and night.

He was moved to a ward, and when we next saw him he was sitting up, but he was just there smiling. I wasn't sure if there was anyone home. Then Adele pointed to a form at the end of his bed, and it read DO NOT RESUSCITATE. I can't honestly offer you details about that moment, for I blanked it out.

I was so shocked at that notice it must have erased my memory in some kind of self-protection. It was hellish, for it spelled out where we were. And Dad was just sitting in the bed, not saying much, just smiling. He was in the hospital for Christmas, for New Year's Day, and it was up and down. Pneumonia had set in after the hemorrhage, and he fought the pneumonia for about nine weeks. There wasn't a day or night that we didn't visit. One night I was sitting with him when he pointed to the ceiling and said, "Look at the garage they gave me. I've never seen anything like it, with all mod cons." The lights and the ceiling had come into his mind as this grand garage. I asked him what it was like and, being a great storyteller, he told me. It was a happy hallucination. He then went to sleep. I didn't think it was good: He'd lost weight but still, still, we thought he could fight it.

I talked to the doctors and said we didn't want Dad to die in hospital, we wanted him home if he was well enough to be transported. We wanted to look after him. The doctors were wonderful, but they never said he only had so long to live or anything like that; they shied away from it. It's a kindness for some folks but not for someone with a personality like mine: I wanted to know so I could deal with it.

The Wednesday he came home, the doctor with him was saying to my dad that he was coming to the end of his life. We couldn't believe it, and I jumped in and said, "No, Dad, it's about medication, and you'll have to go back to the hospital for it."

He said, "Nah, no, I'm not going back in there." I told him he could have it at home, and he said, "Good, good, I'm not going back. I'm fine here."

My daughter-in-law, Fiona, was there, and she was horrified with the doctor, who saw we were not happy with her and so she left. I leaned over to my dad and said, "Do you fancy a wee fish supper?"

That brought a smile. "Yes, lass, yes."

We were around his bed after eating and Dad, who'd managed a not very enthusiastic couple of bites, was looking settled. I wanted to keep him in the room with us, to be alert, and I asked him if he wanted to recite his favorite Robert Burns.

With my dad's generation in Ayrshire, home to Scotland's national poet, schoolchildren always had to learn Burns's work by heart. I asked my dad a couple of times, and then he half smiled and recited "To a Mountain Daisy," which tells how, while out ploughing, Burns had crushed a daisy's stem; I now see that as a metaphor for how so often all forms of life are brushed aside in pursuit of advantage. I filmed Dad on my phone, and it wasn't until he'd finished reciting that I knew exactly what the words meant, and my heart hit the floor and shattered right there and then. I don't know how I managed to keep on recording. Other than missing one line, he was word perfect:

> Wee, modest, crimson-tippèd flow'r,
> Thou's met me in an evil hour . . .

When he finished, he moved his head a little on the pillow and, his lips in a half smile, went to sleep.

Dad had to sit up in bed because of fluid getting to his lungs. When it got too much, he had muscle relaxants injected into his body to help with the breathing. It helped for a time, but then he needed the jabs more often. The nurses came throughout the night, waiting for the family doctor to come in the morning. When the doctor arrived, he said it was time for the morphine to stop the pain and discomfort. My daughter-in-law was heavily pregnant at the time; she adored my dad and wouldn't leave his side. That Friday morning my dad seemed peaceful, and my sister, Adele, drove my granddaughter, Elle, to nursery. She was only going to be a short time. I sat holding my dad's hand in the living room when two nurses arrived. I told them what had happened, and as they were with my dad I took the chance to have a cigarette at the back patio door. I had just lit the cigarette when there was a tap on my shoulder and the nurse said, "It's time."

I was all over the place. "*What?*"

"It's time, he's just about away, honey."

I rushed through and pleaded with him not to go, to please stay.

"Don't go, Adele's not here."

Then the nurse said his pulse was coming back up. I called my sister, who'd just dropped off Elle, and told her to get back but she'd have to be quick. Dad came back and I could hardly believe it, he was so strong in spirit. Incredible. He had one living sister left, Amelia, and we told him she was coming. When she arrived, I played him some soft music in the background and his sister talked to him. He was breathing peacefully but I could see it was getting labored. It came about five o'clock and it was getting dark, and Auntie Amelia said she had to go.

She looked at my dad. "Well, Bill son, I'll see you again soon."

She became upset, and we went into the hall with her and wrapped her up in her scarf. There's a glass door from the living room to the hall, and I remember turning round and looking over my shoulder, and my partner and brother-in-law and Fiona were standing at Dad's bedside looking down at him. When I left the room with Aunt Amelia they were all sitting on the couch. I then saw Fiona's face, which told the story. I went over and she said, "Jen, he's gone."

My sister and I rushed into the living room, and Adele put her ear to his mouth. She said she felt breath, but it was the last of the air he had left that fell into her ear. I put my ear to his mouth and felt his pulse, and he was gone. I cradled him and let out a god-awful scream: *"Dad, I'm not ready to let you go!"*

He'd been waiting for his sister, Amelia. He'd held on for her. And when she'd said cheerio, he was content to go. He could close his eyes and get on the road. I do believe that when folk are dying they are aware of what's around them.

And in just the same way, I think it's a kindness to send their spirit off with as much love and respect as possible. We wanted to honor Dad now and forever. The scene, which as I mentioned hasn't left me since, replays over and over in my mind and heart: the piper leading the hearse into the crematorium and playing "Highland Cathedral," which some folk argue should be the Scottish national anthem. On the pipes it is such an appropriate song. I chose all of the songs, as my sister said she wasn't up to doing it. We were orphans now. Dad, who was ninety-two, died that Friday, January 29, 2015, but there was a holdup on the funeral—a lot of dead people at that cruel time of year—so our service couldn't be held until February 11. Making the arrangements helped Adele and I cope with our sadness, and I'm a believer that being busy brings a bit of calm.

It gave me time to think about the songs, and one of them, played as Dad's coffin was placed on the shoulders of his sons-in-law, grandsons, and nephews and slowly walked into the crematorium, is called "Ae Fond Kiss." Robert Burns wrote it for his platonic love, Nancy, and it was adapted to a beautiful song. We replaced "Nancy" with "Daddy," to personalize the song as a gift to Dad from my sister and me. There wasn't a dry eye, for even the most stoic will open up to a piper's lament. After the ceremony, at Holmsford Bridge Crematorium in Dreghorn, Ayrshire, where we'd also had my mother's funeral, we left to the haunting sound of a piper and "Auld Lang Syne" by the Royal Scots Dragoon Guards.

I know you'll think we hung a big kilt around his funeral, but that was how my dad was, a traditional, hardworking Scotsman who down in the mines had been paid as much for risk as effort. When you work underground there's nowhere to go but up, and he liked to look into the sky and consider a brighter future for his family. He knew there wasn't a lot to leave, but he was proud that we could have "a little something to help."

He'd been careful all his life. What money he had was tied up in the house. We left him—his ashes—at home while the house was up for sale. It took time, but later in the year my sister, Adele, took the house for her son. I guess they didn't want Papa Bill hanging about, so my sister took his ashes to her house. I did get my half, £15,000 in cash, from the house. I had nothing, so for me it was much, much more than "a little something." The money went to pay off commitments and help out the family; my indulgence was a week's holiday in Spain with my son and the grandchildren. Finally, I had cash to invest. Oh, we all know how money can vanish, and that fortune in cash was heavy in my purse, which you'll understand. It goes quickly. When you get something new you want to use it, and when you get money you want to spend it.

I wanted to invest so it wouldn't just dwindle away for this or that supposed necessity. I'd had a lifetime of torment, and I didn't want to waste my chance at family security. I sat tight on it for several months.

Then my best friend told me about the investment of a lifetime.

ONE

In the Beginning

I was brought up on the edge of life. As a child I had this fear of saying the wrong thing, of being in the wrong place. I never knew when I might fall out of the world. When I was growing up, I found out I almost did.

When I was born, in the summer of 1970, at Ayrshire Central Hospital in Irvine, half an hour's drive from Glasgow, my mother was forty-two years old and my dad was five years older. My mother told me—and I so wish she hadn't—that it wasn't long afterward that she nearly killed me. She confessed that caring and coping with newborn me bawling my head off overwhelmed her: "You were only a few weeks old and you *widnae* [wouldn't] stop crying so I just took you through to the kitchen. I'd had enough. I was just about to tip you out of the window when your dad grabbed my arms."

My relationship with my mother was always tense, even before she told me she'd tried to chuck me out the kitchen window. My parents moved to our small town in the late 1960s and settled into a gloomy, gray-colored, purpose-built council block of four flats (public housing). Our upstairs flat had three bedrooms and a fair-sized living room. It wasn't claustrophobia that spooked my mother, it was her nerves. They jangled.

My mother. Margaret—Meg to the family—was troubled in a world of grief. Yet, despite all the difficult times, I still loved her very much. The problems were there long before I was born. My sister, Adele, is thirteen years older than me; she grew up listening to the Bay City Rollers while I was daft about Spandau Ballet. My brother is nineteen years older. I truly was the baby in the family, the intruder. My timing was poor.

What torment my mother had with my brother was all but exploding by the time I was born. I don't—couldn't—know the details. I've had no more than a few words with my brother in my life, and his were not kind. He did not talk properly to my mother for the rest of her life. That cracked her heart and soul.

What I do remember is her begging him, sobbing on the phone, and the repeated words: "Please, Son, *please*, Son, I miss you, I love you." She wanted a visit. She was grieving, but she was grieving for a son that was still living, not dead.

When my mother's demons were truly raging and she was climbing the walls, my father would try and persuade my brother to visit; he never did. I was only three years old when this started happening, but the sense of it got into my bones and has never left. It was heartbreaking, especially for me as a little girl growing up and not understanding what could be wrong. I had a brother but never saw him. When I asked, I was hushed up. The fear was that I'd set my mother off. It was my role to be seen and not heard. I had all those dreams and wishes as a child of growing up with a brother who was loving, caring, and a protector, and they were that—dreams. The reality was a nightmare of emotional pain and suffering, mostly for my mum but also for the rest of the family, who felt the repercussions and had no option but to stand by and watch her suffer in grief. I felt it was so very cruel, and I felt powerless to help.

My mother's rules meant that I wasn't allowed to get dirty. I couldn't invite other kids over. Mother's law also forbade us to play music. We couldn't even put a small perfume bottle on the dressing table; it had to be in a drawer. Dust was the enemy, and every crushed cushion or untidy cupboard could start trouble. I was very lonely.

My parents had no interest in education. My dad left school at a young age, and his dad had died when he was fourteen years old. He couldn't help me with my schoolwork, and neither could my mum. I was an inquisitive child, but they weren't focused on homework and things like that; I was on my own.

I had this rabbit, my playmate, which stayed in a garden hutch my dad built. I took it out in my doll's pram for walks. I came home from school one day to do just that, but there was no sign of the bunny. "Where's the rabbit?" I asked.

"Oh, Bill Carble took it away for some stew."

Bill Carble was a long-distance driver who sometimes stayed over with us and rented a room on his travels. My mother was laughing when she told me; I was distraught. It's still a severe memory, hard to believe all these years later, but it hurt; it seemed callous then and even more so now. My early years weren't all filled with misery, but they were difficult. Mum would take a hankie, dampen it with her tongue, and wipe my face before I went out, a picture of perfection. In every photograph of me as a child I look the cherished part, but it's hellish because inside I'm just this wee girl who is lonely.

My mother was bitter for reasons I will never truly understand. I loved my mum dearly, believe it or not, but she saw things through a dark, dark glass. Still, there was that unconditional bond between us. I think my mother was mentally unwell for a very long time. Her doctors had her on nerve tablets called Ativan (lorazepam), which they finally stopped prescribing when they realized the pills were worse than the symptoms: Lorazepam is highly addictive, and you can get hooked after taking the tablets for only two weeks. She was very funny, although bluntly direct, and once she was off the Ativan tablets she became the loving and caring mum she was always meant to be. It took time.

When I was ten years old we moved to a cul-de-sac in a newly built housing development in the village. The new place had only two upstairs bedrooms, but it worked because Adele had left home and married. The toilet was directly at the top of the stairs, and downstairs we had a small living area and quite a big kitchen. You need to know that setup because that's where a neighbor tried to assault me soon after we moved in.

I started changing into a young woman at a really early age, and when I got my period it frightened the life out of me. I ran to my mother, who started praying to God—this from a woman who doesn't believe in God. I was dismayed, but she went into a cabinet and cut up a towel. "Put that between your legs. That'll do you till I go to the chemist," she said. "You'll get this once a month for seven days." That was the end of that. I wanted to know what was wrong with me, but there was no conversation, no explanation, no understanding.

I was ten years old, and I felt like I'd done something bad. My physical change made me look that bit older, but I was still very much a child.

The evening that would traumatize me for many years happened on a Saturday night when my mother was out for a wee drink with one of her sisters-in-law at the local bowling club. My sister, who lived across the road from us with her husband, Riley, was out with him. It was just me and Dad at home and, as usual, I was fixated on the television.

There was a knock at the door, and I heard my dad say, "Oh, Jim, come in, come in." It was a new housing development, and everyone was trying to get to know one another and make friends. So that's what my dad was doing, and the two of them were talking away while I was still focused on the TV. Jim was a British Gas engineer in his late forties, but he looked ancient to me. He got comfortable on the sofa. I was in my chair but close enough to smell he'd been drinking; he wasn't overly intoxicated, but he was chirpy. Then the phone rang, and it was my mum, who told my dad she was leaving the club. Her walk home took her past a bit of vacant land, which was only five minutes away, but it was dark and she didn't like walking past it alone. She'd phone Dad, and he'd go and escort her past the scary bit. He told our visitor what was going on, and Jim, next-door neighbor to my sister, said, "That's okay, I'll wait till you get back."

As the front door closed on my dad, Jim got off the sofa, came over, knelt down, and tried to put his arms around me. I knew this wasn't right, and I immediately stood up.

In those days you had to get up and go over to the TV to switch the channels. I said that's what I was going to do, but I jumped over his legs and past him, straight out the door and up the stairs to the small bathroom next to my bedroom. I locked the bathroom door from the inside, but, for child-safety reasons, you could turn the lock from the outside, it had a slit in it, and you could use a penny to open it. I knew this, and I was so terrified my hands were sweating, so I got a towel and went to take a firm grip on the lock from inside when it started turning.

I grabbed the lock. I was frightened, but I held the towel round the lock and he kept trying to turn it from the outside. I was crying, saying, "Please, leave me alone!" Then he went into my bedroom. He started banging on the bathroom wall from there, and then he started squeaking the bed.

"It's okay," he said softly, "everything's all right, come out. I'm ready for you."

I was chanting back: "Please don't hurt me.

"Please leave.

"My dad will be back soon."

I heard him go down the stairs and thought he had gone away, but I couldn't move for fear. I was gripping the towel around the lock, too terrified to let go.

I didn't hear him come back up the stairs, but suddenly that door-knob lock started turning again. He must have thought I'd have let go of it, but fear made me hang on tight. He was louder now, more demanding, more agitated, and he went into my bedroom and was squeaking the bed. I don't know what he was doing on the bed, but he kept trying to get me to come out, repeating "I'm ready for you."

There was silence for a time, and then I heard the front door open and shut. I still didn't let go of the lock, didn't move, and then a couple of minutes later I heard my sister and brother-in-law come in.

I rushed to them. I was breathless, trying to tell what had happened, tripping over my tongue. I was in such a state.

Riley, my brother-in-law, stormed out. Adele was trying to calm me down so she could make sense of what I was saying, but I was a wee lassie, upset and blubbering about what had happened.

Just at that moment my dad came in: "Jesus Christ, what's going on here?"

Adele explained. My mother had had some drinks in her so she needed the toilet and went upstairs. From there she said, "That didnae happen. What a terrible thing to say."

My dad, as usual, walked away; he couldn't deal with it. I was half-way up the stairs, looking up at my mother and crying my eyes out. "He did do that!" I cried. "That's what happened."

She dismissed what I was saying, so I repeated it: "He did do that."

I want her to hug and hold me, to protect me from this bogey-man. She could see and hear how hysterical I was, but she shrugged off my distress; it was as if I'd done something wrong. Should I have said nothing? Once again, I felt shame, but this time it was as if I'd brought shame on the whole family.

The man had gone off to his house, and Riley went over there to confront him. Adele told me later that Jim's wife begged Riley to leave things until the morning. Riley was ready for a fight, a real rammy, and told her, "He better no be fuckan here in the morning."

My sister went home and I was put to bed. There was no more talk about it, and I cried myself to sleep. In the morning, when I walked into the downstairs room, my mother was looking out the window across the street at the man's house. She turned around and said, "That's it, no need to talk about it. I've just seen her put him out of the house. He won't be back."

For my mum, that was the end of the story. She would not discuss what this man had done; shame had been brought on us, and it wasn't to be spoken of. I don't know if she couldn't deal with it or didn't know how to deal with it. It was the early 1980s, a time of baloney bullshit and caring what the neighbors might think.

I didn't have any friends. I was constantly watching TV because we didn't have any books in the house and so I couldn't go off to my room and read. Or play music. Nothing. There was no escape for me, and I was getting angry. And I was getting beaten a lot. This was when the doctors took my mother off the Ativan tablets. She stopped taking them cold turkey, and it was hellish. I was the only one at home for her to take her anxieties out on. And she did. I got the full majesty of her anger.

I was deeply unhappy. I was twelve, maybe thirteen, when I found tablets in the bathroom. I took them and I went to bed. I got a shock when I woke up: I was alive! I did feel hellish tired, but that was it, and I could hear my mother and her sisters downstairs talking. They showed no interest in me. I desperately wanted a cuddle, but I knew that wasn't going to be. She'd come off the Ativan tablets, and my cry for help hadn't worked. No one noticed I'd taken the pills.

I started to rebel, to stay out all night. I was in high school and I hated gym because my body had already outgrown the gym outfit, the wee knickers they gave you, and I was embarrassed. I was conscious I was different from the other girls.

I'd had that experience with that man trying to attack me. I had all this going on, so I'd take off from that class and go by a little river at the back of the school, where there was a big cement pipe, and I'd sit in there. It was like my dad's garage, an escape. I started smoking, stealing my mum's cigarettes out of her apron pocket.

When I did go to school, I spent my time between classes having a cigarette. All the smokers would meet up for a puff, and that's when I met Eileen Middleton, who was a year above me at school. We were given one pound each for lunch money, and you could buy a single cigarette for ten pence. I was in my school uniform, and I'd go into the shop and ask, "Three single Regals, please." Three singles was your limit: If you spent more on the single cigarettes you didn't have much left for lunch—you'd end up with a packet of scampi fries and a bread roll. Very jet set. But we often didn't have money, and if I lit a cigarette, Eileen would say to me, "Hey, Jen, can I get two's up on that?" Which meant we'd share the cigarette, half each. It was the start of a long, long friendship.

Although I was having fun hanging out with Eileen, there were many days when I'd skip school. One day I came home and my mother asked, "How was school?" I thought it was strange, as she'd never asked me that before. She was holding a mop—the old-fashioned kind with a wooden handle—and I was leaning over the kitchen countertop and she was asking what I had done at school. I was busy trying to make something up, and she got hold of the mop and started beating me. I was lying on the floor, and she beat me from head to toe with the wooden handle. I put my hand up to protect myself and she fractured my hand, although I never had it tended to.

That night she locked all the doors and I had a panic in me, so I climbed down the drainpipe and ran away. I lived on the streets for three or four days, spending the nights in doorways.

Mum and my sister found me and brought me home, but instead of saying—as you would with your child—"Thank God, I've got you home and you're safe," my mother got a hair dryer, one with an electrical cord wrapped around it, and she started hitting me with it.

Every whack of that sharp plug cut into me and drew blood.

Confused? My thoughts were shooting through the roots of my hair. Weirdly, I felt sorry for my mother. I knew this wasn't normal. Something was seriously wrong. But I was so frightened, so I kept running away.

On the streets, I ran into Callum, who would become my son's father. Callum was a punk rocker and a rebel with a mohawk haircut. I was thirteen, he was fifteen. I ran into his arms, thinking this punk rocker would protect me, but he didn't. It was worse.

Love Hurts

I was with Callum from the age of thirteen until I was twenty years old, but he was difficult. I'd gone from one bitter person to another.

It was a repeated pattern, but this time I felt I was being controlled by Callum. He constantly intimidated me. I was fifteen when I tried to get away from him. One of the girls asked me to go to the disco ice-skating rink, and I loved skating. Callum said, "You're not going."

I said, "I bloody well am. I'm going skating with my friend."

The rink was in the next town, and I had as great a time as you should at that age. Then my friend said, "Look, Jen, there's Callum up there."

He was looking at me and he was raging. I could feel my fear change the atmosphere. He stalked over to me. "You're coming back with me."

"No, I'm not, I'm staying with my friend who I came with."

"If you don't come back with me something bad's going to happen."

"I'm going back with my friend."

I'd started to rebel, and he sneered at me. "See, if anything happens, it's your fault."

It was always *my* fault. I was fearful but fed up with Callum's attitude. We got on with our skating and a couple of hours later went to the bus station for the trip home. Somebody told us that Callum had been stabbed. We couldn't believe it—this is long before mobile phones, so we couldn't check anything—but at the bus stop at home he was standing there waiting for me. He was covered in blood. It wasn't his blood. He hadn't been stabbed. He'd stabbed someone else.

He looked at me. "*This is all your fault.*"

I didn't know what to do. I didn't know whether the person he'd stabbed was alive or dead. In time, Callum was charged with attempted murder and then it was reduced to grievous bodily harm (GBH). He went to jail for six months. In prearranged calls from the young offenders' detention center, he'd phone his father, Eddie, who was a lovely, kind man. Eddie would contact me and say, "Callum's calling tonight."

As a teenager, it was emotional turmoil—things were still difficult at home with my mum, but I kept trying to keep everyone happy rather than pleasing myself. I was caught in a cycle of control. I was fifteen, nearly about to finish school, when Callum was released from prison after six months. One day he came and met me at lunch. He took me to Ayr and told me, "My mum left me £350 when she died, and I'm buying you an engagement ring."

His attitude was that I belonged to him, that he owned me.

I thought that maybe this little sapphire ring would magically change my life into the fairy tale I dreamed of as a child.

We had a small congratulatory engagement party, with no alcohol or anything. It was Callum and me and Eddie and the rest of Callum's family. It's crazy to remember it. How mad was it? Before the party started, Eddie had popped out to the shops and I was buttering sandwiches. Callum whispered something and I said, "What?"

He threw a carving knife at me. It missed, and as it clanked on the kitchen floor, he shouted, "*You* made me do that."

I became like a mouse. I knew he'd stabbed someone, I knew his threats weren't empty ones. And then he would cry and ask "What's wrong with me?"

And I'd end up comforting *him*.

When my mother met "Mohican" Callum for the first time her

face was a picture, and the rebel inside me felt gleeful to have given her a shock. When she discovered we'd become engaged she nearly pulled my finger off, trying to get the ring from my hand.

Callum's sister Lilly was a lot older than he was, an age gap like that between Adele and me. She sent photographs of me to a modeling agency, but my mother said I'd put on too much weight for modeling. I came off contraceptives because I didn't want to put on additional weight from the pill, and I started dieting. I was sixteen years old, and I thought that when I got the modeling job I'd be able to say "I'm out of here."

What's the saying? When you're making plans, life happens. It sure did with me. I became pregnant, so my modeling career was over. My mum wanted me to have an abortion, but I couldn't think of anything worse. That was never going to happen, but she kept on and on about it. I left school and got a job as a seamstress in a shirt factory, forty pounds a week, and I sat dreaming about the life I nearly had.

I came home from work one day and in the hall by the door was a small beige leather suitcase. My mother was standing there. "That's yours," she said. "You've made your bed, now lie in it."

I looked at her in shock, in amazement.

"Are you having this baby?"

"I am."

"Take your case, out of here."

Eddie took me in and I was so thankful.

A few months into the pregnancy I started bleeding, and the doctor said there was no problem, but I had to lie with my feet up in bed all weekend. Eddie telephoned my mum and told her what had happened. He came to me and said my mother was on the phone. I thought she was going to say "Come back, everything's going to be all right." Despite all that had gone on, I still wanted my mum. She didn't show any concern, and I knew then I was on my own. I said to myself, "Jen, you've got two options here—you are either going to sink or swim. What are you going to do?"

I was going to swim. But I was terrified—it makes me cry now to think of it—for I didn't know what to do. How could I love this baby when I didn't know what love really was? And a wee voice came back at me: "Just do the opposite of what you've been through."

Then, a miracle: I was a good five months pregnant when my mother called. "Right, come home."

I couldn't wait to go home. A girl wants her mum even after having gone through all I had. I virtually ran up the road. She couldn't do enough. She got a secondhand pram, and it was a stunner. She fussed about baby clothes. Callum and I got a two-bedroom council house. We'd only been there a week and I was seven and a half months pregnant when I became ill and was rushed to the hospital. I had preeclampsia; my blood pressure was through the roof and I was swollen and in pain. I stayed in the hospital until Lee was born. When I was pregnant, my mother told me that she said to herself: "I couldn't accept at that moment that this was my wee lassie and she was having this baby." But she had to accept it, and in time, she did, and she gave a lot of love to my son, love that I never got. That was some comfort in what was becoming another difficult situation for me.

I didn't need to worry about my own love, because as soon as Lee was placed in my arms and I looked at this gorgeous wee baby boy, an instant love overwhelmed me, and I cried tears of utter joy. For the first time in my life I had someone to take care of, to look after, someone I had to be strong for. This wee boy was my whole reason for swimming. We had a home and a baby, and this was my life. I was seventeen years old.

Callum, myself, and Lee, the family unit I craved, lived in that council house our families had helped furnish and carpet, but Lee was only about eight months old when Callum's behavior became unbearable. I left one evening with Lee and went to my mum's, but her controlling ways were intense too. I sometimes stayed with a friend who also had a baby, sofa surfing with my baby; I was bouncing about like a ball. Callum gave up our house, but he began saying that if he didn't get to see his son he would commit suicide. Eddie offered us the use of his trailer. I felt an overwhelming sense of guilt because maybe I had been too quick to leave Callum, and, yes, his tears and suicide threats worked. The three of us stayed at the trailer park for several winter weeks. I became physically ill from the cold and, tail between my legs, took myself and Lee back to my mum's. I was a homeless single mum. I eventually got the keys to a small downstairs flat for Lee and me, and Callum moved in too. It was one in a block of four, through emergency housing. It was where the council put people of, shall we say, less fortunate circumstances, but it was a home for my wee family for many months.

Callum's only concession to responsibility when Lee was born was to get rid of the mohawk. I didn't drink, but he was going out and drinking vodka, then coming back well blattered, his anger and bitterness overflowing.

Lee was eighteen months old when I suddenly had extreme pains in my stomach and I couldn't walk. The doctor said I had a pelvic infection and put me on antibiotics. I took the medicine and it was fine, but a couple of weeks later I was doubled up with pain again and in bed. Lee wasn't sleeping in his crib, so he was in with me when Callum came home drunk, absolutely drunk. He fell asleep, so there we were, Lee, me, and him on the bed. I was in pain, and it was difficult for me to move.

There was a late-night knock on the door; it was my nephew, who is three years younger than me. I was scared to answer, as it was three o'clock in the morning, and I thought something had happened to him, so I woke Callum up. "*I think something's wrong.*"

He got up, walked over to the closet, opened the closet door, and pulled out a couple of suitcases. Then he said in pure Ayrshire, "There's nobody *fuckan* there!"

"You're in the closet!"

He came across and landed a punch to my cheekbone: "*There's nobody fuckan there.*"

I had our baby boy by the side of me, and I just froze. He fell back into a drunken sleep, and I got up and sat next to this old-fashioned coal fire. I was sitting there rocking in the chair. Callum came in. "Get to your bed."

"No."

"Get to your bed!"

I didn't say anything. He reached out and I pushed his arm away. He grabbed my leg and began pulling, and my backside hit the floor with a thud. The pain in my pelvis made me feel like I was fainting. I didn't have the strength to get away, and he pulled me across the floor into the kitchen.

I managed to get my other leg against the kitchen door frame. I was trying to get back on my feet, and the pain was hellish.

Callum went over, got the biggest bread knife we had, and came back to me.

I was on all fours, trying to get up, and he grabbed the back of my hair and pulled me to my feet. He swung me over and smothered me into the sofa, holding the bread knife at the back of my neck. And he was laughing. He threw the knife to the side and laughed in my face. "Did you think I would do that?"

I just screamed, and then I flew at him. I was like a woman possessed.

The shock quieted him down.

I knew then that it was over. I swore that in the morning Callum would be gone. I took an oath: "My son will never be brought up like this."

I wasn't strong enough to protect myself, but I was strong enough to protect my son. I had somebody else to think of.

Callum and I broke up and he moved out, but his intimidation continued. He'd knock at the door at three in the morning and peek through the blinds, trying to spook me. I was a confused, single, teenage mother, but I was determined not to be trampled all over. I might not win, but I'd put up a struggle. The birth of Lee was the birth of that attitude, to fight from my corner. It was bloody freezing in the flat, so cold you could see your own breath. There was no phone, and all I had left after Callum went was a wee portable television. It was a color set, but it was the coal fire that brightened me. I was lonely, and sitting by the fire in the evenings, the flames were my company.

Other than Callum, who kept harassing me. I'd be sitting there with my baby asleep and my mind wide awake with fears, and he'd peer through the windows and shout through the mail slot, "You'll never get rid of me." One night after I'd put my Lee to bed, I was sitting by the fire watching this tiny TV, when the living-room door opened and there he was. "Told you, you couldn't keep me out."

He used a penknife to open up the old-fashioned window in the bedroom where I slept with Lee. He stood there laughing at me. And then he left. I thought there was no protection from this cruel intimidation, but I finally got him to leave me alone. Well, it wasn't so much me as my friend, who I began seeing. He's six-four and big, a giant, lovable, and funny guy. We started dating. I wasn't really ready for romance, but I was scared. I looked at my friend and I saw in him a chance for protection. We were together and dating for a couple of years, and that's when Callum stopped.

I remained wary of that flat and its rattling, easy-to-open windows. I was never secure there. By good luck, Lee and I got a two-bedroom council house. It had been left in a mess, a real midden—you lifted the carpets, and shit hit you in the face. When my mother saw it she wailed and said, "*Why* are you taking this?" When you touched the wall, the grease stuck your hand to it. I was on my hands and knees scrubbing away, empty bottles of cleanser discarded in the rubbish bags, spraying disinfectant here, there, and everywhere, like John Wayne taking down the bad guys in one of my dad's Western movies.

I was so happy.

I was singing as I scrubbed, high on hope—and most likely the clouds of disinfectant. I'd make this place a lovely and proper home for Lee and me.

I was able to fit in shift work in pubs. One of the better jobs was at a palace of a place in Irvine that was half pub, half Indian restaurant. The snag for me was that it was a good distance from home, and I often had to rely on taxis there and back, which took a chunk of my wages. But in 1993 it was a good place to work behind the bar, and it attracted an easygoing crowd of regulars. Many of them were from the Indian Sikh community; they worked in a network of local restaurants and shops and met up for a pint at the end of their day's work. One evening Veehan, this tall guy with long hair, walked in. Apart from his striking looks, what stood out was his American accent.

At the end of one shift, he asked if I'd like a lift home. I was pleased to accept and save some cash. We hadn't gone far when he turned a corner and smashed the car into a tree. He told me, "Don't worry, I'll get you home."

We picked up another car and tried for home again. This time Veehan was getting around a parked lorry when another car came speeding toward us. He turned the car into the lorry and drove under it. Next thing I knew, I was lying on a grass embankment and Veehan was leaning over me. "I've got to go," he told me, "I've been drinking." If I hadn't already been in shock, I'd have been shocked. A month later I went back to work. Veehan came in and apologized for all that had happened. He took all the blame, and over time we built up a relationship. My mother knew what had happened and she didn't trust Veehan because of the car crash and the racial difference. I didn't see color at all, I just saw this man who was so funny and nice. I thought it best to keep my mother away from him, as she'd be a hand grenade in the romance.

One Sunday morning I was in my bed with Veehan, and there was a knock at the door. It was my mother. I whispered to him, "Be quiet, she'll go away." She didn't and continued banging on the door. Veehan told me to answer it, but I hushed him. "You don't know my mother." My mother hammered away at the door and shouted: "I know you're in there heating the sheets with that black bastard."

What was I to say? *Good morning, Mother, the kettle's on.*

She continued her rant through the mail slot: "You're with that person who nearly killed you."

I didn't answer the door. That was Veehan's first and, necessarily, socially distanced introduction to my mother. Later, when she'd calmed down, she told me it wasn't about his color, but she was angry that he'd put me at risk with the car crash. Veehan was good with Lee, and we were happy. But he also drank so much that it became a serious problem for us. We'd met in a bar, but it took time for me to realize he was a problem drinker. It became impossible, and I couldn't have my son around him. I gave Veehan an ultimatum: He had to stop. I contacted Alcoholics Anonymous (AA), and it helped. I went to meetings with Veehan, and while it was heartbreaking, it did work.

Life with a drink-free Veehan was the glorious result. Nearly three years later I became pregnant, and we were all delighted and excited. Veehan had no children, so this was an important moment for him. I was eight weeks pregnant when it all went wrong. I had an ectopic pregnancy, where the baby grows in the fallopian tube, and I nearly died. My fallopian burst and the pain was god-awful.

I was rushed into surgery and I was a very lucky woman to survive, but I lost the baby. I was heartbroken and so was Veehan. The doctors removed the fallopian tube and explained that, although I had one tube left, it was badly scarred and I wouldn't be able to have any more children. I was twenty-five years old, and I was devastated.

That was 1995 and I was trying to deal with being told that was that, that there would be no more babies. We drifted safely back into our lives without the baby and it was settled, happy. For the first time in my life I felt secure, loved, and I was living with Lee and Veehan as a family should. Veehan loved Lee like his own son, loved him to bits. Then in 1998 I had what seemed like morning sickness, and I thought: "This is impossible." But I had the test and, yes, against all the odds, I was pregnant again.

"It's a miracle," I told Veehan.

Later, I was having tea with my mother when I got this terrible pain—and I knew it was an ectopic pregnancy again. The hospital called me in immediately, and before I knew it I was in surgery, and I lost that baby and the other fallopian tube. That was cruel, the hope and then the loss of another baby. Veehan just couldn't take it. The last two nights I was in the hospital Veehan didn't visit me, and that wasn't like him. On my first night home, my mother was there to help with dinner. Veehan came in and I knew he'd been drinking. My mum went off home and Veehan continued drinking. I spoke to him but he didn't answer.

I said, "I'm away to my bed," and I started to get up. I was cut from one hip to the other, like a hysterectomy wound, and as I went to the door, Veehan pulled me by the hair and I went down on the carpet. I was in a crouching position, trying to protect my wound, and he was kicking me, saying, "It's all your fucking fault. Two children you lost of mine! It's all your fucking fault."

When he finally stopped kicking me I swore to myself: "When I'm better, and I will get better, I'm going to deal with this. And we're finished, that's it." He left sadly and quietly, and there was a vacuum in my heart.

I was back to juggling life again as a single mum. I did go out with a group of friends and they were shocked when I told them I'd never had a holiday. I was twenty-eight years old.

The group decided I *was* to go on holiday, and all the arrangements were made. I was going with a friend, but she became ill and couldn't travel. Jamie was divorced, and when my friend canceled he said, "I'm going away again, and you're welcome to come with me." We went to Spain, where we took a bus and stayed in a holiday park. Within a year we were married and had moved into the wee house we'd bought together. Lee was starting secondary school. I had a husband and a new job—all of this was packed into my pressure-cooker life. I did feel anxious that I'd moved too quickly, but I was so desperate for the stability of a solid family unit.

I tried a couple of jobs and then went to work with the Advanced Computer Group, which involved marketing and innovative computer solutions for companies. I learned IT skills and communications. I was working all out to make all the elements in my life work.

Still, I stumbled in my relationship with Jamie, and after two years I faced up to the marriage being a great mistake. I was at fault. With great grace, Jamie, who went off to live with his parents, agreed that Lee and I could live in the house during our two-year legal separation. When the house went up for sale in 2002, I was officially homeless. Luckily, I had the offer of a council house. I had a month to get it into shape before we moved in, and I was still doing up the house when I got a call saying I should visit my mother, as she was trying to hide a growth on her neck. When I got there, she was on the couch with a scarf around her neck. I asked her why, and she said, "It's just a wee bit cold."

I went over and pulled down the scarf. I'd never seen anything like it my life. It was as though it was a rubber ring and it was growing from the side of her neck. It was massive. I said I was going to phone the doctor, and she said, "Listen, hen, phone them tomorrow, not tonight."

The next day the family doctor came, and although my mother objected, he said she had to have it checked. She went into the hospital, and it was thirteen days before the cancer diagnosis came back. The morning they were to tell her, Adele and I went into her ward and there was a curtain around her bed. When I pulled it back my mother had shrunk; there was this wee, wee woman lying there. They had told her she had terminal cancer. It was as if all the air had gone out of her.

When I asked the doctors how long she had to live, they suggested a month, maybe. We said we were taking her home that day.

My sister was driving, and Mum was silent in the car. She hadn't said one word, but suddenly: "I want to see Jennifer's new blinds."

Adele drove past my half-decorated new home, and my mother looked out and just nodded. We got her home and she had a wee lie on the couch while we got the bedroom ready. She went upstairs and never came down alive again. It took thirteen days.

I'm glad we had that time. There was some balm on old wounds. She said, "Your dad and I are sorry for not believing you about that man Jim going after you that way." She held my hand and looked straight into my eyes and told me: "Hen, make sure you never live your life without love." I was so sad in that moment that my mum was looking back on her life and this was her big regret. I made a promise to her that I would never live without love. She didn't want anyone with her other than Adele and me. We sat with her day and night, and then we got my dad and said we thought her time was near. He came in and kissed her on the forehead, and then he went back to his bed and fell asleep. It was his way. He never wanted to confront bad things.

I went downstairs, and a moment later my sister called me. I ran upstairs, and my mother was the color of cement. I let out a scream: *"Mum!"* She looked like she'd shrunk into the sheets. She opened one eye and looked straight at me, shut her eye, and that was that. There was a kind of peace about her. We woke my dad up and said, "She's gone."

He came through and saw her, then went into his closet. He put on a pair of black suit trousers, a crisp white shirt, his braces, and a black tie, then went downstairs and waited for the undertakers to take her away. Adele and I couldn't understand. Was it the older generation? Was that what they did?

A few days later, Adele told me to have a look in the living room. On the wall, nicely framed, was a big photograph of my dad, aged nineteen. I looked at him. He smiled and said, "Your mother never let me put pictures up."

It was a moment of relief. He was lost but finding himself in the past.

Some of it didn't return. My brother never came round to see him.

What I went through as a child was partly because of what Mum had gone through with my brother, who was her blue-eyed boy. She never heard a bad word about him to the day she died. She really did love him dearly.

When he was nineteen, my brother got into a relationship and was married. One day, he came to the house, gave Mum a Mother's Day card, and said, "I can't come back. My wife doesn't like you, and it's causing an atmosphere in the house."

My mum calmly told him, "Son, you've got to do what's right for you and your marriage."

She never saw him again.

An elderly mourner said they thought they saw him at my mother's funeral, and that was disquieting for us all, especially for Dad, for it was a ghostly thought. My brother had a daughter, Bonnie, and she was the double of me. I was only three years older and I saw her at school, but she knew that her mum didn't want her to be close to her dad's family. There was an uncomfortable feeling, and both of us kept our distance to keep the peace. At the time of the funeral, she was living in Perthshire with her husband and three young children. She came down to us the night before my mother's funeral and explained she'd had a difficult childhood. She told me no more. The following week, four weeks exactly to the day my mum died, I got a phone call at work from my sister: "Jennifer, Bonnie's dead."

I went to my father's house and he was sitting silently in the front room. He was wearing his black trousers, black tie, and white shirt. "I'll wait here, in case my boy calls. He might want me. *He'll need me.*"

He didn't. He never came to see Dad.

Bonnie's husband had arrived home one evening and found her dead in their garage. In a letter she said that she didn't want to hurt her kids the way she had been hurt. I spent the next nine months going up and down to Perthshire. I had to leave my job, to make sure Bonnie's kids were looked after. I fed and cuddled them. I felt I couldn't do anything else. In time, Bonnie's widower met someone else, and that was a blessing for him and for Bonnie's children.

Though I had no money coming in I was surviving, but only one meal at a time, living on the savings I'd managed to gather. It was difficult, and finally when I went to see about benefits I had the money to get a bus to the office but not the return fare. They'd delayed the payments for another length of time: I was stuck. Then I got the phone call that the house I had with Jamie had finally been sold and we'd received £10,000 out of it. I felt guilty because I had ended the marriage, and I didn't want more bad feeling over money. I told Jamie to give me £1,000, and he could keep the rest. With that cash behind us, Lee and I could soldier on.

I decided I could work for myself from home and started Etele, marketing IT services and products. I didn't realize how tough it was working for yourself—it's a bit of a cemetery life, seven days a week, no holidays. Still, it worked well, and within five years I had established my own little office. I was no tycoon, but I was paying my rent and making ends meet. Lee left school at seventeen and went to work in a carpet factory driving a forklift. That changed his life, for it was there he met Fiona, who was in the administration department. Six years later, Lee and Fiona became pregnant unexpectedly, and I was determined to celebrate that and help them in any way I could—to do everything different from what I'd suffered. I invited them to move in with me and offered the words that I would have loved to have heard when I was a pregnant teenager: "Don't worry about anything. Everything, *everything*, is going to be wonderful. I'm here to help."

Fiona and Lee were my main priority. It's scary with an unexpected pregnancy, it's a whole new world of unknowns in which you haven't taken lessons. We soon learned it was going to be a lot tougher than any of us could have believed.

In 2009 I had a hysterectomy, which was not unexpected after my two ectopic pregnancies, and I was told I'd need nine months at least to heal. But I was self-employed, and after six months I felt fine and I started traveling to see clients. Within a week I felt tired, sometimes dizzy, with that feeling of the ground coming up to meet you. No matter how much sleep I had, I felt I had climbed a mountain, my legs were so weary and heavy. I'd started to slow down like an old car with a clogged-up engine.

I was with a client, who said I looked knocked out and I should go home and rest. I didn't argue. I went straight to bed, set the alarm for six thirty the next day, and pulled the covers over me. I slept.

When the alarm shrieked I tried to take the covers off me, but I couldn't move my arm. I tried to sit up. I couldn't do that. I was paralyzed.

I shouted to Fiona in the next room, "I can't move."

I was panicking, and she thought it was a cramp or I'd been sleeping the wrong way, something that would go away when I woke up properly. She was quite calm. But we waited. And waited. I couldn't move.

I was like Lot's wife, stuck to the spot, in my bed for the foreseeable future. I thought it was a good thing I'd changed the sheets the day before! The doctor came to give me blood tests and more blood tests, but they came back showing nothing wrong. Soon I was on all these tablets—strong, strong tablets that leave you feeling like a zombie: morphine, amitriptyline, and all in super-sized measures. I was on 3,600 milligrams of gabapentin, which is one of the highest doses you can possibly get (duloxetine came later) and all my fellow sufferers out there will know from that how teetering-on-the-edge I was.

This went on for six months, and by now Fiona was heavily pregnant and having a tough time with it. But she's an angel and she helped me to look after myself. When you don't know what's wrong with you, it's your imagination that plays games. I thought I had cancer. I thought it was in the spine, as I couldn't move my legs. I could only really move my head, but even my head felt too heavy for my neck. I had a cushion I put into the crook of my neck to take the pressure off it. "Zombie" is the perfect description of the around-the-clock state I was in. I couldn't hold my mobile phone in the first months. At times I could hardly hold my breath. The pain was cruel but the fear was overwhelming. What was wrong with me? I was only forty years old.

After months of continuous blood tests, a tearful encounter with my doctor finally had me diagnosed with myalgic encephalomyelitis (ME). Americans call it chronic fatigue syndrome—CFS or CFS/ME—but it's not simply a condition that makes you exhausted. There's a crossover of symptoms with multiple sclerosis (MS), but doctors know that lesions on the brain cause that lifelong condition.

Doctors don't know what brings ME to your door. I asked my doctor what the next move was.

He looked puzzled and gave a robot reply: "We'll refer you to a pain-management consultant."

His mantra: "Keep taking the tablets."

"They're not helping."

"There's nothing else I can give you."

At this point I couldn't even take daylight. I had to wear sunglasses. My room was blackened out, for the slightest bit of sunlight would bring horrific pain to my head and my eyes. I was in a darkened room morning to night, and that was it. I'd constantly ask what I could do, and the reply was always to keep taking the tablets, what I regarded as my knockout drops.

If I'd reacted to the early warning signs and slowed down maybe I'd have escaped the worst. When I woke up unable to move, that was my body protecting itself from more damage.

It was lonely. I was fully bedbound and suffering excruciating pain throughout the body—bone pain, muscle pain, and nerve pain—and I could hardly speak, as I was embarrassed being unable to string my words together. When people were talking to me I'd be constantly asking them, "What did you say?"

I saw my son getting upset—he and Fiona were looking after me all the time—and I suggested we make jokes about the daft things I was coming out with in zombie-speak. I told him that although I would get better, the jokes wouldn't.

When I did try the stairs it was exhausting. I'd often climb them on my hands and knees, and I came down them on my bum. Fiona arranged for another stair bannister and an apparatus for the bed so I could pull myself up, as well as a contraption to make it easier for me to use the toilet. I felt such a burden to Lee and Fiona, especially since I felt I was never going to get any better. I thought I couldn't do this to my family anymore.

I had heavy suicidal thoughts: "Jen, why don't you take these tablets and that'll be an end of it." Thinking like that engulfed me. I was tired, tired of fighting, tired of pain. Lee and Fiona had a life to live, and here they were taking care of me. I had to fight through that feeling with all I had, and that was a hell of a time.

My granddaughter, Elle, was born around Christmas that first year of my full-on ME. She was the ray of sunshine I needed. I told myself: "I want to live." I wanted to see that wee beauty grow up. She was and is a blessing. I wanted to take her for a walk in her pram, to push her on a swing, things you take for granted. With ME you don't sleep, so Grandma was great for night feeds. They'd bring her through with her bottles all ready, and I could cope with that. It gave me more hope. I wanted to get better and I started furiously paying attention to what I was eating, listening to my body, learning when to rest, how much effort was sensible.

I was two years in bed with Fiona feeding me, washing me, caring for me; and three years when there were days when I could get out of bed and make it downstairs; it was nearly five years before I stepped outside the front door again. It was baby steps—I was progressing, but there were relapses. It was increasingly frustrating. I wanted to walk. But if I walked too fast, I was soon back in my bed again. It was trial and error until I learned to avoid the mistakes.

You can't defeat ME but you can mitigate the effects. It was an ongoing struggle to achieve a good quality of life. I know this makes me sound like an episode of *Casualty* or *ER*, but while trying so hard to be "normal" I was rushed to the hospital with a ruptured gallbladder. The surgeon who operated had an invitation-only party list of his colleagues to watch—they'd never witnessed anything like it: Twenty gallstones had burst out of my gallbladder, and some had gone into my liver bile duct. It was a tricky piece of surgery. The medication had built up that colony of stones and that was madness, taking pills that were poisoning me and still being in pain.

I stopped taking the medication. I tried more herbal remedies, like cannabidiol (CBD), but coming off the heavy meds brought on pains in my head, hellish pains, as well as excruciating sickness and tremors. But that eased, and because I was listening to my body, I was able to manage ME, able to function. I had relapses every few months—stress was *the* big trigger to bring it on—but even the attacks were shorter. The ME attacks my internal organs and goes for my heart, so I have to take heart medication every day.

The other devilment with ME is that another symptom is fibromyalgia, which can mimic a heart attack on the chest-wall cavity. I confused doctors a few times with what were copycat "heart attacks." The ME went for my digestive system as well. On good days I found I was able to go out, go visit Eileen, do a bit of shopping, but I couldn't push it. My full-time job was managing my body. It had to be *full time* or I ran the big risk of my muscles being so exhausted I'd be locked in one spot, all but handcuffed to my bed. I wasn't having that.

A week after Dad's funeral, on February 11, 2015, my second grandchild, Jax, was delivered safely. A joy and another wee beautiful soul for me to worry about. My son and his family, what I wouldn't do for them. I'd go to bed every night and not sleep but think about getting them to a safe place. My mind wouldn't rest. With me unable to work, my rainy-day savings were gone. In the saddest of circumstances, I now had my dad's money, my inheritance.

I wanted a safety blanket for Lee and his family. I wanted to invest in a secure future for them.

THREE

Happy Days

Eileen always has the kettle on. She says I'm super-glued to my phone, and I say she's lost without a cup of sugary tea in her hand. But even a strong cup of tea wasn't any preparation for what was to happen after I popped round to see how she was doing on that miserably wet day in 2016.

Eileen is not a complainer, but at that time she was severely unwell. Her kidney function was very, very low, and with her having MS, she struggled with balance on her left side and needed to use a walking stick. She was all but housebound, and if she did manage to get out of the house, she needed support. She couldn't go out alone. She was waiting for dialysis treatment and could only stand for a few seconds, and even then she needed to hold on to something for support. That's how weak she was. She loved company. She became exhausted really quickly and I was worried for my friend, so I used to go down and visit her at least three times a week, but if I wasn't well, we'd speak on the phone two or three times a day.

I was putting our takeaway salad lunch on the plates when she said, "I had a conversation, this chap Rex that I know messaged me on Facebook. Have you ever heard of digital currency, Jen, Bitcoin?"

I told her I'd heard about it a few years ago but didn't know any details, and she replied, "Rex says this OneCoin—it's a cryptocurrency, like Bitcoin—is a winner and it's grown in worth really fast.

People getting returns of more than 100 percent, and it's something to look at. He invited me to a webinar with a girl called Sally. It went on and on forever! I switched off my video for I was nearly falling asleep, so I don't remember much about it other than your money made more and more money."

MS patients have trouble with memory, as I do with ME. I've got to write everything down or record it so that if I've had a conversation that's important I can go back to it. Eileen and I have lots of laughs together about our memories. She'll say, "What was I saying there?" And I'll reply, "I don't know—you're asking me?" And vice versa. Unless somebody walks in your shoes they might not see the funny side of it or even understand it.

Eileen said that she had no detailed memory of what was said on the webinar, and I said it seemed interesting anyway. She was in good form that day and I went back home. About a week later Eileen called me and asked if I remembered "about Rex and that woman Sally" and the digital currency investment. She told me, "He's just phoned me and said it's going to go up in value again and now is the time to invest before it'll cost more to get in."

I was facing a bleak situation then: I was unwell. I was having relapses and had to take to my bed and draw the blinds to create a blackout, as the light burned my eyes. Sometimes I wore sunglasses in bed. I wasn't fit to work for another employer because of the way the ME just took the feet from underneath me, but I didn't even have the energy to be my own boss. I couldn't commit to clients. I'd lost everything I had because of ME and I just wanted the chance to invest my dad's money for my son and keep it safe for him and his wee family. A few years on and I still get so emotional thinking about it. Eileen knew where I was at and she told me, "I think you should take a look at this—you should at least speak to Rex."

I remembered some of my IT clients had mentioned Bitcoin before and I said to myself, "Digital currency, I've heard of Bitcoin, I think I will speak to him." I asked Eileen to give him my phone number. He called me the same day. His name was Rex Charles. He described himself as a "wealth strategist." He was enthusiastic but not pushy. He explained about digital currency and how this investment opportunity was growing in value faster than Bitcoin.

"For you to really understand it, I definitely recommend that you go to a webinar."

And there was one that night!

He asked, "Would you like to jump on? I'll send you the invite link."

I said, "Aye, do that, that'd be great."

I joined the webinar that evening, and this pleasant lady named Sally Losa was hosting it. It lasted for about an hour and a half. There must have been about another hundred people or more on that webinar. It was ninety minutes of OneCoin marketing, which explained the Bitcoin story, how it had soared in value, and Sally explained what digital currency actually is.

The OneCoin team went back in history to the Stone Age days of bartering goods for goods and how money has changed throughout time. The message was that digital currency would bring a financial utopia, a digital future that would make flat currency obsolete. One-Coin was going to be the global leader, and the only one that mattered, the number one cryptocurrency. Then they played their ace.

They introduced Dr. Ruja Ignatova.

She appeared on a video presentation, which had a buzz about it, with repeated promotional talk of financial freedom. The film shown to prospective investors worldwide was so professional and the insistent message so convincing I felt some people would be kneeling in front of their laptops worshipping this lady and the message she was delivering. She came across as a deity.

For the moment they simply called her a money-world superstar. She had a PhD and used to work for the big-time financial company McKinsey & Company, which advises many Fortune 1,000 companies, institutions, and governments. They showed her on the cover of *Forbes* magazine and on glorious display on two pages inside. She was shown in *Financial IT* magazine making a speech at a European economic summit and explaining what she had achieved in founding OneCoin.

I was sitting in my rented council house and already hero-worshipping this Dr. Ruja and listening as Sally Losa told us the value of OneCoin. Then, more excitement as they explained that as soon as you bought a Tycoon package for £5,000, the package would have a digital value of £48,000 based on OneCoin being valued at £5.25 at that moment. At the same time, I was recruited into the OneCoin WhatsApp groups, where all the chat began about how you could really only change your family's life with the Tycoon package and above. The sales team insisted that as soon as you even looked in the direction of one of the packages, you were a millionaire. It was a powerful pitch. The OneCoin "rules" dictated that the person who first contacted you, in my case Rex Charles, got back in touch, and he did that the next day, his Brummie voice coming loudly down the line: "Hey, Jen, what did you think about it?"

"My God, I'm absolutely blown away."

"Well, now's the time to invest because there's going to be a split happening soon, so the quicker you get in, the better, for your investment is going to grow in value. You don't want to miss out. Do it now and you'll be far, far richer today, tomorrow, and forever." He repeated the point that the £5,000 Tycoon package was—at the time he was talking to me—worth £48,000. It was growing all the time, as were the OneCoin members, who were almost at one million. He said the growth was phenomenal compared to Bitcoin. Then he went full blast into the *Wizard of Oz* stuff, never revealing what was behind the curtain and how OneCoin did its arithmetic.

Rex told me if I bought a £100 Starter package (with a £30 activation cost) alongside the Tycoon package I would receive an extra split when the coins doubled at certain times during the investment period. He said the Starter package came with one split and 1,000 tokens, and the Tycoon came with two splits and 60,000 tokens. In total, if I purchased both of these packages together, I would have in total three splits and initially 61,000 tokens. He said this meant that after all three splits had taken place I would have a total of 488,000 tokens, which would give me 8,561 OneCoins. He gushed that at the current value of £5.65 per OneCoin at the start of March 2016, my Starter package and Tycoon package would have an immediate digital currency value of £48,369.65! Which was exactly what was pitched on the webinar.

However, he said that if I delayed investing, I would get much less for my money because the "mining difficulty" was due to increase, which meant I would get less coins if I decided to delay my investment even for a week or two. He explained that the mining difficulty continually and gradually increased over time, so the clear message was to get in at the early adoption stage. The mining difficulty is the number you divide your number of tokens by to work out how many coins you will receive in your packages. So that meant my 488,000 tokens divided by 57 (mining difficulty) came to 8,561 OneCoins. Rex kept stating, with growing urgency, that the mining difficulty barometer was currently sitting at 96 percent but was about to hit 100 percent. That's when the terror of that dreaded acronym FOMO—fear of missing out—manifests itself and you start to get high anxiety and panic, and you don't think straight. I sure as hell didn't, but blinding as that jargon was, I'd seen the light. I was a believer.

I said I'd thought about it quite enough and I'd like to try the £5,000 Tycoon package. His voice took off: "Jen, that's fantastic—I'll just get the details for you and I'll give you a call back. My God, how exciting is this? I'm so excited for you."

He was excited? I felt I was finally doing something positive with my dad's money. And that cash didn't seem a daft amount to invest, although my dad would have been amazed at the champagne talk and the amounts of money being discussed. He never drank other than a small Bell's whisky on New Year's Eve—Hogmanay to us Scots—but even then somebody else would usually finish his drink. He wouldn't have known a Porsche if it ran him over. He was that old-fashioned working man who believed that if you had a pound you only ever spent 95 pence, or nineteen shillings and sixpence in Dad's mind.

Rex was back in no time with my instructions. OneCoin wanted my money first and then they would activate the package. I had to send my £5,000 to an account in Germany but via a different account held at a High Street bank on the Isle of Wight, and I did this on March 11, 2016. Rex wanted a screenshot of my transaction and then he'd set up my account and give me an activation code and my log-in details, and I'd be a OneCoin investor with my Tycoon package. I told him, "Oh, I can't wait . . ."

As soon as I got the details I activated my package and I was so, *so* excited, I jumped in a taxi and I went to Eileen's.

Eileen has a disabled ramp leading up to her back door, and as I was walking up it I thought I couldn't wait to tell her my news. But then I told myself: "Wait, she hasn't got any money to invest." I thought about that and then I knew in my head what I was going to say to her.

I went in and she, as usual, shouted, "Put the kettle on?"

I told her I'd just had a conversation with Rex Charles. "How did it go?"

She was desperate to hear. She pulled out a chair at her kitchenette table and sat down. "How did it go?" I repeated as I sat beside her: "I've purchased a £5,000 package . . ."

"Did yay? Did yay? Go on. Oh, my God. I'd loved to have done it but I haven't the money."

I told her, "I know that. I'd like to get you a £550 package, what they call a Trader . . . I can afford that . . ."

"Oh, I'll pay you back."

"No, never mind that. Listen, I want to do this and it's a chance for both of us to make a really good investment."

She was so happy and appreciative, and I said, "Come on, let's get you signed up then—you introduced it to me so it's only right you have a package."

I was looking at my wee friend who was so ill, and there wasn't a way I could not buy her a package. There was no way I could invest only for myself when she'd brought it to me and she was so unwell. Of course I was going to get her a package.

And Eileen was the first person I brought in to OneCoin. She made the tea and I called Rex to purchase and pay for Eileen's Trader package on March 18, 2016, the same day I bought myself a £1,000 *Pro-Trader*. Rex was delighted, which made me more excited. We had to send the money right away. It was the same routine, with him giving us details where to send the money and him replying with access codes. We were nervous about doing it, really nervous about sending the payments for the packages, because you had to do it all yourself. Once we were paid up, Eileen was added to the WhatsApp groups, and at one moment I thought they were going to sing *Hallelujah!* When it was announced that "Jen has just purchased her first Tycoon package," everybody in the group started posting these clapping signs, and there was much applause, like cheerleading. I felt there was a cultish side from the first day. Eileen received the same enthusiastic greeting. It was so easy: You purchased OneCoin tokens, and these then generated coins, which went into your account. One day soon, we were told, we could turn these coins back into euros or pounds. It seemed like easy money.

Within one week of being in these groups it was made clear that our packages wouldn't change our life financially—what we really needed was more investment.

Some offers were out of our league but that was okay, good luck to them; Eileen and I were ecstatic with our investment. And the more we earned, the bigger the packages we could buy. Take a deep breath: The Ultimate package was a whopping £118,000 and came with 1,311,111 tokens and seven splits; the total number of tokens at the end of all seven splits was 167,822,208, which, divided by the mining difficulty of 57, gave you 2,944,249 OneCoins. As of March 2016, with a OneCoin value of £5.65, that was £16,635,008.33. The bonus was that if you also purchased a Starter package with the Ultimate package, you could then double that figure. Just like that.

All that week Eileen and I couldn't stop talking about it. I said to her, "Eileen, I'm going to get another one of those Trader packages."

She had a cheeky smile. "Well, I was thinking about a couple of those £1,000 *Pro-Traders*, I'm going to get a loan for it. We can get our money back out in twelve weeks and I can get that loan paid off. You can get your initial investment back out—all we've got to do is be patient for a few weeks."

And yes, that's what we were told: that we could get our original money back after three months. So that was the plan. Ruja said that when all your coins would have been "mined," you'd have your full amount of coins in what was called your back office (your One-Coin account). It seemed perfect: After that time I could take out my £5,000 and Eileen could get her money and pay off the loan and we'd still be rolling in OneCoin investments—at its current value I'd still have £43,000. So it was a no-brainer. We were going to be okay.

The night we did that was really cold, a damp night. I had my big furry coat and my boots on, and I was all wrapped up when I went over to Eileen's. Her living room is small, as it is divided so she can have a bedroom downstairs. She'd fallen down the stairs before, so she has to have her toilet and this bedroom on the ground floor. It's intimate, very face-to-face, and we could feel each other's excitement.

"Can you believe we're going to do this?" she said, putting the kettle on and talking along, as much to herself as to me. "Oh, Jesus, we're going to change our lives."

I was the same: "This is life changing. This is the answer to our prayers. *This is it* . . ."

When we sent the money for the extra packages, it was a scary time. We were to send the money to a different account, in Dubai, and Rex Charles gave us the wrong names. He kept emphasizing that we put the name in a certain way, but with digital banking neither Eileen nor I could get the full name to fit into the space on the computer. We were on the phone to Rex: "Have we done this right? Have we put the name properly?" There was so much apprehension. We wanted to get it done without any problems. We didn't want to miss out. *Don't miss out.*

Finally, when the money went through, Eileen and I just looked at each other and gave a big scream. We thought our hardships were over. We were just hyper, *absolutely* elated. Ruja had made us believe it was really going to happen.

And now it had.

Opportunity hadn't just knocked, it had battered down our door. Eileen and I were giggling like the couple of teenagers who used to sneak a cigarette during school breaks. I can still feel the hairs on my arms and down my back bristling with the excitement. For once I believed my life would change. Ruja had promised and convinced me this would be life changing because OneCoin was in the early adoption stage. This wasn't even the jackpot.

I *so* wanted OneCoin to be the breakthrough of my life. I admired Dr. Ruja, this magnetic personality, this glamorous, high-fashion woman in the monied world of men. She was a gold-plated feminist, a saint in a tainted world, and I was a super fan. She lived in a place so secure, so comfortable, without any worries about the gas bill or a granddaughter's birthday treat. I wanted to be worry-free, and if a beach holiday came with it, then all to the better. But what I wanted most was what I'd never had in all my forty-six years: security. Ruja promised that, and when I watched her and listened to her speak about how I could achieve that dream, I believed her. This is what I *needed*.

Ruja was living my dream, and all I wanted was a sprinkle of her stardust. She was that good. She was selling a Brave New World, a cryptocurrency for the people, for the man in the street, the folk who'd had a windfall, a lucky break, a win on the Premium Bonds or the lottery, enough to be happy with but not enough to change your life. With OneCoin, Dr. Ruja offered the true life-changing opportunity.

Eileen and I were in at the beginning of an amazing thing, a revolutionary investment opportunity. It was a very, very exciting time. That night Eileen lay on her recliner sofa with her legs up and her laptop open and humming on her knees, and I sat next to her on the sofa. We were so happy and buzzing. We'd sent the money and we started talking about our lives. So excited. With our illnesses we both get a lot of pain in our muscles, nerves, and bones, and sunshine does help. Our dream was to purchase a small property in the sunshine that both our families could share and the two of us could get away to, especially in the cruel Scottish winters, when we both feel the pain the worst. That was a huge thing. We got carried away about that and we even started looking at homes in Tuscany, Spain, and the South of France, for that's where our dreams connected. I felt it definitely would become real; it didn't seem so far off. Any moment now.

Gleefully, Eileen and I came to a truly big decision: that we would spend one week at her villa and the next at mine. And maybe the next at a five-star spa hotel. And a week looking after the grandchildren. Just for variety. We didn't want to become blasé with our rich, newly minted OneCoin lifestyle, and although we felt we'd won the lottery with this amazing cryptocurrency opportunity, which was much bigger and better than Bitcoin, it was no gamble. We'd invested in a fabulous business endeavor. In a few years we'd be wealthier than any lottery winner by getting early into OneCoin. We talked over endless pots of tea, and often into the early hours, of our plans for spreading happiness and comfort among our families and friends. I'd find myself in a taxi going home at three in the morning imagining a carefree future, something so out of my reach for so long. One night on the car radio they were playing Susan Boyle singing "The Impossible Dream," and I was humming away. It was my theme song.

Those were glorious days. I adored Dr. Ruja. She was my champion. She was a woman, a woman who had thrived and conquered in what remains very much a man's world. You can trust a woman to do the right thing, to nurture, to look out for families and others. If she'd conjured a halo above her head I'd have believed and applauded even more. I was sold. I'd have to force myself to sleep, and the more I tried, the more I kept seeing myself in a world free of pain and worry. When I did go off, I went to sleep smiling.

I felt so in control and part of the moment, of understanding where we were in the world of money. The futuristic cryptocurrency was my Fort Knox, my security, a solid investment that would secure our financial future. Eileen and I were winners. We were in the OneCoin world. Rex was my direct contact, and above him was Jack Cadel, his immediate superior, and above Cadel were the cousins James and Harry Stone. The cousins were among the top boys responsible for bringing OneCoin into my life. Harry was my "executive" connection, my diamond leader. We were "family." And the family grew. Not long after we invested, Eileen received a call from Mitchell Thomson whom we both knew, but Eileen talked to more through Facebook. Eileen had told him that she'd invested in OneCoin digital currency. Mitchell was into Bitcoin and wanted to know more.

Eileen called me and we agreed to send Mitchell the OneCoin promotional video and that I would talk to him if he had questions. Eileen can stutter at times and said she didn't feel confident explaining all the ins and outs. We organized a Zoom call for the three of us and Mitchell started asking some questions we didn't know the answers to. We'd only just joined, so I said the best thing would be for him to join a webinar like Eileen and I had done, and we hooked him up with a webinar the following day. After that he messaged me and asked to invest through me and not Eileen, although Eileen had spoken with him first and the OneCoin etiquette would make Eileen his "contact." After getting to know Mitchell, I think that Eileen's illness and her health at that time put Mitchell off investing with her.

That's the way he was, and he was very demeaning to Eileen on many occasions. I asked him to explain to Eileen, and when I knew Eileen was okay with it Mitchell bought the £5,000 Tycoon package through me. Sally Losa sent me the bank account details for Mitchell to send the cash to. Mitchell had some trouble with a digital banking machine and there were back-and-forth phone calls before he finally managed to get his machine working.

I only wanted to invest my own money, but when I met my friends and family all I could talk about was OneCoin and the opportunity. I was so hyped up: "You'll never believe this! I invested in digital currency."

That would kick off the conversation, and I'd start enthusiastically explaining what OneCoin told me about the Bitcoin story, and before I knew it I was telling everyone the same information that was fed to me. I was like a disciple, telling people that OneCoin at the adoption stage was worth £5.25 whereas one Bitcoin at that stage could be bought for ten cents.

And Bitcoin (in February 2016) was valued at about $450 US, so I was really excited and telling people how brilliant it was to be in with OneCoin at that launch stage with the value at £5.25 a coin. The potential for growth was immense. That was my message. *Hallelujah!* indeed.

The webinars were with Sally Losa, but by then her partner, John Munero, had started joining her on them; together they comprised my team. They worked long hours and they worked hard. When I told them of my career as a sales and marketing consultant and my experience in multi-level marketing (MLM) I could see the light bulbs flashing above their heads. They told me I had potential, and I was pleased. They grinned and chanted their message, but much of it came over to me as gobbledygook.

It took months to understand the central elements of the One-Coin system, which was overly complicated. You could see your account online, but to start making the glorious amount of profits I had to join a discussion group on WhatsApp messaging led by Sally and John. There were talks of leadership ranks and packs with names of precious stones, OneCoin packages, types of values visible on one's back office—details of your account in coins, tokens, your cash account, business volume, mining operations, and commissions calculated as a percentage, it seemed to me, based on the size of the moon at any given time. They held these webinars three, four times a day. They went on through the afternoon and into the evening, and every one lasted an hour and a half. No corners were cut. Potential investors were shown the same thing I was: the story of Bitcoin, Ruja in her full glory, the promotional video and all the razzmatazz, the glowing Yellow Brick Road to pots and pots of gold over the rainbow. I must explain that this was real upmarket marketing. It wasn't a tacky show using cheap video. It was convincing and impressive, and all the money OneCoin spent was up there on the screen. This was a rich outfit run by rich executives who were going to make their investors rich. They had it to a T. It was a very clever tactic by Ruja.

One aspect I didn't go for was what they called the 90 Day Challenge, which you were given immediately upon joining OneCoin. Everybody who invested was urged to use WhatsApp groups to contact a hundred people a day and attempt to recruit them. There were instructions, a template, on how to pitch OneCoin. It was too high pressure for me, and I didn't like it. Yet, although I disapproved of this marketing tactic, I was a OneCoin loyalist. And the word *was* spread by the people who joined, who became Ruja's evangelists. It was such an exciting time, and it was the first thing you shared when you met friends or family because you were so enthusiastic about this life-changing investment you'd just been given. It was the natural thing to do. You made money while you slept.

So when Mitchell Thomson asked me questions before he bought his Tycoon package—Who was Ruja? When was OneCoin started?—after my webinar induction I had the answers on the tip of my tongue. Shortly after, Mitchell bought another Tycoon package and he even bought one for Rex Charles, the "wealth strategist." That was a few months in. Rex had called me one day and said, "Oh, Jen, I haven't been able to afford to buy the Tycoon package, and to change my family's life I really need that Tycoon package. I was wondering if you could loan me the money." He said he was saving to invest in OneCoin while he worked on the marketing side. I said I was sorry but I didn't have the money to loan. I found it strange. Even if I had the cash, I didn't know this man other than as a voice on the phone. After I said no he approached Mitchell Thomson and he bought his package for him. Mitchell, like Eileen and I, believed—in different things as it turned out, but for now we were on the same hymn sheet.

And I was to do some singing. With no rehearsals. I'd started bringing in big investments because of Mitchell, who was on what was called my downline and bringing in much more money than me. I had a handful of people but wasn't chasing any more. Mitchell was. Because of the cash volume, John Munero and Sally Losa wanted me to move into the MLM structure, as they wanted to be getting the commissions off Mitchell. I wouldn't move because all I cared about was my investment and not commissions. Every OneCoin member was given a downline, which was divided into two teams, each paid for by the weaker team. If you had three £1,000 members in one branch and four £500 members in another branch, someone on commission would be paid 10 percent or £200 based on the weaker (4 x 500) membership. Payments were always made on Mondays, called Happy Mondays, which were even more so for Ruja, as you'll learn. As it was, OneCoin took 40 percent of the commission I inadvertently earned, so in all of this I got £1,800, which, enthusiast that I was, I used to buy more OneCoin packages. Anyway, Ruja's pitch was that the 40 percent she received automatically "mined" more OneCoin tokens for OneCoins to continually be added to investors' accounts. The money, you see, was circulating, and we all benefited. Eileen and I were invited to the first OneCoin recruiting event in Scotland at the Hilton Glasgow Grosvenor Hotel on April 12, 2016. We'd been talking nothing but Dr. Ruja and OneCoin 24/7, so this was a big deal for us. I didn't expect a fuss, but we were ushered into seats at the front of the room. It was the first time Eileen and I met John Munero and Sally Losa face-to-face. Eerily, Eileen said she took on the full body shivers when John Munero hugged her; there was something of the night about him, she said.

Sally told me I was the first person in Scotland to buy a Tycoon package and asked if I would go up to the stage and say that. I was, inconveniently to say the least, speechless at that, but by then the event had begun. They'd hired a bagpiper to tune up the crowd as the leaders banged the drum, as it were, for Dr. Ruja and OneCoin. On stage James and Harry Stone began their presentation, selling the crowd on their new extravagant life and how far they'd come since being homeless. It was a flawless double act. Harry enthused: "I remember my cousin James coming to me and saying, 'I really need to show you this.' And I was too busy with my life and working—I was working seventy-six hours a week—so I said, 'You think I have time to do other things?'"

And James took his cue: "And I said, 'That's why you need to see this.' So I took him to a presentation . . ."

Harry: I saw individuals speaking on stage who were so confident and I thought: "Wow, look at them—look at the strength they have." I was told to share my story—I remember sweating and I couldn't say a single word—I felt like vomiting. At that moment, I knew I needed to grow.

James: They were showing how you could make £20,000 a month and I wasn't even making that in a year. I'd never heard of anyone making that much a month. I'm thinking this can't be true. I didn't believe in the money side of things, but I liked the personal development aspect of it so I got involved.

Harry: I had never really heard of personal development because I was living a mediocre life where the only thing I knew was just paying my bills. I didn't know anything beyond that.

James: Some of the people we met didn't even have an education and they were coming here and finding success. We were sitting way at the back—there were about seven thousand people in the room. Remember?

Harry: I was looking at James and saying, "Do you feel what I'm feeling?" And at that moment, we made a decision: We're either going to make it to the top, or we're going to die trying.

James: I don't know the dream that you have, but the dream that you are holding in your mind is possible.

There was a crowd of about two hundred, with groups standing at the back of the room, and everyone was swept up by the Stone cousins' act. There were pictures of them homeless, though not quite in rags, on a screen behind them as they spoke—and now most people could put a price on their suits and watches. We were taken aback at the amount of cash one person could wear—without adding the Rolex and the rings. We were taking all this in when Harry introduced me. He invited me on stage to talk about buying the Tycoon package. I didn't want to do it, but they insisted. I tried to say no again but they called me up anyway. Eileen gave me a friendly shove.

Before I could gather my thoughts I was up there with a microphone in my hand. I'm a terrible singer, but it was like a karaoke evening in the pub, and there I was. I truly can't recall exactly what I said, but I praised OneCoin and Dr. Ruja and endorsed the benefits of cryptocurrency in offering an alternative to High Street banking. I was regurgitating all the messages flowing in to me through the webinars and the WhatsApp group chats. I was fluent in OneCoin-speak and I must have made sense, for there was lots of applause. And the Stone cousins and Sally Losa and John Munero were happy. That cheered me up, for although I was always going to ask questions, I wanted to be friendly with everyone. Life's too short for anything else. I'd learned that. I wrote a note to myself that evening and it's still on my Facebook page: Incredible event in Glasgow last night, the first launch! It was a packed full house and this is only the beginning, so looking forward to the London event in May. I have photographs of the evening, and there's one with me and Harry Stone giving the "O" sign, the OneCoin salute.

Now people were asking me questions, including Lee, who up until then hadn't paid that much attention to OneCoin; it was just something Mum was involved with. The simplest questions: How did OneCoin work? Most of us are familiar with High Street banks and building societies: You put money in—if you have it—and you have a bank book or regular bank statements. And a bank debit or credit card—if they let you have one. With cryptocurrency there's none of that.

What there is instead is an act of faith—that's if you're like me and not some pure math specialist—for your money goes into the world of mathematics, of algorithms of computer systems, which, not touched by human hand, verify and record every transaction in what is called blockchain technology. The Bitcoin blockchain is a protective shield around the currency; it is a publicly distributed ledger that has never been hacked. It can't be changed. It is what it is. The currency and its value is controlled by specific technology and not touched or interfered with by anything *or* anyone else. In gambling, the bank or the house always wins—the odds are stacked in their favor. I've found that with High Street banks. I was refused a banking facility and a credit card when I was a single—and earning—young mother. Then when I had my dad's money, they were all over for me to deposit and invest. The banking industry is devoted to making a profit, not to people. The blockchain keeps human hands off.

The tech I know now is a world away from what I understood in the first place about OneCoin. At the time I described blockchain "banking" as allowing you to send money across borders without the need of the banking system. This wasn't often that helpful, and more explanation was needed, so I developed this answer to prospective investors:

A blockchain creates digital currency, which is basically an algorithmic digital process that allows one to transmit money across borders outside of the banking system and also store data that is transparent, verifiable, and immutable, which means it cannot be changed. The blockchain, a secure, decentralized ledger, prevents fraud and counterfeiting.

What it came down to was that digital currency controlled by a blockchain was a system for everyone—whether you had ten pence or ten million dollars you could be in—and I understood and celebrated that as democratic banking. When I was talking about it with Lee and with my investors, I was placing lots of faith in Dr. Ruja and her talents as a financial entrepreneur. I was driven by the fear of missing out. OneCoin was the new coin on the blockchain, as it were, and Ruja and her team were very convincing that it would soon be the world's number-one cryptocurrency.

It was as if we were in a race with Bitcoin for the cryptocurrency crown.

Bitcoin, the first decentralized cryptocurrency, was also the longest lasting, but it had weird beginnings involving its enigmatic creator, the so-called Satoshi Nakamoto, whose existence and identity have never been established. There was a lot of faith in play there too. Bitcoin's blockchain was designed so that only 21 million *virtual coins* would exist, and that had its own attraction in verifiable scarcity. Governments and central banks can print more money at any time but Bitcoin numbers stay put. (Bitcoin's value went from less than a penny in 2009 to more than $41,000 US in January 2021, having shot up by 300 percent in value in 2020. If I had bought 33 Bitcoin for the £10,000 I invested into OneCoin, by the spring of 2021 it would have been worth not much short of £1.5 million.)

The continuing legitimacy of Bitcoin was an insurance for my belief in Dr. Ruja and OneCoin and was very much part of our "OneCoin family story." I read articles in financial magazines, and these specialists acknowledged that cryptocurrency was the most interesting and exciting advance in monetary economics in decades. There was nothing to give me doubts, and if anything negative appeared about OneCoin I put it down, as we were told to do, as being the work of Bitcoin haters. If I had a doubting moment I'd say to Eileen, "You think something is going on here?" She'd come right back and say, "Nah . . . look at Bitcoin. We just have to stay invested." We were also comforted by videos of Ruja in action, explaining our path to riches, to what seemed to us like a land of milk and honey, paradise.

All her personal appearances across the world were recorded and circulated on the internet. She was a superb saleswoman, and I could only sit back and watch her on my laptop—with Eileen on the other computer tracking our OneCoin investments going up, always up and up—and feel better and better and better. Ruja's voice on her

2016 promotional tapes was like meditative music and calming, like one of those tapes that help you get off to sleep:

So what is the future of money? In my opinion, the future of money will be outside the banking system as we know it today. One of the most spectacular entrants that I've been following now for five years is Bitcoin; a cryptocurrency, the first cryptocurrency, the biggest cryptocurrency currently, and these people who created Bitcoin—nobody officially knows who they are—have my fullest respect for the innovation, disruption, and value creation that they actually did to the financial market. These people created something new and something really exciting. Bitcoin and the blockchain technology, which makes financial services independent from governments, independent from regulators even and independent from banks as we know them, is already changing the world we live in.

I'm not sure if this is politically correct to say, but emerging markets are out there—we can speak about Latin America, we can speak about Asia, we can speak about Africa—in all these regions, and we have people who are underbanked, unbanked, or just forgotten by the big players. Why? Because they're poor, because they have needs that are not that interesting in terms of the transactions, or simply because some of these people do not have proper documents. I have been in countries where people—every one of them—has a smartphone but no proper ID card. So how do these people bank? If you're an affluent customer, if you have a lot of money, the banks will fight for you— they'll give you cards for free, they'll do their best to make you happy; but the people out there, the mass customers, the ones who actually change the world, the ones who are working for the economy—these people are underserved, and I believe that cryptocurrency can change their life. If we manage to make cryptocurrency actually accessible to people out there who are smart enough to understand the smartphone—if we make it simple—we can become the next mass phenomenon like Google, like Facebook.

Gosh. That was Dr. Ruja speaking at an economic summit, all heavyweight stuff, and she was convincing me and millions of others that OneCoin was the next huge thing. A huge player. Google! Facebook! And all controlled and protected by the marvelous blockchain—which no man or woman could tamper with. I felt like a revolutionary, like I wanted to buy a red beret.

It was the message she was delivering at similar events in Dubai, Macau, Singapore—anywhere with an audience. You could randomly stick a pin in a map of the world and OneCoin would have a salesperson there in person or virtually.

Oh, there had been wee concerns, but the leaders of my One-Coin group were always eager to explain inconsistencies, which were dismissed due to us all being pioneers—soon-to-be amazingly rich pioneers—in a revolutionary new way of banking. With this digital currency the middleman was out and the profits were simply far larger. When in doubt, invest more—that was the message. We thought the ship had come in for us. It wasn't a lottery. We'd put our money to work as genuine investors.

And, like all true converts, during that summer of 2016 neither Eileen nor I wanted there to be any snags. If one of us had a question, the other would dismiss it with the logic of the true believer. Why would all those big-shot money people be involved with the *financial genius* Dr. Ruja if she wasn't the real thing? And all those who questioned her were only jealous because she was offering us, *the little people*, a chance to get on the money ladder. Over time we became more fluent in the language of OneCoin and came to know any detractors as "haters."

I could so understand that. I'd not just invested my dad's money into OneCoin, I'd invested all my emotional being. To me this was an answer to my grieving for my dad. He'd said I never had any patience, that I couldn't wait for paint to dry, but with Dr. Ruja I patiently hung on to the train of her couture gown. I happily nodded along as I was encouraged to keep promoting OneCoin, to keep adding investors. The OneCoin promotional video was on replay in my head:

OneCoin founder, Dr. Ruja Ignatova, was born in Bulgaria and raised in Germany. She completed both her master's degree in economics and a

PhD in law simultaneously in Konstanz and Oxford in only four years. Prior to founding OneCoin, Dr. Ignatova was the youngest associate partner at McKinsey—where [she claimed] she worked for various other high-profile banks, including the state-owned and Moscow-based Sberbank [which, in a move not connected to OneCoin, was sanctioned by American, UK, and EU leaders following the Russian invasion of Ukraine in February 2022], and was CEO for one of the Europe's largest asset management funds, managing 250 million euro in assets. Dr. Ruja has made it her mission to open the door for everyone, uplifting people all over the globe to be able to profit from the same opportunity as any highly knowledgeable or well-educated person with special knowledge in the field of cryptocurrency.

Positive stuff. In the group, it was forbidden to be negative. Every day we were bombarded with the message: *OneCoin is the world's number-one cryptocurrency.* When questions came up about Dr. Ruja or OneCoin, I was with them against the rest of the world. Critics were simply hordes of jealous people, the *haters*.

It felt like being in Scientology or the Moonies. There was no middle place. OneCoin became the religion of us investors, and our dedication to Ruja was extreme, the very definition of a cult member. In a cult, you *believe* above all else. In France and Belgium they took this to Satanic heights. Laurent Louis was a leader and promoted OneCoin "as a pure product of Satan to fill our pockets, thanks to a new currency, the OneCoin." The leaders were never anything but diamond geezers, people to be believed and followed, and like a good cult member I believed and followed. Leaders had an answer to everything, and somehow in this world everything they brought up became credible.

I can't explain why other than by saying that at this time any thought or concern about the credibility of OneCoin was absurd. And I was overwhelmed by the renowned financial specialists endorsing OneCoin and the luxury and wealth around Ruja. She'd celebrated her thirty-sixth birthday in May 2016 at the Victoria and

Albert Museum in London with a glamorous party, guests in ball gowns or black tie enjoying pink champagne, vodka, and sushi and dancing to a live performance by Tom Jones. There were effusive tributes, and more songs and hugs for Ruja from Tom Jones. It was an A-list celebrity event. What a star she was! When I watched the event I wished I was there. It was all more endorsement of what I'd done with my dad's money and with that of all my friends and family. I was anxious to invest because I'd seen her presented as an acclaimed financial consultant and, most of all, because she'd spoken at the Fourth EU-Southeast Europe Summit sponsored by the *Economist* magazine. I couldn't imagine that the *Economist* would host a forum with a suspect speaker.

Dr. Ruja had mansions around the world and was trusted with billions of dollars of other people's money. She was clearly doing the right things with it. I was happy to be a cheerleader and an enthusiastic investor, and the only wobbly moments for me at that time were when I was asked why I couldn't withdraw *real* money from my OneCoin account after the promised three months. It was showing more than £40,000, which was absolutely fab. My fridge was on its last legs; it had limped along on tender loving care, but even high-velocity TLC wasn't going to save it. Eileen made a pantomime show of smelling the milk every time she came for tea. I was keen to get some cash out to buy a replacement.

I asked politely, and thought Sally Losa came back quite aggressively. She made me feel a bit like an unflushed toilet.

I was taken aback by this, as she'd always been so sweet, almost cloying. Previously, it seemed my happiness was her only goal in life. I was concerned, being new to OneCoin, that I was making a mistake and putting my £40,000 at risk.

Was life going to mug me once again?

Sally was quite abrupt, even shirty with me.

I quietly said that the arrangement as presented to me was that I could withdraw money—cash, not OneCoin—after the set time. That was the contract deal as far as I was concerned. It was no panic for me, but I would have liked to get my initial investment back, as I was protective of what my dad had left me.

She questioned why I would ever want to reduce my investment and interest as the profits were storming in.

She was back to her all-smiles personality, and as she said that it made perfect sense to me. The more in my account, the bigger the profit. I let it go and put it to the back of my mind, but it wouldn't stay put. I excused such rattling concerns as me being overly cautious, to acting like an anxious old woman about it. This was a brave new world. I also wondered aloud why the company's bank accounts changed several times a week, and they told me that banks couldn't handle the huge amount of money managed by the organization. Well, of course, how could an old-fashioned banking system cope with this miracle? We were pioneers, part of a new financial world.

The promise was that we would get at *our* riches selling their One-Coin profits on a public exchange for *real* currency. The niggle—and it was only that—was that there was no date for opening the exchange, after which we could withdraw some of our profits in old-fashioned hard cash and get an actual return on our investment.

Still, those all around me insisted that Dr. Ruja, the messiah of our money, was hard at work on that. I was more worried on the timing because Eileen had stretched and gambled on a high-interest loan of £2,000 to invest, and if she didn't pay it off quickly with the interest it would cost her £6,800. Any time we brought up questions and asked for a time frame on a real money return, we were both hit with the marketing and the razzmatazz of the OneCoin family. It was a simple message during the online webinars: What you've invested is just a tiptoe into the big money, and you need to put in more to fill your boots.

The assurances were magnificent. These were experts in multi-level marketing, which I'd had experience in when trying to earn some extra cash by selling aloe vera–based products, operating sales like an Avon lady. In an MLM you get a percentage of your sales but so does whoever recruits you, and it can pay huge dividends. And it was the potential profits that were being explained to us. The excitement and promises just became more and more extravagant. They were fluent in happy-speak. OneCoin representatives raved about the great profits to be made in cryptocurrency. I was content with the answers. My questions had only raised question marks about me.

Cleverly, I was invited to an event at Wembley Stadium, in London, on June 11, 2016, where Dr. Ruja was the star turn. Gosh, I wanted to see that; I even dreamed about it. We were told to order £15 black OneCoin T-shirts before the event, pick them up and pay for them in cash, then change into them before entering Wembley as part of a giant team. Sadly—and I think it was the stress of all the excitement—I had a relapse with the ME and I knew I didn't have the strength to go. Yet, with the genius of OneCoin's multi-level marketing, a dazzling package of the event arrived electronically: I watched the Wembley event live on Facebook sitting in my bed. There was footage of the crowds of fans, almost all in their newly bought One-Coin black T-shirts, flipping through the merchandising market stalls outside Wembley. Oh, I wanted to be there. I could sense the excitement of what was going to happen next. Two Finnish OneCoin "stars" warmed up the video viewers and the thousands in the crowd.

One had a cute line of patter as he brought on Sebastian Greenwood, who gave an Oscar class in enthusiasm before introducing his "sister." And then . . .

Dr. Ruja paraded onto the stage of a packed Wembley to a rock star's reception of cheers and applause. Her floor-length red ball gown glowed in a blaze of pyrotechnics as flames shot from the stage to Alicia Keys's "Girl on Fire." Immaculately groomed, her necklace, brooches, and dangling earrings sparkled. I thought that if cash dressed up for the evening, this was what it would look like.

All this money, the rent of the place. Wembley Stadium! The cars, the red carpet, the glamor and glitz, the dazzle of lights and diamonds, the—I don't know—the money involved. No one would spend that for nothing. Amid all the hoopla, I was name-checked as a OneCoin success story, which sidetracked any of my doubts. It's another marketing tactic: If she can do it, so can you. You don't have any choice: It's the "Come on Down!" moment when Dr. Ruja's cheerleaders choose someone to applaud. In my head I was up there with Ruja, strutting my stuff alongside her. She was winning me over with every syllable she uttered. What kicked off crowd hysteria was her announcement about a new and upcoming blockchain that would be "the Bitcoin killer"—and see OneCoin become the market leader.

I'd learned so much more about how cryptocurrency worked, for myself and to be able to explain to my investors, to those on my downline, whom I felt very much responsible for. Most were like me, trying to build some future security for themselves and their families. The message about Ruja was that she wasn't doing it for the money alone, she wanted to make economic history. I watched in some awe as Dr. Ruja spelled out her "vision" at Wembley: more than one million merchants and ten million members into the network. Within it, OneCoin would be surrounded by support groups: education (OneAcademy), exchange (OneCoin Exchange), community (OneLife Network), partnerships (Merchants), payments (OnePay), currency trading (One Forex), investments (Fund), charities (One World Foundation), applications (CoinCloud), and entertainment and games (Coin Vegas).

I'd joined a new world. And I spread the word to everyone I knew or met. What many stumbled with was the "mining" aspect of One-Coin. I explained it was nothing like my dad down a pit shaft for the day digging coal. Instead of money produced by countries, conjured out of thin air, digital currencies are coined not by governments but via algorithms—they're "mined." Mining happens electronically when a computer solves a complex mathematical problem. The more coins mined, the more difficult the math becomes for the computer. If you think of it like the book *Treasure Island*, it's like searching for the gold without a map: You have to work bloody hard to solve the puzzle. The more mining, the more coins, and vice versa.

All that collective energy makes the coins really secure, as it would take an unimaginable amount of computing energy to hack the system. The bonus—if one was needed—was that the idea of digital currency is that the blockchain means there can only be so much of it. Scarcity inflates the value, and for me, OneCoin had only gone one way: up.

Watching the Wembley event, any concerns I had went out the window. Again, I was comforted that Ruja was a woman, and that was important: a *woman* giving people like me a chance to leapfrog the banking system. I was one of the forgotten in the past, but now I was emancipated. This was a gender-equal world. We were winners. And there was testimony to prove it.

Harry and James Stone appeared on stage to tell their word-perfect story of how they'd had nothing, were destitute—and here they were a year later in designer suits wearing Rolex watches and the shiniest of shoes, driving Porsches with their private number plates. Dr. Ruja was such a star she had a fleet of luxury cars and a $12 million super yacht, *Davina*. I was mesmerized as I sat in bed and watched the event. I was there in fully focused mind, if not body—especially when Dr. Ruja and Sebastian, who I was told was her right-hand man and a flamboyant OneCoin entrepreneur, were on stage at Wembley. My dreams weren't dreams anymore. The two seemed so devoted to the future of OneCoin. This was so real, they were real. If they could spend millions on a business presentation like that, what were the limits?

Ruja had arrived in my life on an internet cloud, magically, like on a flying carpet. I thought my prayers had been answered. I was ecstatic, and my heart was thumping. I'd never known such happiness. My dad's gift was safe to infinity—which seemed to me to be where OneCoin was going.

FOUR

Manic Mondays

felt like a tycoon.

Even when I was stuck in my bed with the bedroom blinds drawn to stop the light stinging my eyes.

I had the edge in this digital business. In my marketing career I had learned multiple computer skills—I was the one who was asked to fix the bugs in the office IT system—so I was comfortable working online, with webinars and Zoom conference calls. To me, it was like being around an office table. And with my ME, having on and off days, fighting to find the energy to get going, being able to operate from my iPhone was a real bonus. My iPhone was truly a lifeline. Even lying in bed, I talked, I texted, I emailed, and I signed in to online meetings. My greeting call was *WhatsApp?* It wasn't difficult to see why new investors were attracted: Like me, they saw a once-in-a-lifetime opportunity. If I or anyone else hesitated, the friendly OneCoin cheerleaders above us would point out the millions who had missed out on investing in Bitcoin. It was an ongoing cavalcade of self-acclaim. The online seduction was passionate. There was never a *good* moment, always a *brilliant* one; never a *great* package of OneCoin investment, only a *classic opportunity*. And like everyone else, I didn't want to miss out on what seemed to me to be a fate-inspired new life. I had had the money at the right moment to join the OneCoin family. It seemed like a close family, as they were always in touch.

James and Harry Stone had 200,000 members in their downline, and we were told they earned £450,000 per month. They were very much the head boys in my zone. Beneath them in the hierarchy was Jack Cadel, who controlled Sally Losa and John Munero. Sally and John were my mentors, always there to help. I always want everybody to benefit. It made so much sense to me, the *family* implication, that we would all profit from one another's endeavors. I was this one wee Scottish person running my OneCoin chain and there were thousands more like me all over the world doing the same.

Forget Santa's little helpers—we were Ruja's. The money was pouring in every day, every week, every month. It was a flood of money going to Ruja. When I had questions, it was Sally and John who would set my mind at rest. Or almost at rest. There was always a niggling doubt. Anyway, I'd been constantly told that doubters were simply people who didn't understand the absolute genius of OneCoin and its deified creator, Dr. Ruja. I wasn't going to be one of them. To make more money—money, not OneCoins—I was encouraged to bring in new members on commission. I was a willing evangelist for this currency, which was going to save the world for folk like me, people who spent their time on the sidelines, shoved away by the sharp elbows of the men in suits. Sally and John had maneuvered me into a group where I could earn a commission and they would benefit too.

I thought I was helping everyone I spoke with. They told their friends and their families, and my little group grew and grew. Young or old, well off or poor, we were all keen to better ourselves financially in some wee way. All the small investments added up to £250,000. And that included investments—a mixture of Pro Trader, Trader, and Starter packages—I'd bought for my immediate family. I got one for Lee, one for Fiona, and one each for my two grandchildren. My sister, Adele, who'd initially been a OneCoin skeptic, became a convert. With money I owed her for the lawyer's bill for handling my dad's estate, she asked me to buy her grandson a package. The family that invests together sticks together. We'd all had our turbulent family times, and it was the OneCoin family that was helping us bond and, in time, reward us.

All this money was coming from my group in a tiny corner of Scotland. Part of the marketing was to grade OneCoin representatives by a precious stone fandango. It had a crown diamond sitting at the top, and dancing around that were a black diamond, blue diamond, emerald, ruby, and sapphire in a sliding scale. I was Miss Sapphire—I sounded like a men's magazine pinup—before I went on to be a double ruby for the business volume I'd created, cash that came almost entirely from Mitchell Thomson's efforts. I'd told people about the cryptocurrency in order to spread good news, not to earn a commission when they bought into it.

I felt I was being lady bountiful to all my wonderful friends and family. There was a very complicated compensation plan—much like multi-level marketing—which I had no interest in. That's how many people made a lot of their money: by recruiting other investors. They were the salespeople recruited by OneCoin because of their ability to create the excitement and encourage more and more investment. And they were good, very good. Much of my life was now spent on OneCoin webinars, which I could handle no matter how my ME was treating me. The webinars attracted people from around the world who were intrigued by cryptocurrency. Many of them were annoyed at missing out on Bitcoin and nagged by FOMO. I'd explain if I joined a webinar that Bitcoin wasn't a match for OneCoin. What we were dealing with was a cryptocurrency that could be used to buy and sell, to trade globally and instantly. It was a solid investment.

There *were* tricky moments. OneCoin bank accounts were closed or changed. Dates for exchanges, for retrieving some of my investment, were put back. But it was like a stuck traffic light: In those moments, it wasn't green but it wasn't red either. It was always amber in the OneCoin world. Action was always *imminent*.

And it made sense there would be teething problems in a revolutionary new banking system. Who could doubt that? We were warned about those who might challenge OneCoin. The hierarchy was always alert to defend OneCoin against attack by those they branded disillusioned Bitcoin followers—the haters.

But there were enthusiasts too. On one webinar a nice-sounding guy named Barry took part. He'd been invited by an American he met on Facebook, but as a fellow Scot when he heard my accent he felt more comfortable talking to me. He'd lost a lot of money when his property investments in Cyprus had gone badly wrong. He was fighting to come back from that loss and was attracted to digital currency, having seen Bitcoin jump in value from a few cents to, at that time and as Barry put it, "a couple of hundred quid." What Barry wasn't comfortable about was sending money via an American connection, making a "faceless" investment. He hooked in with me—amazingly, he lived not too far from me—and in time bought packages for himself and his children worth about £15,000. Like all of us investors, he uploaded images of his passport and other ID details of himself and his children, to comply with the OneCoin "Know Your Client" (KYC) investment requirements. The OneCoin family's data bank was becoming very rich too.

Barry told me that he wouldn't have bought his first packages if not for his direct contact with me. He was perplexed when he bought a £5,000 Tycoon and had to send his money to Dubai. The High Street banks, we were told again, could not keep pace with this new financial movement, with the future. The United Arab Emirates (UAE) were part of the future of banking the unbankable, a secure place in which to do business, like the free ports of Singapore and, from 2014, Luxembourg. We were told to remember that we were financial revolutionaries. Which is how my friend Wes, who then lived near Liverpool, also saw himself. He was looking for an investment and was pointed toward OneCoin. When he went on a webinar, he discovered I was a member. He was delighted when we talked, and he told me his story:

I'd been in the networking industry about seven years, and when another networker, a role model in the industry, told me about OneCoin I was happy to have a little look. I inherited some money from my grandmother and wanted to do something positive with it. I was impressed and confident about it when I discovered Jen was involved. I trusted her, knew her to be a good person. I also respected the financial skills of the guy who first told me about OneCoin. I watched the marketing promotions, these guys in expensive suits and flying around in fancy cars. They said it would take twelve months and you're going to be the richest you've ever been. What wasn't to like? I was keen and I drove over to Manchester to meet Sally Losa and John Munero, who were Jen's immediate connection. We had coffee at a lovely cafe in Manchester's city center. I was only going to put a little bit of money in but, honestly, they absolutely blew my mind. I was looking to make some serious income, and they sold me on OneCoin. I went immediately for the £5,000 Tycoon package. After our coffee and chat, the two of them walked me to a branch of my bank in Manchester and waited with me as I transferred the money from my account direct to their account. I was excited to be involved, I couldn't wait to do it. In all I invested £9,000. I have a big presence on Facebook, so I preached the OneCoin gospel and brought in more people and much more money.

Because I had been unable to happily accept the applause when they announced my name at the Wembley event that had galvanized the OneCoin world, I was strongly invited—ALL MEMBERS MUST ATTEND—to be honored at the second Scottish event in a suite at the Glasgow City Hotel on June 21, 2016. It wasn't a big hullabaloo. Eileen and I took our partners, as well as Fiona and Lee. I was in touch online with Barry and Wes much of the time, and they were under orders too; to my delight, I saw them in person at this gala gathering. The agenda was the same—upbeat if, sadly, no bagpiper—and the Alloway Suite in the hotel was packed. It was congratulations all round and telling people to bring investors for a quick sale. Again, I was presented as a success story. The OneCoin operation was in overdrive. It was a controlled evening, and following it Jack Cadel invited us, including Wes and Barry, to dinner at a restaurant on

Sauchiehall Street. We all paid for ourselves in sterling, but Jack was making a point about the future spending power of OneCoin. The owner was part of the OneCoin network, a merchant who would soon take payment in our revolutionary new currency. Soon you could pick up the check in OneCoin.

Now, I'm the sort of person who likes to know exactly what is what. If I didn't understand something or thought it unusual, I would question it. This, I was told, labeled me as "being difficult." And that irritated me a little. I was an ardent believer, I only wanted clarity on some points. Difficult? *Moi?* I shrugged it away. When we were on our webinars, we would always be alerted to haters, the OneCoin detractors. These people were dismissed as disenchanted Bitcoin investors or those who'd missed out on the wonderful Dr. Ruja's initiative. They were jealous of her staggering success. The greatest sin was buying Bitcoin or any other digital currency. That was treachery. No one, especially Ruja and all the sparkling diamond leaders, would ever soil themselves by investing in Bitcoin. The OneCoin mantra was to not ask questions or your account—my £48,000—would be frozen. Worst, you'd be kicked out of OneCoin. When I first saw it happen to someone I was shocked and asked why they were being punished for simply asking what seemed to me like legitimate questions. The answer was that they were not true investors but trolls, haters, and that was why they were removed.

To me, that was terrifying, as my OneCoin account was my family. I'd been lonely during my life. I didn't want anything to go wrong, to be alone again and to lose connection with my dad's money. Which is why, when our leaders insisted on us attending a OneCoin "training" weekend seminar in September 2016, Eileen and I happily took the train down to London. We were still buzzing about this life-changing new adventure. When Eileen had taken out her loan with its outrageous interest, she'd arranged for a few hundred pounds extra to cover her expenses for the trip to London and the hotel. One-Coin wanted to teach us how to sell more OneCoin. The Saturday was a smaller event run by my direct "colleagues," Jack Cadel and James and Harry Stone, who were carried to the stage like some conquering generals. Their job was to boast about the fortunes to be made from OneCoin. They gushed about making *multiple six figures a month* as they paraded around in their sharp suits weighed down by bling. They spoke about a "Dr. Zafar" from Asia who operated in the UK from his "Diamonds Club" training OneCoin promoters and recruiting investors. He worked so hard on behalf of us all that he had supposedly earned $749,000 in one day. All the promoters repeated Ruja's boast that OneCoin had more than three million investors around the world. For our day we were told to try and bring potential investors, people who hadn't invested in OneCoin. It was the same hype, the same motivation—not the full Ruja fireworks, but still the great selling of dreams. For us OneCoin champions it was like a dose of adrenaline. We also heard again the Stone cousins' story of going from nothing to millionaires.

One of the early cheerleaders of OneCoin whom I embraced was the gregarious and always flamboyant man I knew as The Dutchman. Behind the image he was effective, enriching himself and Dr. Ruja's empire by millions and millions. He approached the selling of OneCoin as if it were shampoo or diet pills—with the big advantage of not having to spend money on packaging.

He proved to be a multi-level marketing genius, and with OneCoin he was earning more than $2 million each month, two-thirds of it in cash. He introduced us that weekend to Ed Hartley. Ed Hartley was everything I imagined an American salesman to be. He was so pleasant, with such a friendly nature I felt he should be wearing a ten-gallon hat above the amused smile that was always across his face. He instantly struck me as the sort of man who could make any concern you had disappear like a magician's trick. I liked the way he was promoting OneCoin: You knew he was selling, but he came across as an honest broker who believed in his product. That Saturday was a tough day. The pressure was on for us to get out and spread the OneCoin gospel. Eileen, who was waiting for a transplant and was operating on 10 percent or less kidney function, was walking with a cane and tired easily. She managed amazingly to keep up, but, as I said, we were both still running high on hope. Much of that was focused on the presentation by the much-heralded Ed Hartley. Anticipation kept us lively.

Ed Hartley certainly had a reputation for delivering the goods on stage. He'd been doing it for more than three decades and was in the top 1 percent of earners in the network marketing industry. He'd run teams of forty thousand people and created more than $6 million in earnings. I could see why Dr. Ruja was keen on him. He'd just come aboard, and his reputation was such that it was a big deal that he had chosen to visit the UK on one of his first OneCoin missions. He was much more subtle, but he had that special something. People ended up standing on chairs. He was a motivational speaker, and a good one at that.

He really lifted that room, and when he left people had smiles on their faces and it was in general a happy atmosphere. He inspired people, but he was a fairly gentle giant of a human being, tall and impressive. The event went on for hours and hours, and it was past eight o'clock when it eventually finished. Eileen and I were both drained, but we talked on about Ed Hartley and how good his turn was. But we were so tired we went straight to bed because we had to be up early for Sunday's training day. That was the first day they made a song and dance about OneCoin and OneLife being all about *education*— "profit" and "investment" were now taboo words. I thought I was hearing Tony Blair—education, education, education. The speakers came on, emphasizing education again and again. I remember looking at Eileen and asking, "What's this all about?" As they trained and enthused us to sell, sell, sell, they said it was for compliance reasons. That didn't seem right to me, because previously the pitch had been enthusiastically about investment and profit. I learned that investments presented as an "education" package could get around international laws and currency exchange regulations. It was presented to us as an innocent way to circumvent red tape and allow the usually unbankable a chance to improve their lives. On paper, they would "buy" the education package and get their OneCoin free.

It was a long and tiring Sunday. We'd only had two fifteen-minute breaks: It was hard work making an *easy* fortune. We were bombarded by different speakers, people showing us how to promote OneCoin; this was all for people who'd already invested in the UK and there was a huge emphasis over hours and hours on this type of training. It was mind numbing—and then Ed Hartley came on about four o'clock in the afternoon and again he raised the ceiling, boosting it with his energy.

He walked in with a smile that enveloped the room. He had the place laughing—there hadn't been much laughter going on before he arrived; it was more like a dull drone. He brought cheer and made us think he could change our lives. He talked of people having belief in themselves and to have dreams and go for them. He told inspirational stories enhanced by his smile and his charismatic energy.

I was feeling pressure from my immediate OneCoin contacts. They didn't see me as a team player and they resented me for that. I'd had a bust-up with Mitchell Thomson, who was rude to Eileen, and I had to walk away when we had words about something daft, a OneCoin logo. "I never want to see that man again," I told Eileen. And I didn't.

Sally and John frowned upon me for asking questions, and my heart kind of went with Ed. I thought: "Here is a good soul, the sort of person to follow. And I know he's a busy man, but I'll reach out to him for help. Maybe, in time, he can become my mentor, my guide in OneCoin." I was thinking of my downline of investors, since we didn't have John or Sally to ask any questions. I broke off with them. Eileen and I felt they weren't telling us the truth, that they were sly. Something did not feel right at the time, so we began not to trust them. I was so sickened with them, and Eileen became the go-between, but she wasn't as ardent and direct as I am with questions. I needed a line into somebody to get updated information. And out of all of them, I felt I could trust Ed, that maybe he was the knight in shining armor. I wrote to him later, and he responded immediately, on November 3, 2016, saying he was traveling in Asia but would be in touch as quickly as he could. He was keen to help. I looked forward to meeting up with him again.

Despite dutifully turning out for "training," when I got back home from London I heard yet again that I was being "difficult." Sally put my "minder," Harry Stone, on to me. He told me he would like to offer me a "gift": that he would purchase another Tycoon package for me. When I asked him why, he said it was because when I joined, Sally and John had placed me on the wrong side of their networking structure, which meant I was placed on their investor-only side and not the networking side of their structure. With Mitchell Thomson on my downline and networking his ass off, it meant that Sally, John, and James and Harry Stone were not receiving the high commissions they would if I was in their networking structure.

When I joined I said I only wanted to invest, so they placed me in their weak commission side. (There are two legs in this structure, a left side and a right side, and one of these sides is called a weak leg and the other is the qualifying Business Volume [BV] leg—the side that brings in their commissions.) Harry wanted me to move to their BV side, and he told me, "Jen, this is a unique gift I'm offering you. It's another Tycoon package for you and your family's financial future. It's a blessing, and I hope you accept it. That way everyone wins, it's a win-win situation."

It did not feel right in my gut. I said to him, "Harry, thank you for your kind offer, but I need to think about this. I'll come back to you in the morning with an answer." All night I thought about it and how I felt so uncomfortable with what he'd said to me. In the morning I still had this horrible feeling that it wasn't right and it didn't sit well with me at all, so I thanked him but refused his offer. Within the hour Sally messaged me, and despite swearing to myself that I'd never speak to her again, I asked for a Zoom call.

I wanted to see her as we talked.

Her face flickered and then focused on my computer screen. She had fire in her eyes. I acknowledged the connection and waited for her to speak.

She came over loud and clear, and the message was that I was behaving despicably. Everyone was doing everything to accommodate me, and all I was doing in return was creating problems where there were none. I was being *difficult*.

She told me how ungrateful I was by not accepting Harry's gift. I looked her straight in her virtual eye and told her exactly what I thought about her.

I felt that she and her partner were not being straight with me. I wasn't getting any updated OneCoin information—we didn't know what was going on. I told her I knew about the sly move she had attempted so she and the others could share in the commissions that Mitchell Thomson was bringing in.

I said I was going to keep asking questions. My concern was for all the other investors in my downline who were as much in the dark as I was.

And she was doing nothing to help. *She* was the *difficult* one. She looked away from her screen and said nothing.

I said, "I think we are done here now, Sally, don't you?"

I shut down the Zoom meeting, and that was the end of that conversation, and the so-called gift was never raised again by any of them. This meant they could not get those commissions they wanted so badly.

You can imagine that after that it wasn't so nice to communicate with them. I thought they were simply being greedy, no more than that.

I left the call with a shrug of my shoulders. Eileen and I had each other, and we talked ourselves out of our doubts. We were winners. Eileen still needed dialysis; her kidney count was down to six, which meant they were barely functioning at all. Yet, with all our health problems, beneath the daft dreams, we both believed that OneCoin offered us a *serious* and secure financial chance at a new life. And to my surprise, I was a big deal. Mitchell Thomson had switched his network to OneCoin's MLM system so that he could earn commissions and was now bringing in piles of cash—but on my downline. My status, inadvertently, was such that I was offered three nights for free in a five-star hotel in Bangkok. That was to be my honor.

Not that generous an honor. I still had to buy the roundtrip air ticket to Thailand and pay £100 for entry to the OneCoin Second Anniversary Event on October 1, 2016. I wanted to bring Eileen with me, but her doctors told her such a trip was too risky, so I decided to go it alone. I was beating myself up with stress, concerned about what had happened with Sally Losa, John Munero, and Harry Stone, accused of being "difficult" for not accepting Harry's gift. I'd also just received the all clear after a breast cancer scare. My body was in a relapse. How the hell was I going to get to Bangkok, stay there three days, and then come back? I didn't have the energy to pack a suitcase. I was in pain and my body muscles were exhausted. My doctor advised against the trip because of my health. I had to lie in bed and wait to get better.

I'd recently made friends with a girl named Clara Tuffin through OneCoin. She was very entrepreneurial—she had that spirit and she loved OneCoin. I'd sat up many nights as she told me her domestic problems, and I offered as much sympathy and advice as I could. I had been there. She kept talking about the Bangkok event. She was desperate to go. I scrimped and saved up £300 in living expenses for Clara and gave her my airline ticket in return for her relaying back to me information and news for the investors in our group.

She needed to renew her passport, so I paid for that and she was off on her adventure. She knew I was fed up with Mitchell Thomson and John and Sally and how difficult it was for me to get information for the group, to know what was going on with our investments. She was delighted and promised all—that she was going to *do it for the team*—and before takeoff she sent me a video of her trip to the airport, all smiles and thank yous. When her feet hit the tarmac at Bangkok it all changed. I got not a word of news, and eventually photographs of her out with John, Sally, and Mitchell arrived on my computer. Nothing on the buildup to the event. Behind the scenes, she had left my group for John and Sally's—like they tried to do to me to cash in on Mitchell Thomson's business volume. I couldn't believe I'd been so naive. I felt heartbroken that she had treated me the way she had. She'd played me for an absolute fool.

Her fourth and last night in Thailand was Clara's fiftieth birthday, and she was on her own tab, as her new pals had left Bangkok. She sent me a video message from one of the city's swankiest hotels. She'd filmed her deluxe room and bragged how gorgeous it was and what a wonderful time she'd had and how much she was enjoying spending the night in such extravagant surroundings. I watched from my sickbed. I couldn't believe the sheer audacity of her sending me this video now that she was on her own. The previous days she was so nasty in communications that this came at me like a bolt from nowhere. The video was really a dagger to the heart, something that still sickens me so much. I never knew people could be so downright bad. I sure was naive before I joined OneCoin and met all these horrible characters that ran through the very core of it.

On the film Clara was chatting away from five-star luxury surroundings, a true heaven, especially compared to her home circumstances. Before she said goodnight, she told me the money I'd given her had paid for her room.

FIVE

Remembrance Day

I was irritated by Clara's behavior in Bangkok, but that disappointment didn't spread to Dr. Ruja. From my bed I watched a OneCoin Facebook live stream of her presentation. She was fabulous, resplendent in a floor-skimming purple dress as she walked to the stage to the echo of Sebastian's wonderfully enthusiastic introduction. She announced something historic was about to happen.

The buildup was immense as Dr. Ruja told the yelling and whooping crowd how they were part of the greatest financial revolution since a caveman bartered the first wheel. Ruja could have read out a telephone directory and received applause. Everyone was hysterical.

Such was the noise and the bamboozling math with which she blinded us with her trickery and promised the impossible. She revealed on stage, projected on a massive digital video screen, that there was to be a new blockchain, which would increase the number of OneCoin available from 2.1 *billion* to 120 *billion*. She had discovered a new algorithm that enabled OneCoin to have the largest blockchain in history! Then, twenty-one minutes and twenty seconds into her speech, Ruja announced to much fanfare that the new blockchain had been activated. Amid yells of joy, she then said every investor's coins would be double. I could all but sense the sheer delight of such a happening, the vibration of the news throughout all my group. Double! For me alone, that was £96,000 value in OneCoin. Happy days. The security around this news in Bangkok was tight. Senior OneCoin leaders were invited to join her in a larger conference room before the event began but were met by bodyguards who took away their mobile phones. Ruja spent the time speaking with them and in deep conversations with global bankers. She also said they would be joining the American market as soon as the proper paperwork was complete. We OneCoiners *were* going to rule the world. I thought she looked a little nervous on stage, but who wouldn't with such a phenomenal breakthrough? And we'd heard she was going to have a baby, although I couldn't see that lovely telltale bump.

I was so wrapped up in the video. Everything seemed to be so on track. But on the screen there were flash messages from an outrageous American posting notes that OneCoin was a fraud. Here was another person we'd been warned to block. I'd had my moments over the bank accounts being closed and getting some cash back, but this idiot bloke was off his head. Bloody nuisance. He was another person jealous of the success of OneCoin and its investors. Later—after being presented with what were, to me, his crazy claims—I remembered the name of this highlighted *hater:* Tim Tayshun. I was so brainwashed, I wasn't ready for what he was saying. I'd been told to shut out people like Tim Tayshun, that they were mentally unstable haters. I may have been upset by Clara's antics in Bangkok, but this bloke would have been immolated if he'd heard the words I was calling him. I was fuming.

He was more than five thousand miles away in California, in San Juan Capistrano, a beach community south of Los Angeles. Tim Tayshun was appalled by what he witnessed at the OneCoin show at Wembley in June 2016, when my name was announced as an example of a happy success story. There were other people honored along with me, but Tim would pick out a few names, note them down, and, in time, attack. He'd started studying OneCoin in March 2016, by co-incidence when I first invested. As a cryptocurrency enthusiast, he'd been contacted through Facebook to check out OneCoin for a man who wanted to invest. Almost instantly, he was certain it was a fraud: "I knew it was going to be the biggest scam in the world," he claimed.

He believed OneCoin was fake and that people like me who were investors and inviting others to join were just a bunch of, as he put it forcibly, *fucking scammers.*

Now, I will curse and swear if I want to, but my first reaction to Tim was: "How dare you? I am not a scammer."

He first found me through Facebook and left messages—I don't have them as Facebook removed them—because I'd been singing the praises of OneCoin on the site. He'd spent the previous eight months howling online that OneCoin was not legitimate. He had, as he said, been *rattling cages, antagonizing and disrupting* the OneCoin global operation.

His tactic, as he'd done during the Bangkok event live feed, was to post links to information that would discredit OneCoin and Dr. Ruja, our Boudicca-like leader and, to many of us, the female emancipator of us disciples of digital currency.

How dare he?

"You're a fucking scammer."

"No, I'm not."

"You are disgusting, you scammer."

This was all happening suddenly, out of the blue, late on the Friday night of November 11, 2016, when he'd popped up on Facebook Messenger: It was a cold evening, and I still feel the chill of it; and it was the beginning of what was a battle over a long weekend from hell. It's dated and time-stamped on my mind. I was horrified. I told him, "You don't even know me."

He went on bombarding me with messages saying he could prove it was all a fraud. He sent information, but by this time my head was spinning, and I couldn't even look at it. I went to bed and got up the next morning and Tim was still up—California time—and still at it, still attacking me with messages. He kept it up all Saturday and then went to sleep, and when he got up again it was Saturday evening for me and early afternoon for him and he was starting again. He was not giving up. He was like a dog with a bone. I even phoned Eileen. "I've had a terrible weekend," I told her. "I've got this guy going at me." I couldn't really talk to her or explain much. I was all on edge with this going back and forth all the time. I was so worked up and angry with him.

When I woke up on Sunday morning he'd started again. He'd sent dossiers of material, but I couldn't read any of it. It was late Saturday evening for him, and more messages were dropped. I was fed up with him, and it was getting very nasty going back and forth.

I messaged again: "Fuck this. I've had enough. I want to see you on Zoom, I want to see you face-to-face. Here's the link, you're welcome to join me. I'll be there."

Tim came flying into my view, his face filling the computer screen, a big American man with a big deep voice: "Dr. Ruja is a fraud. She's been convicted of fraud . . ." And off he went. "This is a criminal. Do you understand what I'm saying? I'm not an asshole, okay? I understand what I'm talking about. I've investigated OneCoin. I understand OneCoin more than 99.999 percent of every member there."

I was livid. This was nonsense, and I asked him, "What is your name? Is it Tim? Is it Timothy? Is this Tim Tayshun? What's your correct name?"

"Timothy Glenn Curry."

I was furious. "Why are you messaging me as Tim Tayshun?"

"That's a nickname I've had for twenty years."

We had a back-and-forth, and I told him that when I joined One-Coin in March, I knew about him then. I'm embarrassed by the argy-bargy now—I have it all on video—but at the time my voice held nothing but contempt for him. I had taken a look at some of the material, and he'd predicted people would commit suicide over OneCoin. I told him I thought that was disgusting. But he was patient, and he tried to explain.

When you and I got into cryptocurrency we got into it for the same reason: Cryptocurrency can bank the unbanked, bank the more than 2.5 billion people who don't have the means to be banked. I promise you this. All you need is a cell [mobile] phone. Now, OneCoin is a company that prints its own money. There is no government in the world that is going to allow a company to do that. OneCoin is not registered anywhere in the world as a money services business. In order to print money you have to have an MTL, which is a money transmitter license.

The reason cryptocurrency in general can accomplish that is because it's decentralized. It's not a company, there is no CEO, there are no employees of any cryptocurrency in the world other than OneCoin.

This upset me, and I was on edge anyway. I was worried about the time, as I had to be at a baby shower in Glasgow. I was looking over at my television, which was on mute but showing the time and the Remembrance Day parade. I was already late. But the information was hammering at me. I explained that I had ME and I had to take the information in small bites.

It gave me a moment to come back at him about Bitcoin being hacked, and that in turn put him back on the attack: Bitcoin had never been hacked—although exchanges, virtual banks that hold digital currency, had been. Bitcoin as a protocol had never been hacked. Tim forcibly but patiently, like he was talking to a toddler, explained what cryptocurrency banks should or should not have.

I was wild. I loudly told him, "I chose to go with a centralized cryptocurrency because I felt secure where my money was going."

"You're foolish. I'm sorry," he responded, "but Ruja's a criminal."

But I was back at him: "Do you realize that the messages you have sent me have been abusing and harassing?"

"I'm only trying to help you."

My cheeks were bright red now. "You're not helping me, you're upsetting me. I'm a single parent."

"And you've invested ten thousand dollars in this and you're going to lose it."

"I'm happy with that. I made a decision. If I'd bought shares, any investment, if I chose to buy gold . . ."

"And you'd have more chance of winning. This is a scam."

"I do not believe it. One hundred percent in my heart I do not believe it is a scam. All that you have written to me, it's abusive and wrong . . ."

"If I see a woman getting her purse robbed on the side of the street, I'm going to tackle the guy that's robbing her purse."

"I've got a caring heart. I care for everybody—everybody, not just my family . . ."

"You've been deceived by professional criminals, professional con artists. You have to understand you've been deceived."

"What you have to understand, Tim, is that you have your opinion and I have mine."

"It's not an opinion, it's a fact."

"You say it's a fact. Well, see, in that dossier you sent me last night, you made up a fact about a specific number of suicides that will happen!"

"There's going to be at least a dozen suicides that will happen over OneCoin. I promise you that. Absolutely promise. I swear to God. I bet you one thousand dollars, one thousand dollars."

"That's absolutely shocking that you can say that."

"This is the biggest scam in the world right now. Do you understand that?"

"After I read about the suicides, that was it for me, I couldn't read anymore. That discredited it."

"Think! Dr. Ruja was convicted on twenty-four counts of fraud, or was she not? Let's start there."

"I haven't read that, but let me tell you, everyone in life can have a bad run and can go bankrupt . . ."

"She was the treasurer of another crypto con—$50 million went that time, and this is much bigger than that."

I became even more embarrassed. "What about all those entrepreneurs, the big guys in life, who have tried something big and it hasn't worked? You're going to knock them for that?"

"She's a fucking scammer, she's a fraud. She was not businesswoman of the year two years running in Bulgaria—the title doesn't exist! She hired a PR person who specializes in . . . Listen, I'm telling you the truth . . ."

"I'm going to say something to you here: People have got a lot to say about Dr. Ruja—"

"She's not a doctor, it's a fucking lie, she doesn't have a PhD."

"Where's your proof in the pudding?"

He responded, "You're looking me in the eye? We're having this conversation right now. Tell me what you need, and I promise that anything I have claimed I can back up with facts. I'm not a blogger. I don't get paid to write shit . . ."

"What do you do this for? Why do you do this? You say you want to protect people, but you're actually hurting people."

"That's number three. There're three reasons I'm doing this. The third reason is to protect people. The second is to protect what I want to do in the future. I'm not entirely altruistic, okay? The first reason is because this shit is going to make a bad impression on all of crypto-currency, as regulators are going to say OneCoin was a billion-dollar scam, OneCoin was similar to Bitcoin. OneCoin is not a cryptocurrency. There is no blockchain, and I can prove it."

Very definitely I told him, "Yes, there's a blockchain, Tim."

"How?"

"I can prove it to you."

"Well, prove it to me."

I paused for a moment. I was shaken, and I had to get out of this conversation. "You know what? I've got to go. You prove it to me, send the information to me, and I'll see it when I get back. You prove it to me . . ."

"I'll fucking prove it to you."

"You need to stop harassing people, and you need to stop upsetting people because this—"

"I'm not willing to do that because you people are scamming money and this company is going to collapse."

"This is obnoxious, I've never met anybody—a person like you . . ."

"I don't give a shit . . . it's a fucking scam."

"Just the way you are speaking, it's disgusting. And people are to take you seriously? Oh, come on."

I closed the connection. I struggle now to watch that video. How could I have been so certain? Because I wanted to be? I was dressed like an Avenger that day. I remember looking in the mirror: I had on a black high-necked sweater, a black and white skirt, and black knee-length boots. I looked the very image of a strong, confident woman. But I was shaking—and now I can't say if it was anger or fear.

I was worried about being late to the baby shower for my daughter-in-law Fiona's sister. I had to take a train, but there were no taxis to the station as the weather was hellish. I was traveling with one of Fiona's friends, Jack, and we had to walk through that right cold wind and rain.

I was so late after all that with Tim, and when we got to the station our train had been canceled because of the severe weather. I was so fed up by that point. I was really flustered, pissed off, and Jack being Jack said, "Shall we get something to eat, Jen?" We went to the Corner House, which I like. I talked to Jack throughout over pâté and haddock and a strong cappuccino, which I needed. I remember those little details but not a word of what he said or what I said. My mind, my whole head, was somewhere else. All that kept echoing was: "*Dr. Ruja is a fraud.*"

After that early lunch, I *had* to go to Eileen's, which was only a five-minute walk away. I phoned her to say I had lots to tell her and to "have the kettle on." When I'd talked to Eileen after Tim first came at me, she'd told me to block him. She said he was a worry and to cut him off, as I didn't need the aggravation. Something stopped me doing that, I don't know what. Distressing as it was, I wanted to hear him out. I did—then abruptly stopped direct communication with him. I do know that video talk was the beginning of the journey into OneCoin hell, when all my nightmares and worst fears rained directly down on me like stair rods. It was only later, when I found myself even more surprised to be alive, that I truly realized I was up against a global conspiracy operated by some criminally powerful and ferociously determined individuals, people from Eastern Europe with names like cavalry charges.

SIX

Fake!

I haven't told you about Gordon. He's one of the reasons I'm able to tell you anything at all. I first saw—well, I first *heard*—Gordon late one Sunday afternoon at the end of January 2012. My sister, Adele, and some of our girlfriends decided I should get out of the house. I was feeling better at that time and learning to cope, to function and control my ME a little. We didn't go far, only to the local pub where a karaoke session started up. When I heard this wonderful voice, I turned my head to the stage and there was Gordon with his beautiful smile.

He still has it but, as you can imagine, it's not been easy for him to always put on a brave face for the past decade. A few years older than me, Gordon had been married for many years and separated for five years when we met. A superb craftsman, a skilled carpenter, he'd worked hard all his life, and after that pub meeting we started dating. We had sort of clicked together. He also got on with the rest of my family. Elle was starting to crawl and walk a little when Gordon and I met. He became part of the family. He helped me with my father, with the most difficult and intimate tasks, when dad was dying. When he had to help Dad with his toilet he told him, "It's okay, Bill, I've done this before."

My dad eyed him:

"No wi' me, you havenae."

Gordon has been there throughout, but when my dreams about Dr. Ruja and OneCoin began to fester I shielded him from them. I did the same with Lee and Fiona. I didn't know what to think and I didn't want them sensing the worst, especially around Christmastime in 2016. Tim from California was bombarding me with information, and I read and read; I desperately wanted to understand what the hell was going on. I couldn't ignore it. It was a torment.

I tried to stay positive, and the OneCoin leaders kept bouncing back my questions again and again, labeling Tim a "hater" and a "Bitcoin discontent." As they said that, I could hear Tim's voice bellowing and echoing: *Fake!* He'd gone on and on about all legit cryptocurrencies requiring a blockchain. He force-fed me information. It was hard to digest, like all unwelcome truths. He went on and on and on that an incorruptible computer record of all transactions was needed to prove that the currency is sound. The blockchain technology makes it impossible to counterfeit new currency and guarantees there is a finite number in circulation. Without the security of the blockchain and the fiendish mathematics, which I hope I properly explained earlier, the price can be rigged or faked. Fortunes could be made or made to vanish on a whim, depending which button is pushed, what numbers tweaked. When I'd first invested, Gordon told his older son, who said it might be a scam. When Gordon mentioned that to me I dismissed it, saying I wouldn't invest in scams. Me? I was in my bed much of the time and didn't talk about OneCoin much with Gordon. Doubts were now doing somersaults in my head. It was an absolute hellish time for me. At home I went into a cocoon. I was only confiding my qualms to Eileen. The thing is—and I know you will understand this and not think I was being silly—I didn't want Tim's accusations to be true. It wasn't as if I'd gambled dad's money, I'd *invested* it for the future. After all the bumps on the road, One-Coin had to be the real thing, something I could trust. And there was a crowd of us involved, including Barry and Wes. Yes, Wes. He explained what unfolded:

I was moving smoothly in OneCoin, building teams and building fast, and by March 2017, I'd already brought a lot of people into the company. The rumors started with people saying it was a fraud, it was fake, but along with my team we spent hours and hours defending the company on Facebook. I had no idea a blockchain was needed, I was pursuing the vision I was sold. I was just hell-bent on achieving my goals and I walked blindfolded into this dreadful trap. My partner, who worked in networking, tried to warn me but I wasn't listening. I wasn't listening to anybody. I only started to pay attention at a OneCoin event when I was told in detail that OneCoin had no blockchain, which meant there was no safety valve and it could all explode at any moment.

When I came back from the event, I was really worried about it, because Jen is one of my closest friends. And because I knew how much we defended OneCoin, I was thinking: "Oh my God, if I broach this to Jen I might lose a friendship over this because Jen had so many people she cares for and looks after properly." I had to tell her. I called her on a Saturday morning about 7:30 A.M., I was that anxious. It was March 4, 2017. I started out with: "Please don't hate me . . . but I've got something to tell you." She listened and started realizing the truth, and she told me, "Look, I'm gonna make a cup of coffee. I'll call you back." And, of course, she did. We're both emotional people and we ended up really upset that weekend. How are we going to tell our teams? What are we going to do? I decided to go on Facebook Live, I was so angry about it. I decided to out it, and I did a couple of these Facebook Lives, naming names and torching all the OneCoin claims and promises.

A few days later this American guy Tim's name came into my inbox. I'd been defending OneCoin to him in the past but he wasn't there to gloat. He messaged me with a warning:

"Bro, you need to stop what you're doing because your life will be on the line."

It was scary for Wes. And it got scarier for all of us. Wes took down his Facebook Live posts but we agreed we had to alert our groups. The concerns about the lack of a blockchain were solid information from a group of blue and black diamond leaders—despite their daft jewel ranking, they were informed executives bringing in millions and millions of dollars—who'd heard this at an event in Asia. I already had red flags flapping in my mind when Wes called that morning and I told him my worries. Wes continued putting pressure through Facebook and I sat silently in the OneCoin group watching and listening to what was being said. Eileen and I had started to wake up. She became our fifth columnist on the groups, alert to everything being said and proposed. I felt a bit of a traitor, since it wasn't honorable to people I believed were my friends, but it was clearly necessary to protect those who had trusted me.

This was when I truly began to question the wonderful world of Dr. Ruja. Who the hell was she? I went back to my OneCoin beginnings and Rex Charles. He wasn't the confident self-styled "wealth strategist" I'd first encountered. He now had doubts and was downsizing his involvement with OneCoin. Rex had seen that Anonymous, the internet group of cyber chatters, hackers, and activists, was raising issues around Dr. Ruja and the OneLife Network where investors and merchants "trade" in the cryptocurrency. I was close to losing it with Sally Losa on some calls, but I tried to stay on focus to get information. I wanted to know what they knew. Here are my text messages from March 8, 2017, as they appeared on my WhatsApp, and how Sally replied to me:

Jen McAdam (JM): We really need to know facts about any corruption as we don't want any part of that if it's true. Rex said he has doubts and will no longer be promoting OneCoin. He said he sent a list of questions to James and Harry before they left to speak to Dr. Ruja and he has asked others [I never thought to ask who the others are] but he still isn't getting any answers to his questions either. Today he said he has faith in OneCoin still but unsure to network it still. That chap from the Anonymous group has said that within the next three weeks to two months OneLife Network will be shut down and any cryptocurrencies in the UK which are not regulated will be shut down also. He also went into other things that are way beyond me and said that [redacted] has already had three death threats. He also said that City of London Police are on this and have been for months. Arrests will be made. I'm very scared, Sally. It might not be true, but I'm really scared for everyone. What're your thoughts on that?

Sally Losa said it was "worrying" and that she'd try to find out what was going on. She called me the endearment "hun" in her message, but that didn't comfort me.

JM: Okay, would appreciate the answers, the phone isn't stopping with people upset. We need answers, even an update from James and Harry, for everyone concerned.

She said she was meeting with Harry and James the next day, and would let me know what they said. She asked if I wanted to talk to them at that moment.

JM: I'm happy to join a webinar when they update everyone on the whole team. I'd appreciate if you update me after your meeting with them tomorrow. Thanks for getting back to me, Sally.

The next day:

JM: Hi, Sally, any updates yet?

Sally said the Stone cousins were running late. She said they'd not met. She asked me, "Do you have any proof that I can show them, hun?"

JM: Ask them if there is a blockchain and where it is. Why do they feel OneLife Network may be closed, hence why they are building in a new business opportunity? What concerns are there within the OneLife Network? We who have bought packages and also have a team so rightly and honorably deserve answers. We need truthful and honest answers now; that would so help at this moment in time for everyone. Looking after your teams is what they so need right now. Yes, there is a lot of evidence to back it up, which I've read and heard with my own eyes and ears, but this is not from a lot of people that have contacted me and leaders within the last five days. James and Harry should speak to the leaders close to and above them.

That was that. No more communication from Sally Losa apart from a voice message warning me off, forwarded from the European leader who boasted of earning $725,000 a month since beginning network marketing in Spain in 2007. He was close to Sebastian, having worked with him previously, and his links stretched to Panama. From there OneCoin planned to "invade" South and North America. There were to be branch offices, as it were, in Bogotá in Colombia and in Miami. I was all over the place. I was told not to believe anything from outside the OneCoin family. I was still grasping on to hope, grabbing for it like a falling trapeze artist.

The warnings kept arriving on my phone from throughout the OneCoin network. All the way from the bottom to the top. They were all making it clear through direct or intermediary messages that I was to be very careful. The warnings were stark: Stop asking questions or your account will be frozen. I'd seen that happen and that was the last thing I wanted, as my OneCoin account was my family's future. It was a cult, and in my mind I *was* a cult member. I had feared being on the outside—but what was really going on inside? It was like a torrid conspiracy thriller where you have to flip back through the pages of the book to find the clues you missed before.

The only answer from all of my immediate leaders was that anyone disputing the sanctity of OneCoin was a *hater*. I was given the runaround. What made me furious was the high-handed manner in which they said the "mining" details were private, details investors like me "didn't need to know." They denied that the UK authorities were investigating OneCoin—those were more rumors being spread by the ubiquitous haters. With all this, I was still not convinced about anything. The only thing I knew for certain was that I was confused. And angry. And on the brink of hysteria worrying about the futures of all the many people I'd encouraged to buy into OneCoin, people I believed I was helping create a golden future. I couldn't sleep, and through the wee hours I researched online, trying to find evidence, answers, anything that would stop the mental ache. Wes was still piling on the pressure on social media, but there was the thundering sound of silence from the UK OneCoin leaders. Except I did hear that Dr. Ruja was mad at me. Well, vice versa.

I messaged Jack Cadel saying it wasn't acceptable and I wanted answers about the blockchain and how and where it operated. He came back with a voice message on March 10, 2017. He addressed the questions I'd posed to Sally Losa in my text, starting with: "Are the City of London Police investigating OneCoin? No." He then offered this oxymoron: "We make a lot of money per week without letting anybody know about it. We have not kept anyone in the dark." He then went on in a monotone: "Is there a blockchain? Okay, Jen, there is a blockchain. Questions like this were asked even when the company was first born and they were proven."

He said that Dr. Ruja and her goons kept this confidential for security reasons, to protect the blockchain.

With his next words, Jack fell over himself in an attempt to explain away all the concerns. He said in the voice message: "And plus, as an application, it doesn't need a server behind it. So it's our blockchain technology, an SQL server with a database. Anything else maybe only Ruja can answer."

He was telling me by voice message that OneCoin was operating through an SQL server, a common database management system that could be accessed by anyone. I knew from my IT training that this "blockchain" was nonsense, that I was dealing with some awful bastards. I was in my bedroom—I'd only that minute risen from bed—and hearing this voice message took my legs from me and I fell to my shaking knees on the floor. This was the moment I knew 100 percent that OneCoin was a fraud and we'd lost all our money.

Even now, I feel that sharp, heavy, choking pain in my throat and heart. It's still so very raw. I felt a fool. I was ashamed.

I could no longer deny what was going on. I finally realized the truth. I'd learned through research and from the information battering I'd gotten from Tim what a proper cryptocurrency requires. OneCoin had none of it, no protected third-party algorithm to authenticate it as a legitimate cryptocurrency, verify it as something to buy or sell. Dr. Ruja created the currency priced at what she felt would sell it. But it was valueless, it didn't exist. You couldn't even play Monopoly with it. Even toilet paper has value, and look what we do with that. I couldn't speak. For the first time in my life I knew what being dumbstruck felt like. My emotions went into orbit, shock, disbelief, dismay. I was gagging on my words, choking on my guilt. I wasn't so worried about myself but about all the people who had followed me into OneCoin. A quarter of a million pounds! In my world that's the sort of money you buy castles with. Maybe it was pennies for Ruja, with her illicit billions, but for me and the people around me that was a fortune. What was galling was that I couldn't get any reaction from all these OneCoin people who had told me they were my best friends forever.

Wes and I confronted them about the lack of a blockchain. It didn't matter. We put pressure on James and Harry Stone, who'd helped to introduce OneCoin into the UK. We were going to shake the leadership until somebody answered us. I immediately tried to warn my OneCoin world. At the same time, Sally Losa, John Munero, and the Stone cousins went on promoting OneCoin as the number-one profit-making digital currency. I found something deep inside me and I knew I couldn't accept this nonsense. I felt responsible for all the investors, especially those who'd scrimped or sold assets to get the money to buy into OneCoin. I was composed by now. I'd arrange a whistleblowing webinar. That was my strategy to alert all my network. I took charge of myself. I asked Wes to bring his group online too. We had a message to send.

I made contact with Mitchell Thomson and told him he couldn't go on promoting and selling OneCoin. We had to sound the alarm. He told me I was a horrible person and I didn't want to see him succeed. I got nothing but nasty messages from him:

> *I am very saddened that the money from my Tycoon Plus went into your direct sales earnings when I could have signed up under a leader like Sally who actually cares about helping people in a selfless manner. She helps me and Clara Tuffin. You have also been extremely disrespectful to Sally and I think you need to go have a long hard look in the mirror. Why not go spend some OneCoins and buy a nice house on the other side of the world—or buy yourself a Mercedes and sell it if you want some flat currency right now.*

He said he was working with John Munero and Sally Losa and told me not to contact him again. He said I was unpleasant, and I was this and I was that. I've never seen or spoken to him since. It was difficult enough for me to confront this mess, but constantly having the door slammed in my face stung. It didn't get better. I noticed Harry Stone was removing me from the WhatsApp leadership groups. I hurriedly posted a message to Jack Cadel's group to notify members of the issues and concerns I'd discovered over the weekend—the fundamental shock being the lacking blockchain. I had to get in quick because they were intent on transforming me into an invisible woman. I was a heretic. On the horizon, the troops were gathering.

Wes came on the line and said he'd been talking to Tim "Tayshun" Curry, the crypto enthusiast and compliance professional. Well, I had a moment. "Ohhhh, my God, Wes, I have to tell you I blocked that guy in November. He's a mad American." As it turned out, he was not so mad. He was flamboyant and fun, but most of all he was a dedicated follower and fan of cryptocurrency. So much of what I'd come to understand about the OneCoin operation came from the dossiers of data Tim sent me, which had taken me more than three months to study and digest. His resolve was to go after any person or company who abused and threatened the future of digital currency. He ran a bar-restaurant in San Juan Capistrano, and as you'll have gathered from our earlier confrontation, he was not shy about coming forward. That made two of us, but after our bust-up conversations I was hesitant about contacting him again once I'd uncovered the truth about the blockchain. Wes broke the ice. Unbeknownst to me, Tim had been talking about my involvement in OneCoin with Lynndel Edgington, a fraud scheme investigator who ran Eagle Research Associates in California and later Arizona. An activist, Lynn is known in the scam-busting world as "Eagle 1," and he has worked with the FBI for more than twenty years. He lectures at police conventions throughout America and beyond. When I reopened communications with Tim, the two of them were already intent on bringing down Dr. Ruja and all her associates. They were in constant contact with the FBI and also with the UK fraud squad. I had thought all things policing in London involved Scotland Yard, but the City of London Police are very much their own entity. Based not far from St. Paul's Cathedral and a walk from the Thames, they go after white-collar crime, as money is the other river that flows through London. Tim's contact with the City police was DC Kieron Vaughan. He passed on his details and said he would brief him before I made contact. It all felt extraordinary. I'd had a turbulent life, but that was domestic—I hadn't been calling the cops, never mind the FBI. My closest contact with the authorities before all of this was trying to get the council housing department to fix the plumbing. I felt like Dorothy in *The Wizard of Oz*, right out of my comfort zone with a wicked witch snapping at my heels.

My savior, I prayed, was to be DC Vaughan. And he tried to be, but he had to follow procedure, which dictated actions that in 2022 I still cannot comprehend.

I messaged him on March 27, 2017. I got a positive response but we didn't immediately connect. We played telephone tag for a couple of days, and you can sense my frustration in this email as I tried to hurry him along:

> Hi Kieron, I'm in a situation where I also have a team and they require updating also as I have updated them regarding my concerns about OneCoin. This is people who I've also invested and a few over £20,000 each. I dearly want to keep them updated as just now we are lost on what to do next.

We spoke the next day for about an hour and a half. He confirmed that the UK was investigating OneCoin as a criminal enterprise. He told me they believed it was a Ponzi fraud scam and advised me not to invest any further and to tell others the same. He didn't say how determined they were in making inquiries, and at the time I didn't think there might be reason to ask that. Apparently, the American authorities were also looking into Dr. Ruja and OneCoin, and the FBI was involved. That was the final nail in the coffin. The need for me to explain all this to my group became urgent. I had to warn them. I spoke to anyone I could, including a man I knew who ran another big OneCoin group in England. He was concerned but, like so many investors and recruiters, didn't seem to want to accept the truth. Wes and Barry alerted their contacts, and Barry filed a complaint with Action Fraud in the UK. As promised, I sent more information to DC Vaughan. Most important, I announced an urgent webinar for 9:00 P.M. London time, April 5, 2017:

> !! Please share and invite anyone who has purchased OneCoin packages especially within the UK. After a 90 minute telephone call to the London City Police Fraud Investigation Unit last week, I can confirm that there IS a massive Police Fraud Squad Investigation within the UK and they believe also that OneCoin is a massive Ponzi Fraud Scam!!!! They are also working alongside other FOREIGN POLICE FRAUD Investigation Units. Updates from the telephone call with DC Kieron

Vaughan last week WILL BE SHARED on the webinar, plus much, much
more. This is very SERIOUS and EVERYONE needs to call the UK
Fraud Investigation police unit now!

Of course, I'd decided to remain silent in the OneCoin groups
to gather as much information as possible, but Eileen was treated
disgracefully when she asked a few technical questions and was told
she'd be banned. This was very scary for investors, because if they
were removed they had no connection to their investment or information. The OneCoin operation had no telephone contact and rarely
responded from its email address. The only way an investor could
get information was within the groups. This was the platform One-
Coin used to filter down misinformation, where the brainwashing
began and where the fear wrapped around you. This was where the
financial dream slowly turned into a financial nightmare, and by this
time it was all too late. It was the perfect place for me to burst Ruja's
OneCoin bubble. I had to be quick because I knew it would be only
seconds before I was removed. I was still very much in shock and you
can hear me stuttering on the video of that webinar, an event and a
day I will never forget. I still can't believe I did it.

Before I went full whistleblower on the webinar, Tim was keeping Lynndel/Eagle 1 in the loop, and he was briefing the FBI about
what was going on. Lynndel later told me that Tim talked to him and
questioned how I would react—if I would even go ahead with the
webinar. He wanted to know if I "had the balls." Tim had dealt with
people brainwashed into groups like OneCoin and didn't know if I
could handle it. Lynndel said he believed I wouldn't be intimidated,
that I had it in me. He was right—I wasn't taking it anymore. But so
far I only knew a tiny bit about what I was dealing with. Tim agreed
to join me on the webinar and share his knowledge. Unbeknownst to
me, he invited two other cryptocurrency experts, Norwegian Bjorn
Bjercke and Crypto Xpose from Finland, who in public hides his
identity, as well as members of the Anonymous network. There were
many people behind the scenes on that webinar. John Munero and

Sally Losa and other leaders were present, and I believe Ruja and Sebastian joined too. They wanted to know what was going on. At that minute they'd taken more than £100 million out of the UK—small change compared to the cash cascade from the Americas and Asia—but with me rocking the boat there were future billions at stake. Dr. Ruja's take at that time was upwards of $20 billion.

The OneCoin world was tuning in that night. In the queue of attendees before we began, I noticed a man nodding his head to the beat of the webinar background music, Sam and Dave's "Hold On, I'm Coming." I remember that so vividly, as it brought a very much needed wee smile to my face. I played DC Vaughan's taped voice telling me that the UK fraud office was conducting a criminal investigation into OneCoin. Throughout the webinar I could see Bjorn's head nodding all the time, and I thought he was a victim and he wanted to speak. I opened up his microphone, and he explained who he was and how he believed OneCoin was a crypto-gangster network. This was when I first heard those words "criminal network" in such a way it terrified me. I don't know how I kept calm. I was breaking into pieces with fear and shock. As he spoke, I noticed that many of those who had not identified themselves on the webinar were leaving the stage—the person I thought was Ruja included.

She knew about Bjorn Bjercke. My IT background was enough for me to realize that an SQL server couldn't protect a ten-cent investment, but Bjorn was a world expert. Here was the twist: He was the IT genius Dr. Ruja tried to recruit to legitimize OneCoin by belatedly creating a blockchain for it. Bjorn soon taught me to know my enemy. He provided my first detective lessons.

SEVEN

Battle Stations

I wasn't sleeping well before the webinar, and my goodness, my nights didn't get any better following Bjorn's revelations. If I got off to sleep, I'd fall into nightmares of running down alleyways to escape masked gangsters. I'd suddenly wake up in a tremor as evil monsters hovered over me. They'd tear off their masks and it would be my OneCoin leaders snarling and pointing at me, screaming, "Hater!"

Wide awake, I'd sit in bed, fire up my laptop, cradle my phone, and use them both to contact victims around the world. Time differences meant nothing. I was awake for every message alert, every buzz and question, every scream for help. Being awake and listening to the stories of outrage was its own horror. Other victims had their nightmares. They were upset and worried, especially after what Bjorn had revealed about the mafia men allegedly backing Ruja. There was fear of the consequences of making a noise. Some said they would wash their hands of the whole enterprise, shrug off their losses, and remain silent: *omertà*, as the Italian branch of the mafia would say. Many warned me to write off OneCoin as a bad experience. What could we little people do up against a network of fraudsters and gangsters? Others were embarrassed to be part of a fraud. It was hard enough to admit it to themselves, never mind anyone else; many weren't going to tell their family and friends or colleagues at work. We were all asking ourselves, *How could I be so stupid?*

OneCoin didn't like me attacking them. They were quick to go after me. A OneCoin diamond leader broadcast on the WhatsApp network: I heard Jen is on Section 29. The men with the white jackets are coming soon. This sniping was the start of many accusations that I was crazy and would be locked up under the UK's Mental Health Act.

I was *crazy*—but in a good way. I was mad as hell, and there was no way I was going to "shrug off" the abuse of my trust.

As a group, we victims were in shock, but there was a camaraderie of paranoia, and I believed we could help each other. I set up a WhatsApp OneCoin victim support group, but it filled quickly—WhatsApp only allows 257 members in a group—as the stories of doom and disaster increased. I arranged more groups. It wasn't only investments and money that had been lost, but livelihoods and, in many cases, lives themselves. I was running on empty but I couldn't ignore the commitment I felt. I was weakened but, even asleep, I had my phone in my hand and if it pinged I had to look. I learned that even a kind word from me in my little corner of Scotland might save a life. Victims seemed to identify with me—I was one of them. There was also the pain when I never knew if the victims I was in touch with survived. Following that April webinar a message appeared on my computer screen late in the evening from a man in the south of India. He and a group of thirty-two other victims were planning a suicide pact. They had lost their futures to OneCoin. The contact telephone number showed on screen and I called it. It rang. And rang and rang. I called all night and for days afterward. I got no answer then and I never did. I still think of them every day. All I could do was gather more and more information about Ruja and OneCoin to show people who were still investing what a scam it was. Information and social media were the only weapons myself, Tim, Bjorn, and Crypto Xpose had. There were people who sold their houses, sold their land, entered a lifetime of debt to buy into OneCoin. OneCoin waited until farmers in Uganda sold their livestock and crops, then went in and talked them out of the cash that put their families' food on the table. I'd never heard so much misery, and so very often the stories of beaten-down hope had me in tears. Bjorn was always asking me to slow down, but he soon learned I got more energy from every victim story I heard. He told me that even after the webinar I went through a realization process. I spoke to him for hours and he explained most people in my position descend into denial and eventually apathy. I reacted in quite the opposite way. I had empathy for everyone who had run aground around Ruja and most of all those in my network. As the misery heightened, so did my work. I was happy to work all day, every day, often from my bed, to stop Ruja.

Someone hit back, posting pornographic images on the victim support group sites. The images I saw were disgusting, which did what they intended: shock and upset those looking for help, particularly the older and more religious victims. They couldn't stand the blasphemy and depravity and left the forums. It took a strong stomach if you encountered this filthy stuff. I won't detail it to you, for I could not be responsible for implanting even sketches of such images in anyone. With WhatsApp you could remove the offender but the posts themselves stayed in place. I contacted WhatsApp to report what was happening, but they never replied. One WhatsApp account wasn't going to accommodate a world of victims, and in time I opened up a Facebook group to allow the thousands of victims to be supported on one platform. We opened up groups for individual continents and countries: America, Asia, Australia, New Zealand, Europe, Africa, Pakistan, and India. I monitored them all. The pleas for help came in—almost as quickly as the death threats to me. I alerted Police Scotland to some of the threats. Officers came to see me, but I don't think for a moment they comprehended the scale of what was happening. Crime around my neighborhood is more misdemeanor than felony, wayward behavior after too many drinks on a Saturday night. In time, I endured vile verbal sexual abuse and intense intimidation. I was upset, but what had I to lose? OneCoin had taken everything from me. I was concerned about my son and his family, that they might be hurt or used against me. I told my son how worried I was. He told me, "This is who you are,

Mum. Don't stop, fight on—you have come this far. Don't stop, Mum, fight on." That was good to hear, but I don't think Lee or any of us knew then the power of the evil on our doorstep. Later, when Lee and I were in his car and "Dreams" by Fleetwood Mac came on the radio, neither of us said another word. Tears blinded me, feeling my son's pain, his dreams shattered into pieces. Afterward, he sent me a note with no words, only the link to Lanie Gardner's beautiful cover version of "Dreams." Yes, thunder only happens when it's raining.

I fought to become immune to the constant messages of "Fuck you and your dead daddy . . . and his fucking money" but the threats of rape and notes like "You won't be around much longer" never stopped being disturbing. I hid my worst fears from all the family and disguised them as well as I could, but in doing so I tormented myself even more because I was bottling a lot up. Bjorn monitored it all and said he was fearful for my safety, as well as for Tim, who was also more public than him or Crypto Xpose.

Although we'd broadcast far and wide that OneCoin was a fraud, it wasn't shut down. I felt frustrated, angry, and pissed off. I suffered sickness and sadness thinking about all the other victims, especially the ones who were suicidal but not saying a word. I don't think we will ever know the true extent of the suffering of OneCoin victims. What we do know is horror enough. I settled in my mission to get justice. I didn't volunteer to be brave. There was no one else stepping forward, and I wasn't going to let Ruja off the hook. I became a fraud investigator using my bed, my laptop, and my mobile phone. Well, phones: I had to keep replacing my phones because I wore them out—which is what I intended to do to Ruja.

Wes and I went for OneCoin on Facebook, but they blocked us; on WhatsApp, but they blocked us; on Telegram, but they blocked us. Wes became a target for abuse as well, and in the middle of all this his twenty-one-year-old son had to have a heart transplant. Understandably, he had to escape from the OneCoin mess. But let Wes tell you how he saw it at that moment:

When I walked away, Jen kept going and going and going. I don't know if anyone in OneCoin ever cared how she felt but she battled on. She had death threats but she kept on. And evil messages. I had a big following on Facebook with people from all over the world, and when Jen and I started the alarm bells that March–April in 2017 there was a post about me being a pedophile. I'd only been with my partner for a short time, so that affected our relationship with me not able to get close to her two daughters because they were fourteen and sixteen at the time. My inbox was rammed with death threats from OneCoin followers who wouldn't have anything bad said about Dr. Ruja. They wanted to silence us and could do that by destroying us in public. Even when I stepped back, Jen was there for me during my son's successful operation, crying our eyes out some nights, and I encouraged her to step away too.

It is very, very dangerous, and with all the things that happened with Jen, I begged and begged her to stop. She never would. She's completely selfless. I continue to be amazed and impressed how Jen kept it together at that point and became such an advocate for the victims of OneCoin. She took a massive part of her life to do this for all the people who were betrayed, and somehow she needs to be looked after.

That was nice of Wes, and he was correct, for after my conversation with DC Vaughan and the revelations that OneCoin was part of an organization known officially to law enforcement as the Eastern European Criminal Network, I did need looking after. I had gone full throttle looking for answers, but I'd stopped listening to my body. I forgot to manage things.

I'd escaped any relapse until the pain I took one afternoon in my chest. Gordon came home from work and I could hardly breathe. He didn't know what was going on. This was a shock. I was standing there unable to move from the pain. I was resting my head on a kitchen unit when the phone in my hand rang. It was Eileen. "I can't talk," I said to her. "I'm in so much pain."

She shouted, "I'm on my way!" And she was, just like the Seventh Cavalry.

Bless her, she got a taxi, and when she got to my place the pain had me doubled over and every breath I took felt excruciating in my chest. She dialed 999 for an ambulance. The paramedics arrived like a SWAT squad. They gave me morphine for the pain but that didn't stop it, so they gave me a stronger dose, which eased it and allowed me to get to the hospital. The doctors ruled out a heart attack proper but said it was the fibromyalgia mimicking a heart attack on my chest cavity wall. The doctors asked me if I was under any stress, and I thought: "STRESS! If you only knew the stress I am carrying right now." I didn't say that for fear of not being believed; they might think that I was off my rocker, mentally unwell and imagining these extraordinary happenings. The doctors said it would likely happen again and to always call the ambulance. I'd need morphine for the pain—and you never know, it could be the real thing. It was a difficult time. I couldn't stop searching for the truth about OneCoin, but I knew there was a health risk if I pushed myself too hard.

I was so lucky with Gordon and Lee and Fiona. Gordon was always there for me, coming up with tea, cooking dinner, and giving me the strength to fight on. My family knew my body was raging against me, but I didn't share any of this with the other victims.

Maybe that's what did keep me going and kept me alive, giving me a focus away from a body that wasn't too well. I'd get so frustrated being stuck in my bed, unable to get down the stairs and being so reliant on others. I knew they loved me and it was not a trouble for them, but I beat myself up nevertheless. And I was fearful to tell them about the gangster element, because they'd think Al Capone would be chapping the door.

Many people wonder why I didn't walk away from OneCoin and Dr. Ruja with all the criminal connections. Why suffer such heartache—literally in my case? They ask me, "Were you not scared?" The answer is that ME prepared me. When you've been bedbound, imprisoned, and in excruciating pain day after day, month after month, after a time there's not a lot that can frighten you. When you've had to ask yourself if you'll ever get out of bed again, the thought of Ruja and her goons threatening me wasn't so terrifying. I was making it personal with her. With Ruja, I looked back at my life and saw that since I was a toddler I'd been running away. I decided to pick that wee girl up in my arms and tell her, "We're not running anymore, honey." I was so tired of hiding from the people who wanted to hurt me.

I was now fully aware that the OneCoin phenomena was only that: digits on a screen, Monopoly money that could only buy toytown OneCoin packages. The real money was hiding elsewhere. It certainly wasn't being paid out to investors; the opening of the much-heralded and long-promised exchange that would allow OneCoin to be turned into cash, dollars, euros, pounds was still "on hold." Even the more dedicated OneCoin investor-believers were agitating about that.

While I was gathering a resistance movement against Dr. Ruja, she was jetting around the world, selling her vision of new banking for the future, hopping from New York to London, Macau to Dubai to Singapore, filling out arenas, pulling in new investors. OneCoin was still growing fast.

Dr. Ruja and all the others at the top of OneCoin were making so much money they had to pile it up in cash in offices and apartments in Bulgaria, Hong Kong, Dubai, and South Korea in preparation for it to be washed through America and Europe. Ruja had boasted of being on five continents, operating in more than 180 countries, and for once, she was telling the truth: The world was her target. And her monetary laundromat. The eventual destination for much of our money was an international bank haven where secrecy of business and banking are absolute, and you can hear the silence. Bank accounts are not numbered but internet coded. My money, like most people's, probably went the long way round, maybe by suitcase or bank transfer, laundered through New York and California banks, Europe, Southeast Asia, India, the Persian Gulf; millions here, more millions there.

Sometimes the money circulated among European banks, was withdrawn in small bills, deposited in a Western Union office, sent by the platform over the Mediterranean, received in cash by an intermediary in Dubai, and finally deposited directly into the OneLife sanitized account. That's where the real money went, and it was then transferred back through Singapore and Hong Kong into America, going through US banks coast to coast. Truly, it was a financial soap opera, with America as Ruja's laundry basket.

It all seemed so out of my world, and the fearsome news of violent gangsters being involved was the biggest worry for me. I talked about it with Eileen, but she's a fiery wee thing and wouldn't take nonsense from anyone. She was up for a fight like any good Scottish foot soldier. Gordon was supportive, but his focus was always on me and my well-being. Sometimes I think the whole OneCoin thing went over his head—or that's the way he wanted it, as it was the only way he could cope with the frenzy around the house day and night. But my son, and Fiona, and their children?

I got Lee round for a cup of tea and a chat after work one day. I looked him in the eye and told him all about the perils of OneCoin. I explained I was concerned about his family's safety if I continued going head-on against Ruja and her nasty pals. He was as reassuring as he had been before the mafia entered the picture. "Oh, go away, Mum," he said. "You're not going to stop now. No one else has taken this on. You've got to be careful, but I know you won't stop."

One night when I'd been nagged to take a few days away from monitoring the group, a text trail arrived showing a young man was suicidal. Desperately, I tried to reach Mohammed, a member of an Asian OneCoin investment group. He wrote to this group:

I humbly request you all to do something! Or the last option for me is SUICIDE. I know no one get affected by my absence.

A fellow investor replied:

Hahaha, rest in eternal peace as we enjoy our OneCoin.

I tried to join Mohammed's group but, being Jen McAdam, a hated and taboo person in the OneCoin world, I was booted off before I could message him. I posted a message on my own networks:

> You said you are feeling suicidal. Can you talk with me please? I do understand how you are feeling. Please chat with me, Mohammed. Please, you are not alone even though you may feel you are at this moment in time with your thoughts. We have many OneCoin investors from around the world who also feel as you do but have found strength and support with the OneCoin victim support groups. Please do not take your life because of OneCoin. They have taken our money but they do not deserve our lives.

I tried and tried to make contact but with no success as the hours went by. It was late into the night and Gordon, bless him, was concerned for he knew how easily and quickly stress could fire up an ME attack. I'd doze off a little but snap awake and be on the phone again. He kept asking me to try and get back to sleep. He murmured to me, "Jen, you can't save everyone."

"I can try," I replied.

EIGHT

The Witch of Wall Street

With the help of my new friends, I began to swap information with authorities, including the City of London fraud police and the FBI. Our team—Tim, Bjorn, Crypto Xpose, and myself—shared everything, including the death threats. The other three were by my side virtually, and I leaned on them from the beginning—and I still do, for the fight is not over. We've been our own detective squad on a round-the-clock schedule, with Tim operating in a time zone eight hours behind me. None of us got much sleep.

In the early days of my battle with Dr. Ruja, there was so much information for me to comprehend. The details ricocheted like gunfire, and evidence of one piece of villainy led to another, as it became clear to me that my financial loss was small change in the ongoing fraud zipping across countries and continents. I discovered how sophisticated and connected my tormentors were. I believed Dr. Ruja and Sebastian, the son of a British journalist and his Swedish wife, would be found to be professional fraudsters. OneCoin was not their first rodeo. Their mission seemed to be to fool all of the people all of the time. They'd fooled me, and I was shaken by how skillfully they had achieved that.

With much great help from American scam-buster Lynndel Edgington, I was able to put together a picture of Dr. Ruja. This was a woman with a steel spine. The only weak spot I noticed was that she quickly became flustered if things did not go her way. Little things: if her wine was served in the wrong glass, if she was given Coca-Cola not Pepsi, and vice versa. It was real diva behavior. I've studied so many videos of Ruja, on stage, on parade, on the everlasting bullshit trail, and I think I know what makes her tick. She has little mannerisms: touching her hair, pausing for a tiny moment, before she delivers, in a slow monotone, another great lie. Her giveaway tics were most apparent to me on the Bangkok event video; or maybe that was because she was telling a whopper: the switching on of the new and improved blockchain and the coin split that would multiply the fortunes of all OneCoin investors.

By October 2016, Bjorn was world renowned as a blockchain specialist. Only two days before she spouted the nonsense at the Bangkok event, Dr. Ruja had contacted him through a Japanese recruitment agency. On the first call he was tested on his qualifications for the position and he was clearly perfect for the job. He was not given the name of the company and told only that it was a cryptocurrency that had been in business for more than two years. On the next call he was offered the job of global chief technical officer (CTO), with a salary of over $280,000 year. He would be bought a home and a car in Sofia, Bulgaria, and a house and car in London. Bjorn thought he'd won the lottery. He told me he was super keen, and finally he was told the company was OneCoin and that they wanted him to turn their SQL servers into a blockchain. He knew it was a scam—"You can't run cryptocurrencies on SQL servers, you need decentralization," he insisted—and asked for the weekend to consider the offer. He telephoned them on the Monday to reject the offer but got no answer. His calls were never returned. He put all this aside until February 2017, when he saw that the OneCoin leaders were boasting they were going to replace Bitcoin as the world's number-one cryptocurrency.

Bjorn posted comments online, including the news that he'd been asked to create a blockchain for Ruja and, vitally, that OneCoin was operating on an SQL server. Lynndel spotted this immediately and, much to Bjorn's surprise, was in touch with him within ten minutes of his posting the remark. Lynndel explained that the missing key to the OneCoin puzzle was proving that a blockchain didn't exist. He put Bjorn in touch with Tim in California. Tim being Tim spent three hours on the phone with Bjorn, testing him out on blockchain technology. Eventually satisfied, Tim told Bjorn that he was working with American authorities and with police in Europe, including the German cops, whom he wanted Bjorn to speak with. It all went very James Bond at this point, and Bjorn delighted in telling me how he was spirited under the radar into Germany. The German police were keen to interview him, so they bought him an e-ticket and told him they'd pick him up at the airport at Düsseldorf, the home of the head office of the nation's financial fraud investigations. He was told to just be on the plane. When he landed on a Tuesday in March 2017, all the passengers were told to remain seated, and police were at the gates. Bjorn never imagined this was anything to do with him, but a police officer marched into the plane and straight to his seat.

The plainclothes cop showed ID and then escorted Bjorn off the plane, into the airport terminal, immediately down a staircase to the tarmac, and into a waiting unmarked car with tinted windows. Bjorn missed immigration and customs. He arrived at a hotel at seven that evening, was instructed to stay put and enjoy room service, and be ready to go at seven the next morning. He was introduced to a policeman who sat outside his hotel room all night. The next morning, showered and shaved, he opened the door to his room and a new, fresh-faced police escort was there. A phone call was made, and by the time they got through reception the black BMW's passenger door was open for him. He said the fifteen-story gray and brown Düsseldorf police building was like the Pentagon. They drove through huge gates, which closed automatically behind them, and stopped in front of another set of gates. Magically, the gates all opened and another police escort was waiting as they moved forward. Bjorn said he felt like a Cold War pawn but he enjoyed telling me about it. Especially his walk through a maze of corridors and through doors that closed behind him with a whoosh of electronic locks. He finally arrived at an interrogation room.

He was quizzed about Dr. Ruja and her brother Konstantin, Sebastian, and a group of world-class con men. It was made clear to Bjorn by the German detectives that the con men were well connected—which shook me up. My OneCoin upline went from Harry and James Stone, the UK, to their controller in Europe, to the global controllers, the aforementioned con men. I was in their direct line.

His interview went on all day through a lunch of coffee and sandwiches. The Germans were hesitant to give him too many clues to their targets, but to get answers they had to share information.

The main message was that OneCoin was a huge global fraud featuring some of the world's most successful hustlers. Hence the risks the German authorities took by spiriting Bjorn into their country. They drove him back to the airport at five that afternoon and straight onto the tarmac. They had him in control all the time he was there—or never there. He'd been in no-man's-land.

The Germans wanted deniability, as they had no authority to interview Bjorn. He was like an innocent from an Alfred Hitchcock movie, a regular guy caught up in an international conspiracy. What he'd learned and soon after revealed in my webinar was the depth of the gangster involvement in the fraud we victims had been drawn into. Because Bjorn was so aware of the dangerous people involved, he was very protective of me. He'd call up all the time. He and the others learned to sense the fear in my voice. God, I wanted their support and care, but a couple of times Bjorn was terrified I was suicidal. At the same time he believed I was in danger of being murdered. From his perspective, I had taken on a huge responsibility for righting the wrongs perpetrated on hundreds of thousands of victims, and I was shaking the foundations of Ruja's supremely productive money machine.

Dr. Ruja had the means and the contacts to stop us. All four of us got threats, and there was a blast of information spat out on the internet to OneCoin members about the critics and the haters like me, Tim, Bjorn, and Crypto Xpose. Many of the people I was trying to help were turning on us, and I was told that Ruja had personally targeted me. I needed to know everything about her. It took some digging and lots of help, but the gloriously flamboyant Ruja as the front for OneCoin had left a trail of broken bank accounts. She likes to break hearts too, if she can. I learned she needs control over her men as well as her moneymaking. Her erratic behavior reflected the story of OneCoin, soaring to dizzying heights and then exploding every which way—with the detritus dumping on the lives of all her victims.

"Ruja loves herself," I was told by a contact in the IT world. I tracked him down, along with other prime sources, with the author and journalist Douglas Thompson as a witness. We wanted corroboration. I decided to call this young computer innovator named Vlad, who knew we were recording our 2021 Zoom conversation and only spoke with us on the understanding that we would not publicly reveal his identity. He had been approached by the German fraud squad but, as they would not grant him anonymity, he was too frightened to cooperate with them. Why? He claimed, "Ruja is connected to the real big Bulgarian mafia and the serious mafia guys." Vlad provided previously unknown and remarkable detail and insight into Ruja and the OneCoin saga.

It filled in the gaps of the dossier I was compiling. The constant excuse to not act on my evidence was lack of evidence—goodness, millions of people had been robbed. The other was no jurisdiction—but it was happening in front of their eyes. I gathered information for the authorities and for the victim support groups, for I knew that, God willing, in time we might be able to fight for justice. I'd like you to know as much as possible about Dr. Ruja—at least what I have been able to discover over the past five years. It's to give you an idea of what I'm up against. She's a decade younger than me, born on May 30, 1980, in the northern province of Pleven Sofia, Bulgaria. She's of Romani heritage. Her parents, Plamen and Veska Ignatova, emigrated to Germany in 1990 with her and her brother, Konstantin, six years her junior. They settled in Schramberg, a town in the Black Forest industrialized district of Baden-Württemberg. Ruja was diligent at school and earned a law degree at the neighboring University of Konstanz in 2005. Her brother drove a forklift for a Porsche logistics plant near Stuttgart. He said he had "a small life." Konstantin liked German beer, tattoos, and having fun. Ruja found her fun in duplicity.

Four years after she graduated, a steel foundry in the village of Waltenhofen, in southern Germany, got into financial problems. Gusswerk Waltenhofen GmbH, specialists in heavy-duty steel molds for casting parts for the car and metal industries, was facing bankruptcy. Exactly 140 jobs were at risk, and management was flummoxed as to how to save them and their business. A messiah arrived, magically, with an answer. Dr. Ruja had grown up in a nearby town, had legal and business experience, and, best of all, had cash to invest. Her father, Plamen, was a metalworker by trade and was familiar with the steel industry. The workers went full out on production, working long hours for their new boss, their savior. The business boomed—for a time. Suddenly, the profits could not be seen. Consultancy fees, paid by Ruja to her father and vice versa, were colossal and wiped out any future for the factory. Ruja's parents slipped quietly back to Bulgaria, while she ghosted the factory and was gone with more than $1 million. There were workers' demonstrations, but as they went on, Ruja sold the business for much less than it was worth. She did not share that cash. Instead, she stiffed debtors for another $160,000. The new owners, having been sold a bag of tricks, went bankrupt in two years.

The company paperwork vanished with Ruja and her dad. The German courts caught up with Ruja and her father in April 2016, when they were convicted on twenty-four counts of fraud. She was fined $20,000 and given a two-month suspended jail sentence; Plamen Ignatova was fined nearly $14,000. To me it seems slight punishment, but that is what the court records say. The judge was enamored of

Ruja and described her as "this young woman for whom I foresee a socially positive future." She is that convincing.

This Eastern European money world was like the location: foreign to me. It seemed that if you stole a large enough amount of money you got a slap on the wrist. But even more shocking to me was that everyone involved was corrupt. It was explained that Bulgaria, a European Union state, provided a bridge between Europe and Asia and served as the outlaw nation perfect for black market businesses, money laundering, and siphoning funds to offshore accounts. Bulgaria certainly had an intriguing list of people running many companies. I'd gone through the paperwork hassle of UK legalities setting up my one little IT business, and that took time enough. When you look at Ruja's business lineup, it's a fanfare.

The Commercial Register of Bulgaria lists her as the executive of thirty companies and the owner of five more. In turn, this is part of Clever Synergies Investment Fund (CSIF), a private investment group created and operated by Tsvetelina Borislavova, who was not connected to OneCoin, a onetime girlfriend of Bulgarian prime minister Boyko Borisov, who has been dogged by claims of mafia links. I looked him up, and he sounds like a real tough nut. These people were in the business of making elaborate offers you can't refuse. It was an environment in which Ruja flourished. From this safe zone in Sofia, Ruja took her crooked ambitions on the road and almost immediately met a fellow traveler, the affable and corrupt Sebastian Greenwood, who'd become a master of the global con game, a man renowned as an artist because of the aplomb with which he relieved his victims of their readily available assets and all they could sell or pawn.

The ultimate flimflam man, Sebastian was greedy: He wanted not just the gold, he wanted the pot it came in. Dr. Ruja and Sebastian were the perfect illicit coupling. His father, Terry Greenwood, had worked as a journalist on the *South London Observer* and met Sebastian's Swedish mother, Lisa, on a holiday in Spain. The couple have never spoken publicly about their son and OneCoin, Terry

Greenwood telling friends he was reluctant to speak on the telephone as he was certain he was being "bugged by the FBI." The couple, who have not been implicated in any wrongdoing, made a home in the south London suburbs before moving to Sweden, where they started a family and set up a news and public relations business, Greenwood Communications, in Riddargatan, Stockholm, which has no links with OneCoin. Sebastian spread his wings from there. He boasted of operating in fifteen countries, and he did—leaving a trail of distress throughout Southeast Asia and Africa.

Those continents provided him with millions of victims for his increasingly sophisticated operations, which he carried out with an engaging manner and smile and an utter lack of sincerity. When you looked behind the chubby smile of Karl Sebastian Greenwood and stripped away the veneer, you discovered more veneer.

Ruja loved him.

In the early months of 2013, Sebastian and Dr. Ruja clicked together. He had created Loopium, which was an electronic scam modeled on PayPal and aimed at Southeast Asia and Africa. He promoted it as "an innovative new way of receiving and sending money globally for those in need of alternative banking methods 24/7/365." It was linked to a platform called Wave Crest. Two Norwegians, who have nothing to do with OneCoin, were employed to lure investors to wire funds into a remote Norwegian bank and to an American shell corporation, neither of which could have any idea what was really going on. Dr. Ruja was brought on by Sebastian as the legal and financial adviser for Loopium. Her dubious expertise was deployed to create a legal framework to find "havens" for cash in Gibraltar and Cyprus. She arranged money transfers, often more than $575 million at a time, from Swiss and Hong Kong accounts. It went pear shaped for everyone but Dr. Ruja and Sebastian.

Wave Crest and many other companies said they were duped out of hundreds of thousands of euros in lost payments. The couple left bills and wages unpaid and disappeared after Ruja liquidated Loopium "assets" in Gibraltar and Cyprus on April 8, 2014. Two weeks earlier she'd registered Zooperium Consultancy Service in Gibraltar with the same virtual address. The best way to explain it is that the companies are like Russian dolls, one within another and then another. How do you solve the puzzle of these confected companies hidden in the world's tax havens?

Perseverance, as it turned out. Follow the money. Which is what Ruja has done all her life. She and Sebastian marveled at the success of BitCoin, created by Satoshi Nakamoto in 2009. There's a YouTube video that startled me when I first saw it: Ruja and Sebastian, together as always and introducing their amazing cryptocurrency, BigCoin—which, when you say it quickly, could be Bitcoin. The presentation was filmed at the Shangri-la Hotel in Hong Kong in July 2014. It's not the Ruja razzmatazz affair I'm familiar with now; this is a shy Ruja with straight hair and little makeup, standing on a small stage before a small crowd in a simple dress.

The marketing on the video, however, is familiar. Flagged up are posters of a giant golden coin with a central letter *B* and the message "The Future of Money." BigCoin was on offer for Prosper Club members, who could instantly purchase $2,000, $3,000, and $5,000 (US) packages. It was quickly clear to prospective investors that Big-Coin wasn't going to get any bigger. Dr. Ruja and Sebastian hadn't papered over the cracks and BigCoin wouldn't buy you the time of day. Nevertheless, it was a triumphant, $50 million profit rehearsal. BigCoin went through a remarkable metamorphosis and became OneCoin. Documents at Gibraltar Companies House show that on September 1, 2014, the corporation CoolsDAQ Limited, formerly Zooperium Consultancy Service Ltd., changed its name officially to OneCoin Limited. Through Prosper Ltd., CoolsDAQ was the internal exchange developed by Ruja and Sebastian for BigCoin. One-Coin Limited in Gibraltar has one shareholder, OneCoin Limited in Dubai. We could have kept juggling files and more and more company names would have fallen out, but you get the idea. It was all done with elaborate care, and other people's money paid the lawyers.

It's not only me but government regulators and investigators who understand these many years later that OneCoin was far more than a multibillion-dollar con game. They disguised the scam as an "educational package" rather than a "once-in-a-lifetime investment opportunity." The offerings of money and futures and hopes by me and the other victims was window dressing. Dr. Ruja was operating out of small offices in Bulgaria in early 2014 when Vlad, my connection from the IT world, was contacted. He ran a small business with only a few employees, and he said he was offered not much money to create a website for Ruja. It was to promote a cryptofund. He took the job, thinking it was "not a big deal." He was careful as he spoke; you can hear him thinking before offering his memories of his "crazy times" with Ruja. It was extraordinary to listen to his story of the scrappy beginnings of one of history's greatest frauds. His firsthand story reflects on the competence of all of us, as people and as governments, and reveals that the absurd financial success of OneCoin can be possible. He made some startling allegations:

I'd heard about Ruja from her personal assistant, who said she was an entrepreneur, a smart businesswoman, a very well-educated lady. I was really impressed because when I went into her office there were diplomas and certificates all over the place. She said she was getting investors, but she personally did not care so much about money. This was why we needed to work cheap. We came to an agreement and started from scratch; the first lines of software code for her cryptocurrency platform were written by my company. I thought she must be being frugal when she asked me to help kit out her second office from IKEA. In my dad's car we went to IKEA to buy the furniture. I have a picture somewhere of my dad and I putting the flat packs together in the office. After we did so, she asked me to work for her company full time and we worked for several months on this project, but it was tense. Ruja constantly delayed our payments and made enemies of the software developers, forcing them to work fourteen hours a day if they wanted to be paid.

When I asked about money, she tried to make me the chief executive officer [CEO] of one of her multiple companies. She wanted to give me one million tokens for coins. Even in the beginning she had something like twenty companies incorporated in Bulgaria; since the very beginning she has never been checked or audited by the government. This is why she did it [in Bulgaria] and not somewhere else that's open for this sort of dirty business. With her connections and relationships in Bulgaria she can do anything she wants. I can give you one very small example. Sebastian Greenwood did not have a driver's license. Ruja made one phone call, and the next day he had a driver's license. The next day! His driver's license was delivered in a smart cream envelope. Ruja and Sebastian have this instinct to know what to do. And they are shameless.

He then made allegations which, despite all that had gone on before, startled me. Could this be true? He went on:

Ruja told me: "These people are stupid and I have to take their money. They're all stupid people and they will invest, they will give me." She became more and more boastful like that, especially because she was drinking a lot, in the morning every day, like it was normal at eleven o'clock to have already drunk a bottle of wine. Yeah, there were times when we went to lunch at a place behind the office and Ruja would drink two bottles of wine and carry on drinking back in the office and at night. She paid men to sleep with her, and there were the parties. There were prostitutes and wild things involving Sebastian and the Finnish guys. Several times my young [team] would turn up at the office and find many hungover people sleeping on the floor. Ruja didn't try and hide any of this. I don't think the people behind her gave her so much money at first, but they gave her enough to cover the expenses and the wine. That made it more difficult when she began arguing about money and payments. One night, with the lawyer of my company, the three of us went to dinner to sort things out, but before we could try she'd drunk so much red wine she was unable to talk. For me, she was not the mastermind, she was the face. She was on Facebook and showing pictures of her brother and parents—everybody knows about her. She's not from the capital, she's from the provinces. She has a provinces personality—a redneck in English, something like that. Not sophisticated.

When I asked her if what she wanted me to do was legal, she told me, "It's not your business to ask questions, it's your business to do it."

In Bulgaria, you can pay the government and police to ignore what's going on; they are all connected in every sense of that word.

Her brother, Konstantin, who was being paid a few hundred dollars a month to work for her, owns buildings in Sofia worth around 50 million euros. There is no one in Bulgaria to check this. And no one will ever check. You know, this is why I don't raise my voice. Every day was a scandal, every day was the problem. Her assistants threw keyboards at me and screamed all the time. She was screaming at software developers. Screaming was her pastime.

And she didn't care anything about lying to people. The books and educational material she sold with her OneCoin packages were copy-pasted information from internet; if you open her books and write in Google, you'll find the original sources. She didn't care about this. The books sold as informational materials were compiled in three or four hours. I helped her find a girl whose job was to browse the internet, find information about cryptocurrencies, and copy and paste the text and format so it looked professionally done. The books were part of packages costing thousands of euros or dollars or pounds—books compiled by this girl who was paid £50 for the job. Ruja paid £50,000 to a concierge service for such things to be named as Bulgarian businesswoman of the year.

Ruja's favorite movie is The Wolf of Wall Street. *I'm not joking, she watched it again and again. She wanted to be Leonardo DiCaprio's "Wolf."*

On camera, Vlad showed us screenshots of emails, copies of documents and other paperwork he'd done for Ruja. I said what he told us would be sure to identify him to those in that circle in Bulgaria. He said that was not a concern, as he had not revealed evidence of any wrongdoing. But he had to me. I pressed him on that, and he told me, "If no one speaks, no one knows."

What stopped me in my tracks was the realization that I was now accepting this conversation, this talk of crime and corruption and problems being "disappeared," quite matter of factly. Only five minutes before, this was an alien world to me. I'll not say I am a quick learner, but I am a steady one. I gather information and I go through it until I understand it, until I have no questions. But one huge question remains: How could this happen? This mammoth financial organization built from an IKEA flatpack. Perhaps I'd helped Ruja scale up the OneCoin operations with lavish new offices in Sofia when I bought my OneCoin package. Three weeks after I invested, she and 150 office staff moved into a converted and renovated six-story house on Slaveykov Square, close to the city center and Serdika Metro Station. An assistant was very hands-on, lavishing care on the offices and the shell companies; she was spinning webs within webs like a spider. There were polite policemen there. And killer fashion: Ruja's ever-present and sharply dressed guards, who can't legally carry guns, conceal their weapons in Prada-style man bags slung around their necks. On the second floor, Ruja sat in a tidy office and next to her, in a separate office, was a colleague who acted as a secretary and a courier between several banks in Sofia that held the accounts of scores of companies set up to disguise the source of all funds. An assistant seemed to be the on-call laundry lady for Ruja. On the third floor, alongside her office, was Ruja's treasured possession—her safe. The office rule was that when Ruja was in the office the safe had to be stuffed to capacity with cash. This massive lump of steel was the size of a small room on my housing estate but had better soundproofing and thicker floors and a security door opening into it. Inside were shelves and another safe, this one the size of an ultramodern fridge. It held millions of hot money she planned to cool.

On a promotional video for opening day at the office, Ruja appears with a pair of gold scissors and cuts a red ribbon, which had been held tight across the entrance. Her staff are lined up in the background. The doors open, offering welcome to a get-rich world. The rooms are white leather furniture and marble floors, large mirrors reflecting recessed lighting, walls of smart TVs, and slogan-posters with words like "global," "growth," "sustainability," "safety," "powerful," "blockchain," "loyalty," and "ability" arranged in one order or another. A wall-sized photograph shows a mining pit with the cartoon figure of Bob the Miner, the OneCoin logo on his helmet. This display of grandeur was clearly designed to attract rich catches. On opening day the special offers, tailored for the China market, were a Supreme package costing more than $215,000 and the even more limited Super Combo for more than $260,000. They sold 1,191 of these packages valued at more than $160 million. Available free were black pens with the OneCoin logo in white. Of all the offers available, I heard that at least the cheap ballpoints worked.

I'm a coal miner's daughter, and here's my dad (*third from the left*) taking a moment for a photograph with his fellow underground workers.

This is Dad and me having a cuddle—a memory of moments I so much miss.

Mum and Dad with their grandson, a rare picture of the three of them together and one I cherish.

Love at first sight—I'm seventeen years old and the single mother to this beautiful and wonderful baby boy.

My baby boy was growing up when I posed with him in the back garden.

Here's the man, my dad. It's because of him that I found the strength to never give up in my David vs. Goliath battle with Ruja and OneCoin.

Here she is, my forever friend Eileen, who was with me at the start of the OneCoin story and remains by my side today.

Left: My fellow justice fighter, Bjorn Bjercke of Norway, a world-renowned blockchain and Bitcoin expert.

Below: The superb Tim, with whom in the early days I heatedly traded words. He's known as USA Timothy "Tim Tayshun" Curry, veteran Bitcoin and blockchain enthusiast and educator.

Above: OneCoin central—the Ruja HQ in Sofia, Bulgaria, where suitcases full of millions of dollars in cash were delivered every Monday.

Right: This is Ed Hartley, whom I saw as the epitome of the American salesman, in action in London. A kind man, his life ended tragically after OneCoin.

Above: A moment I'd prayed for, and a day I will always remember, June 30, 2022, when US attorney Damian Williams announced Ruja was on the FBI's notorious Ten Most Wanted Fugitives list.

Right: This is me in November 2022, gazing up at the apartment block in Kensington, London, where Ruja bought a penthouse to mastermind her global ambitions. In 2023, it was announced that the property had been seized by authorities, as it had been proven to be purchased with fraudulent funds.

The brown-eyed Ruja is a European pinup too. They have her on most-wanted pictures all over the continent.

UNITED STATES DISTRICT COURT
SOUTHERN DISTRICT OF NEW YORK

- X
                        :

UNITED STATES OF AMERICA
                        :

      - v. -   :   SEALED INDICTMENT

                         :   S4 17 Cr. 630
RUJA IGNATOVA,
      a/k/a "Cryptoqueen,"   :

FBI TEN MOST WANTED FUGITIVE

RUJA IGNATOVA

Conspiracy to Commit Wire Fraud; Wire Fraud; Conspiracy to Commit Money Laundering; Conspiracy to Commit Securities Fraud; Securities Fraud

DESCRIPTION

Aliases: Dr. Ruja Ignatova, Ruja Plamenova Ignatova, Ruja P. Ignatova, "CryptoQueen"

Date(s) of Birth Used: May 30, 1980	Place of Birth: Bulgaria
Hair: Dark Brown to Black	Eyes: Brown
Sex: Female	Race: White
Languages: English, German, Bulgarian	

REWARD

The FBI is offering a reward of up to $100,000 for information leading to the arrest of Ruja Ignatova.

REMARKS

Ignatova is believed to travel with armed guards and/or associates. Ignatova may have had plastic surgery or otherwise altered her appearance.

CAUTION

Ruja Ignatova is wanted for her alleged participation in a large-scale fraud scheme. Beginning in approximately 2014, Ignatova and others are alleged to have defrauded billions of dollars from investors all over the world. Ignatova was the founder of OneCoin Ltd., a Bulgaria-based company that marketed a purported cryptocurrency. In order to execute the scheme, Ignatova allegedly made false statements and representations to individuals in order to solicit investments in OneCoin. She allegedly instructed victims to transmit investment funds to OneCoin accounts in order to purchase OneCoin packages, causing victims to send wire transfers representing these investments. Throughout the scheme, OneCoin is believed to have defrauded victims out of more than $4 billion.

Ignatova served as OneCoin's top leader through October 2017. On October 25, 2017, Ignatova traveled from Sofia, Bulgaria, to Athens, Greece, and may have traveled elsewhere after that. She may travel on a German passport to the United Arab Emirates, Bulgaria, Germany, Russia, Greece and/or Eastern Europe.

On October 12, 2017, Ignatova was charged in the United States District Court, Southern District of New York and a federal warrant was issued for her arrest. On February 6, 2018, a superseding indictment was issued charging Ignatova with one count each of Conspiracy to Commit Wire Fraud; Wire Fraud; Conspiracy to Commit Money Laundering; Conspiracy to Commit Securities Fraud; and Securities Fraud.

My nemesis, Dr. Ruja Ignatova, the fake, so-called Cryptoqueen, stripped of her glamor and shown in all her guises—and to my great satisfaction—as a most-wanted fugitive.

The Grand J[ury]

     1.   From i[...]

[...]018, in the Sou[...]

[...]GNATOVA, a/k/a [...]

[...]nd unknown, wil[...]

[...]onfederate, and [...]

[...]tle 18, United [...]

     2.   It was [...]

[...]JA IGNATOVA, a[...]

[...]own and unknown[...]

[...]tending to devi[...]

[...]taining money a[...]

[...]etenses, representations, and promises, would and did transm[...]

[...]d cause to be transmitted by means of wire, radio, and

[...]levision communication in interstate and foreign commerce,

Approved: _____

CHRISTOPHER J. DIMA

Assistant United St

JULIETA V. LOZANO

Special Assistant U

Before: HONORABLE DEBRA FRE

United States Magis

Southern District c

- - - - - - - - - - - - - - - - -

UNITED STATES OF AMERICA

- v. -

KONSTANTIN IGNATOV,

Defendant.

- - - - - - - - - - - - - - - - x

Tattooed from tip to toe, Konstantin Ignatova, the gofer and cipher for his sister, Ruja, and the OneCoin promoter in Africa and America.

: COUNTY OF OFFENSE:
: NEW YORK
:
:

SOUTHERN DISTRICT OF NEW YORK, ss.:

RONALD SHIMKO, being duly sworn, deposes and says is a Special Agent with the Federal Bureau of Investiga charges as follows:

COUNT ONE
(Conspiracy to Commit Wire Fraud)

1. From in or about 2014 through in or about Mar in the Southern District of New York and elsewhere, KON IGNATOV, the defendant, and others known and unknown, w and knowingly did combine, conspire, confederate, and a together and with each other to violate Title 18, Unite Code, Section 1343.

2. It was a part and an object of the conspiracy KONSTANTIN IGNATOV, the defendant, and others known anc willfully and knowingly, having devised and intending t a scheme and artifice to defraud and for obtaining mone property by means of false and fraudulent pretenses,

COVINGTON

BEIJING BRUSSELS DUBAI FRANKFURT JOHANNESBURG
LONDON LOS ANGELES NEW YORK PALO ALTO
SAN FRANCISCO SEOUL SHANGHAI WASHINGTON

Covington & Burling LLP
The New York Times Building
620 Eighth Avenue
New York, NY 10018-1405
T +1 212 841 1000

Honorable Edgardo Ramos
United States District Judge
Southern District of New York
40 Foley Square
New York, New York 10007

Re: *United States v. Mark S. Scott, S10 17 Cr. 6*

Dear Judge Ramos:

We write on behalf of our client, Mark Scott, with res
defendant's Reply Brief in connection with his Supplemental
trial based on (now conceded) perjury by cooperating witness

As noted in our letter of November 8th, the parties are
raised by Mr. Scott's motion and the Government's post-filin
evidence produced by the Government last week that Irina Dilkinska was in India on the date of
a supposed meeting with Mr. Scott that Konstantin had testified to during trial. These
discussions will continue with the incoming Chief of the Criminal Division of the U.S.

American lawyer Mark Scott, who worked closely with Ruja and her lover,
Gilbert Armenta, in moving ill-gotten monies around the world.

```
- - - - - - - - - - - - - - - - - - - - - X
                                           :
UNITED STATES OF AMERICA
                                           :
        - v. -
                                           :
KARL SEBASTIAN GREENWOOD,
                                           :
              Defendant.

- - - - - - - - - - - - - - - - - - - - - X


                   COUNT ONE
        (Conspiracy to Commit Wi

    The Grand Jury charges:

    1.    From in or about 2014 through

2018, in the Southern District of New Yo

SEBASTIAN GREENWOOD, the defendant, and

unknown, willfully and knowingly did com

confederate, and agree together and with

Title 18, United States Code, Section 13

    2.    It was a part and an object of the conspiracy that

KARL SEBASTIAN GREENWOOD, the defendant, and others known and
```

Sebastian Greenwood's indictment paperwork. Sebastian (not pictured) was extradited to the United States from Thailand to face multiple fraud charges for his allegedly leading role with the OneCoin scandal, to which he's expected to plead guilty.

Daniel Leinhardt, who joined the victim support group and worked tirelessly to help his family and other victims since the OneCoin troops invaded Uganda. His story broke my heart.

This is the easygoing Ted from Spokane, Washington, a friendly man and regretful now that he was not immune to the temptations of Ruja.

Abid Wadood Mufti, former head of telecommunications for the United Nations in Peshawar, Pakistan, opened up his own OneCoin victim support group after losing much of his family's financial future.

My friend Layla fell victim to a friend who targeted his own Muslim community, from London to Bangladesh and all points in between.

NINE

Meet the Gang

When I was a Ruja groupie, I saw such displays of wealth as evidence of success, a bit like the days when fat-cat businessmen and self-styled tycoons walked around smoking giant cigars. Whatever Ruja's abilities and skills, she enhanced them with the people she surrounded herself with. People like Frank Schneider, an acknowledged specialist and her go-to Mr. Fixit. He was a spy, a former chief of operations in Luxembourg's CIA-type intelligence agency, another member of the fiscal twilight zone. Here was a man with connections worldwide: He'd worked with Europol, Scotland Yard, and both the FBI and CIA in America. He knew how to access and wield power. More pertinently for me, he was an expert in covert intelligence operations and wiretapping. At a glance, Frank Schneider belies his alleged reputation as a chilling operator who cleans up a scary mess for his employers and at the same time turns a lifelike mine into a real one. Schneider is a short man with a moon face and a receding hairline, and when he wears his spectacles he appears as an innocent schoolteacher. I was to quickly find out how fast Schneider moved. He had to, for his paymaster Ruja was in a hell of a hurry. She couldn't spend other people's money fast enough. She and Schneider focused on operating out of London and in New York, where millions in OneCoin turnover funds were moved. Ruja's plan was to make her home in London and create a Persil-white "family office," which I learned is an unregulated setup to juggle funds and make investments for those cursed with too much money.

In April 2016, the same month she "blessed" the new offices in Slaveykov Square, Sofia, she bought a three-year lease on premises at 1 Knightsbridge, London, as the "family office" headquarters of yet another company, RavenR Capital Ltd. Just as prime and just for her was a penthouse property home in Kensington not far from Kensington Palace.

With the help of $23 million sent from Munich, she paid $18.2 million for the penthouse suite, with its customized decor—high-end luxury treatment created by the Candy Brothers, Nick and Christian, carried out after a fire when the place was owned by the singer Duffy—and a swimming pool. Lawyers questioned the provenance of the more than $23 million, but Dr. Ruja's evidence and answers satisfied them, and the deal was completed. While Eileen and I were worrying about when we might cash in some of our coins, good old Ruja was paddling about in water wings next door to British royalty. Cryptoqueen indeed. Her London base included some impressive artwork, including *Red Lenin*, by Andy Warhol. Several of the paintings were sourced from the Halcyon Gallery in Mayfair, London. That gallery is owned by Ehud Sheleg, who had been Conservative Party treasurer for eight weeks when he was knighted by UK prime minister Theresa May in her 2019 resignation honors list. Sir Ehud Udi Sheleg is a director of the gallery, which is half controlled by his family trust in the British Virgin Islands. It's been reported that Sir Ehud donated £2.7 million to the Conservative Party and raised funds for UK prime minister Boris Johnson when he was mayor of London from 2008 to 2016. For a time there, Dr. Ruja was in close proximity to *Red Lenin* and other works from the Halcyon Gallery. She loved it in London and was seen at all the smart restaurants. Her motto was "If you've got it, flaunt it." The big celebration was that thirty-sixth birthday bash I told you about at the Victoria and Albert Museum, a venue just a comfortable stroll from her penthouse. With hindsight, that display of success was money well spent by Ruja, like the advertising space she bought from *Forbes Bulgaria* magazine through its BrandVoice service: with some digital tweaks, it magically transformed via Ruja's marketing as a genuine US *Forbes* magazine interview, with her on the cover and two pages of editorial inside that she had shown in her marketing presentation. She tried it on with other unknowing glossy financial magazines—all glitzy paid advertisements for OneCoin, a make-me-rich endeavor reliant on new money flowing in all the time. Her riches tempted millions of us with the hope of another life.

I gloried in it by proxy, as did millions of others. She was Dr. Ruja, and we flashed the OneCoin hand signal, an O made by thumb and forefinger, as a salute to her. I cringe today at photos of me doing that. All smiles and the big O. How stupid. Especially since I learned the O hand signal is used by Satanic cults and white supremacy movements and is classified as a hate symbol. I gave it not a thought at the moment; this wealth and charisma overload was part of an exceptional marketing effort by Ruja and the aggressive salesmen she brought on. A senior American promoter and OneCoin salesman attacked me when I began asking questions. He shouted loud and clear that OneCoin was legitimate and people like me were liars. He was one of the most ardent defenders of OneCoin, posting videos branding me, Tim, Bjorn, and Crypto Xpose as mad haters. He seemed to me to be manipulative and sociopathic. When he realized we were winning our argument, he put up his hands and pleaded personal innocence. I sent him a Twitter message in 2020: Take a trip down memory lane with me. I couldn't find many happy memories for him. One big bump was when he was jailed for nearly ten years after defrauding investors of $7.5 million in high-interest loans targeted at the poor. The American was on parole when he joined Ruja's OneCoin gang in 2015. In a world of like attracting like, he went to work with "Dr. Zafar," who, when he operated alongside my upline partners James and Harry Stone in the UK, boasted of being one of OneCoin's biggest earners, making $900,000 a month. You'll recall that Eileen and I first heard about this frighteningly effective "star" when we went to what I now think of as our indoctrination meeting in London. "Dr.

Zafar," which is a nonsense title in the OneCoin world, was responsible for much of the £100 million that vanished from the UK before he returned to Asia.

Zafar and the Stone cousins were the biggest promoters in the UK, and Zafar was one of the biggest OneCoin pushers in Asia. An appalling man, he would exploit anyone he met and go anywhere for a sale. He allegedly plundered more than £2 million out of Ireland in a whirlwind trip. Promotions were allegedly staged in Dublin hotels and follow-up seminars were arranged. Disgruntled investors were told not to talk. One victim, Edward O'Sullivan from Tipperary, did speak out. He said the OneCoin team had said they had two thousand people who had invested an average of £1,000 each and emphasized this success at meetings. Edward said the people he met at meetings were men aged from fifty to sixty-five who were told: "We like to welcome *Toms* to the meeting." Edward asked, "What do you mean by 'Toms'?" They answered, "We like to invite people who will *T*rust you, who are looking for an *O*pportunity, and have the *M*oney." Edward accepted that he'd lost his money, his initial £910 payment and the seven £110 Starter OneCoin packages for his family. I understood that and his ongoing frustration that there was no retribution. Edward, who continued to despair when I spoke to him in January 2022, telephoned Ireland's financial regulator but didn't get very far. America's financial police and the FBI eventually took a different view of the goings-on in Ireland, and that attitude changed. But it took time, as you'll discover.

I was on the phone all the time to DC Vaughan at the City of London Police, but as far as I could understand there was zero action from his financial investigations unit. He was, as ever, very nice and understanding, but that was never going to be enough. It was more evidence that laws and government regulations are out of step with network marketing bandits like Ruja and her gang, one step behind the fraudsters. I'm sure all this frustration, my feeling of momentary hopelessness, brought on the ME attacks that again took me to my bed.

It was such an exhausting business. I'd lie there trying to rest, and another heartbreaking story would present itself to me. There wasn't a message that wasn't upsetting. When I could sit up in bed and look online, OneCoin was flourishing. What was I—just me and my phone—going to do? I can't imagine the state I'd have been in if I'd thought that Frank Schneider was thinking about how to gag me. Possibly not so bloody minded and righteous. I don't know. I had no clue I was appearing on memo sheets named as a "problem." At the same time, in my naivete about consequences, I was desperately spreading the word that OneCoin was a scam, raging at promoters who were selling it as hard as ever. They scrambled to say they were promoting "educational packages"—to get around financial regulations—but monitored promotions dispute that. Eagle 1 went to a meeting at a hotel in Downey, a city southeast of downtown Los Angeles. This was not Ruja's initial plan—she wanted to hit Hollywood and Beverly Hills and go for "star money"—but SEC regulations meant she had to play things under the radar in America. When Eagle 1 arrived at the meeting, it was crowded but quiet. He quickly found out why: OneCoin leaders were selling to the local deaf community. Eagle 1 pretended to be deaf and didn't take notes until the signer "spoke." The packages were sold and bought via an interpreter, a signer. OneCoin established their own ASL (American Sign Language) group on Facebook and employed an ASL-fluent person as a US promoter/salesperson. OneCoin used the same tactic with the deaf in the English Midlands and with other groups or communities they could corner. In Muslim areas, local leaders were paid and recruited to "sell" the false message of OneCoin being friendly to Sharia law. Most targeted were groups that could be cajoled into a corner: the Muslims with their respect for loyalty to each other, the Orthodox Jewish communities unaware of the worldly perils they were being invited to endure. Fraud has no prejudice, and the only deity is real currency.

I'll grant Ruja and Sebastian and their early promoters in Sweden and Finland had an advantage with their timing. Cryptocurrencies were the latest financial trend, and the world was waiting to cash in on "the new Bitcoin." The market was there. In Africa, South America, the Middle East, and Asia, they targeted so many remote and forgotten communities. Investors had little knowledge of English or access to the internet. They bought what they were sold, as did more than one million OneCoin members in China. Remember that each member had a downline, which could be two or two thousand other small investors. There were some awful stories—like the trusted minister in Uganda who sold OneCoin to his congregation in return for a shiny black Range Rover with tinted windows. If anyone asked questions, they were threatened with their money being frozen and banishment from the OneCoin "family." Vietnam, Pakistan, Malaysia, Taiwan, Indonesia, India, Thailand, Colombia, Brazil, Australia, New Zealand, and the Pacific Islands were all early OneCoin boom zones. Ruja tried to sneak into North America by the back door using a virtual private network (VPN) for investor payments so the US authorities could not follow the money trail. At first, they tried an upfront pitch to America on Independence Day in 2015. Sebastian franchised that operation out to American MLM specialists who then claimed in their literature:

> OneCoin has acquired 180 banking licenses, to legally own their own banks, their own branch, and their own office, inside all 180 countries that we operate in. One of those countries is the United States of America, right? Right now OneCoin is going through the Securities and Exchange Commission approval process of having their banking license inside the United States approved. (OneCoin Ltd. in Dubai and OneLife Network Ltd. in Belize)

That was all lies. Although you'd think using encrypted internet traffic and disguised identities would be a turnoff, Americans were as fearful of missing out on the cryptocurrency boom as everyone else, and many millions of dollars were lost to Ruja. Huge funds came from California's nerd headquarters, Silicon Valley. The marketing was in overdrive. OneCoin blitzed America with online video presentations detailing how to make VPN payments to accounts in Dubai and Southeast Asia. It was all a hard sell.

The promotions were not subtle. I caught up on the video of one meeting headlined in London by a Scandinavian promoter. The Scandinavian was a seasoned salesman, proud that the OneCoin show had opened in Finland in 2014. That was due to Sebastian, who lived for a time in Tampere in southern Finland. On August 11, 2014, One-Coin's Finnish-language website was launched. On September 27 the same year, the sales campaign began at a Helsinki hotel and the local audience was told: "We Finns have hit the jackpot—we are among the first to join." Later, the same bullshitters would say in the same hotel: "Ruja has a motherly position toward Finland because the first event of the network was held here." Well, she'd given birth to much misery, but you'd never anticipate that watching her favored Scandinavia OneCoin recruiter and salesman in action. I couldn't tell which hotel it was in London in 2016, but there were about one thousand people there, an impressive crowd. A OneCoin promoter appeared on stage in sunglasses. I'd heard the line before: "Do you know why I wear shades? Because the future looks so bright." The Finns were enthusiastic OneCoin fans: Within eighteen months they'd invested a conservatively estimated $46 million.

Like so many others, the Finnish victims did not speak out. According to one local agency, the reason was "fear, as OneCoin has forbidden investors to talk to the media under the threat of losing their virtual currency if they comment on the company's behavior in public." I knew the threats had been more than simply losing one's money, for many lives were at stake, especially in "Wild West" areas in India and Pakistan. And it wasn't only people like me who might speak out who were at risk of being silenced. The local OneCoin promoters were also targets for vigilante "justice." One member of my victim support groups explained how his OneCoin group in a Pakistani village had sought out the promoters "and taken them to the hills." There were other such violent stories from Mexico and Colombia.

Meanwhile, the financial investigations unit of the City of London Police were making telephone calls to America; they're probably still waiting for Dick Tracy to answer. The more I virtually stamped my feet and really did scream at the claustrophobic walls around me, the angrier I became. As always, it moved me onward. And I was inspired by the victims. The WhatsApp International Group was the first group I founded, which opened with thirteen members, and that same core group is still there. We're in our thousands now, and the Facebook OneCoin Victim Group is huge too. The WhatsApp group has always been the most attacked, with vile abuse and threats to our lives. But we were strong together; early on one of the victims told me, "Through your activism you've started a movement." I was stunned, as I'd never thought about it that way. I even had to look up the word "activist" to see what the correct definition was and not just assume I knew. I can now see what he meant, because each day more and more victims joined the groups and stepped outside the OneCoin fear they had been in. I saw and felt the victims' voices becoming stronger, which made Ruja work harder to disrupt our "Braveheart" army. I led an ill-equipped bunch of ordinary people, fighting for fairness and justice against teams of experienced money manipulators from around the world, and what we lacked in resources we made up for with noise. If I was crippled in my bed, I would copy and paste information into emails to victims' groups and post them on social media. We shouldn't have had a chance, but I kept niggling away, a pajama-clad guerrilla warrior.

Finally, my campaign was getting the attention of authorities who were now reading and acknowledging the material I was making public, and Ruja and Sebastian must have been resentfully aware that governments that couldn't be bribed would spike their grandiose plans. Ruja couldn't clean our money fast enough. It seemingly had to be laundered through the legitimate financial system, and vehicles for that ranged from properties like the London penthouse, a bank in Zimbabwe, and, potentially, an oil field on Madagascar. Onetime US presidential son and brother and Texas businessman Neil Bush was reportedly on the board of the Hoifu Energy Group Limited, which has headquarters in Hong Kong but is incorporated in Bermuda. It's owned by Chinese billionaire Dr. Hui Chi Ming, who has provoked controversy in the past—he was accused of doing environmental damage to oil-rich Madagascar where, I was astonished to discover, you could once, with little effort, scoop up sapphires simply by running your hand through the earth. Dr. Hui was the East African island's consul in Hong Kong, advising the prime minister, president, and others on economic and Asian affairs. In September 2016, before her insane blockchain announcement in Bangkok, when I was still on Team Ruja, he was attempting an oil field deal to be financed in cash and, according to later US district court testimony I read, "a very large portion of the purchase price" in OneCoin. The Chinese billionaire, who has never been charged with any wrongdoing, was working personally with Ruja, and the two met with Neil Bush in Hong Kong. Bush, who was later interviewed by the FBI, was paid $300,000 to attend. I was taken aback by all of this. Ruja and Sebastian certainly had amazing connections. I looked up the FBI interview report to confirm what I was reading. It reported, "Bush recalled that the head of Hoifu Energy, Dr. Hui Chi Ming, received a bunch of cryptocurrency for an oil deal in Madagascar. Bush had a residual interest in the cryptocurrency from the oil deal. Bush met the woman from the cryptocurrency company, Ruja, in Hong Kong with Dr. Hui." The FBI files report that the Chinese mining tycoon had told Bush he would be entitled to 10 percent of the profits if Dr. Hui secured a deal to sell the cryptocurrency. However, Bush declined the option and did not invest. He has never been implicated in any wrongdoing. I don't think Ruja can blame me for that one going wrong: I had to look up how to spell "Madagascar" and find it on the map in the Indian Ocean.

By April 2017, she was raging on about me. My campaigning was threatening all her international deals. She had spent millions to ensure she looked the part of a financial genius, so she didn't want me revealing she was all fur coat and no knickers. We had and still do have internal leaks from OneCoin leaders telling us other leaders had issued very serious death threats because we were affecting their business and it was not appreciated. Given the mafia-gangster connections I had been warned about, this was and continues to be a constant intimidation. I've never stopped looking over my shoulder and probably never will. Those "what if" thoughts are always there. And more disquieting is whenever someone involved with OneCoin and Ruja goes "missing," as so many have. I heard of Ruja's determination to make me go away from those within OneCoin who were increasingly disenchanted and were as keen as I was to see the dethroning of the self-styled cryptoqueen. Several of them were anonymously feeding me information before the victims' webinars, which I was holding more and more—support sessions for all the anxious members needing help. They were lost, and they just didn't know what to do. And I was about to be hit with something way out of my comfort zone.

Ruja had instructed her Mr. Fixit Frank Schneider to deal with me. I was in remarkable company, but I'm not sure I liked that. Schneider was not new to international financial and political skulduggery and scandal. As a government agent, Schneider was a central player in a political furor involving Luxembourg's secret service, SREL (Service de Renseignement de l'État), which the Luxembourg media said resulted in then–prime minister Jean-Claude Juncker leaving office in 2013. Juncker, who was never charged with wrongdoing, appeared as a witness in the trial in which Schneider and two other former agents were charged with illegal security agency activity, which they maintained had his approval. They were acquitted. One accused agent, Marco Millie, the former boss of the SREL, said he could prove Junker had approved the wiretaps, carried out in 2007, because he had covertly recorded a conversation with his then–prime minister using a modified wristwatch. Junker, who said he couldn't recall authorizing the "bugging," had become the European Commission president embroiled in the long negotiations over the UK leaving Europe. Juncker got Brexit to sort out, while Frank

Schneider had me in his sights. I must have seemed like a fly on his car windscreen.

He was a veteran of run-ins with the world's intelligence services and seriously bad people. To my astonishment, he'd also gone to university in Scotland, which felt too close for comfort. On his company website he's listed as a founding partner and chief executive officer of Sandstone, which offers his CV: "Frank gained an MA in Economics and History from the University of Edinburgh and has held several key positions in business and government, including Director of Operations of Luxembourg's intelligence service. Today, Frank maintains a global network of professional intelligence contacts and manages major client accounts on a day-to-day basis." He flags up on the Sandstone website a quote from 1560 by Francis Walsingham, spymaster of Queen Elizabeth I: "*Knowledge is never too dear.*" On the public forum they detail their expertise, and here is an edited version:

> *We consist of a hand-picked team of creative analysts, consultants, and information specialists. Our compliance and litigation support is based on a high-end operational approach with a unique pool of specific research resources and a global network of direct human connections and investigation professionals. We speak over a dozen languages and have a broad base of knowledge in political, economic, financial, legal, and technical areas. . . .*
> *As a Luxembourg company, Sandstone operates from a politically and historically neutral base—an advantage when operating in complex international environments. We also benefit from the country's favorable professional secrecy legislation, giving the company a strong judicial foundation to guarantee utmost client confidentiality and discretion. . . .*
> *Every day, we are asked to help in potentially controversial, dangerous, and morally complex cases. We handle highly sensitive information and we give advice in often extreme situations. But whatever we do, we are committed to the highest standards of business integrity and accountability.*

Well, I never. They do make themselves sound important. Through Frank Schneider they brought in other heavyweights, including a public relations consultancy called Chelgate, whose chairman is Terence Fane-Saunders, which sounds like the name of an elaborate ice cream. While I was forging ahead in the campaign to stop Ruja, it was the job of Terence Fane-Saunders, known as TFS, from his offices based in Southwark, London, and Chelgate, to manage her reputation. Neither TFS nor Chelgate have been accused of any wrongdoing. Simon Harris, a onetime Chelgate employee who was close to the OneCoin account, told me and Douglas Thompson in a long-ranging interview on August 13, 2020, that his former company was reportedly paid £40,000 a month through Schneider to work on the account. Schneider also hired a prominent London legal firm, renowned in the UK for acting for libel claimants, to represent Dr. Ruja and OneCoin. The gloves were off in an arena with which I had absolutely no experience.

TEN

Death of a Salesman

I'd had the death threats, trolls, and abuse, and now into my home came the electronic advance of a registered letter, dated April 26, 2017, from the Carter-Ruck law firm of London EC4. When their email declaration of war arrived, I had no sense that Carter-Ruck was infamous, regularly known in *Private Eye* magazine as "Carter-Fuck." I understand now.

I don't think I would have cared had I known in that moment that they'd represented the most powerful people in the world, for they wrote: "We are instructed by our clients OneCoin Limited (One-Coin) and Ruja Ignatova in connection with a series of defamatory statements published by you about our clients."

Defamatory! I'd spent months studying the material sent to me from Tim Curry in California. He was the first to show me that One-Coin, showing little faith, was the first cryptocurrency that didn't accept cryptocurrency. He convinced me that only by widespread disclosure would OneCoin collapse and fewer people would be hurt and financially destroyed. I'd contacted all the people I could in One-Coin. I'd raised awareness like a fire brigade. When I'd finally seen the light, I'd gone back to Tim and asked for contacts, and the City of London criminal fraud experts had told me they also believed that OneCoin probably was, as Tim had so colorfully put it, "a fucking scam."

By then I'd heard so many, many stories of the misery brought upon individuals, communities, villages in India, townships in Africa, and disadvantaged groups from America and across Australia to the Pacific Islands, where desperate people watched as the sea level rose and the earth on which their homes are built eroded. It's an ugly metaphor that those islanders, as their past was drowned, were encouraged to put their future in OneCoin and Ruja.

All that considered, I thought any comments I'd made to be reasonable. In retrospect, I was too bloody reasonable. I wasn't in the mood for Carter-Ruck and the following letter, which spelled out their clients' discontent.

You should be aware:

• Our clients refute all allegations that they are operating a scam or an illegal pyramid or Ponzi scheme; and

• No evidence of criminal conduct has ever been put to our clients and no adverse findings of wrongful or criminal behavior has been made by any authorities. Our clients will cooperate fully with any official enquiries.

• The statements which you have published, however, go way beyond what may be considered to be legitimate debate and are causing very serious harm to our clients' business. Our clients therefore have no choice but to write to you in connection with these very serious matters.

In my day, I was a bit of a rock chick, and I love my music. I looked at the letter again and I thought: "I'm not having this."

I knew from OneCoin leaders that Dr. Ruja often anonymously joined one of our webinar support groups; she wanted to know what was going on, what was being said about her and about OneCoin. She liked to spy.

She has this Bulgarian Romani background and I streamed in a rock song to match my mood and attitude, "Gypsy Woman." With that blasting, I went all-out Janis Joplin, swinging my hips into the kitchen, where I had a bottle of Jack Daniel's whiskey. I grabbed a big glass and poured a giant slug of whiskey. I drank it in one gulp. I doubt I needed the courage, because I was so angry. I then posted a voice message on the webinar group:

Ruja . . . You . . . can kiss my ass.

It had been a battle. Now it was war.

I blush a little at that now, but I was mad as hell. I also directed the message to Carter-Ruck as I spoke. I was in shock and furious, as I could not understand why a solicitor acting on behalf of what I believed to be the Eastern European Criminal Network was trying to shut me up. I never had another letter after that initial threatening one accusing me of defamation. If the strategy was to silence me, it backfired. At the time I was still floundering with inconsistent reports and information. I so wanted all this conflict and unpleasantness to simply go away, for life to return to normal. I saw my family— especially my son, Lee—being careful around me, worried not only about my health but the frenzied state I would get myself worked up into. Always, whenever I was feeling overwhelmed, Eileen rescued me with a cup of tea and an encouraging message: "Let's get the bastards." And that's the censored version. It was a sentiment to follow, especially after I watched the video link of Ruja in action in Macau on May 7, 2017.

For that, which OneCoin styled the "Macau Event," she wore a tartan dress. The cheek of it! I was certain she had worn the tartan to personally irritate me and *only* me. The sheer audacity of her brought me thoughts of walking up on that stage and giving her a "Glasgow kiss," otherwise known as a headbutt. Watching her on stage was toe-curling for me, and more ominous for others who got badly burned, including two of her chief executive officers (CEOs).

Pablo Munoz, an American citizen based in Florida, was brought in as a OneCoin figurehead in late 2016. All anyone knew of him was that he had been an executive with Avon Cosmetics, having joined them from Tupperware in 2013. He didn't create any public waves other than make a few presentations for the South American market. His contract, according to the OneCoin whistleblower network, was worth nearly $2.9 million a year. The OneCoin event in Macau went wrong when underworld gossip suggested the Chinese government was going to make arrests at the event. It was tittle-tattle, but Munoz, apparently an unpleasant and paranoid gentleman, was freaked by this. But he didn't want to upset Ruja by not appearing without good reason.

He said his car had been in an accident with a cement truck on his way to Miami International Airport and his injuries were so severe he couldn't walk. A photograph supposedly of the incident appeared, but it was easily identified as a car crash image copied straight from Google. Shortly afterward he was no longer listed as OneCoin CEO, and he has never been heard of again.

When Munoz, who's never been accused of any wrongdoing, didn't turn up in Macau, Pierre "Pitt" Arens was named OneCoin's new CEO. He was a banker from Frank Schneider country, Luxembourg, but he didn't have much more luck getting on with Ruja. Gossip within the OneCoin "family" said Arens, who has never been accused of any wrongdoing, saw himself as this smooth banker who didn't like having to report to his Bulgarian employers—who had him on the usual 2.9-million-dollars-a-year contract—but soon they were just ignoring him. He had his photograph taken for promotions. He continued to strut around the offices and acted the big boss ordering office staff around to get him coffee. He had nothing else to do, said the staff. He was another "legitimate" hire for OneCoin, just expensive window dressing. His mistake was to start asking questions about the business, and Ruja didn't like that. He was spooked at hearing intruders in his garden at night and began believing he was being checked too carefully at passport controls. He missed a vital One-Coin meeting of weekend promoters in Portugal in October 2017 and left the company after only five months. He asked the company for double his money for "stress and risk and reputation damage"; One-Coin asked that he return his $120 mobile phone. Like Pablo Munoz, the banker hasn't been heard from again.

That summer of 2017 I didn't think I could be any more shocked and physically upset. The death of Ed Hartley, the man who had so enchanted me and Eileen when we met him at his appearance in London, took my emotions to a different level. It was painful to discover what had happened to this most charismatic of men. I don't know if he was always as honest as he should have been, but he seemed to care—and he saw Dr. Ruja and OneCoin for what they were. He left OneCoin not long after I wrote to him in November 2016, and a few months later he was dead.

His body was discovered in the parlor of a back street "beauty shop" in Ho Chi Minh City. He was in Vietnam promoting World Cryptocurrency Investment (WCI), the company he set up after leaving OneCoin, where he said things had "started to blur up quite a bit." I don't know what Ed Hartley found out about Dr. Ruja and the evil empire, but it was enough to make him get out not long after he arrived as the golden boy. It seems that, like others, he tried to go quietly, but he'd clearly seen the possibilities of marketing digital currency, and that's what he was doing when he died on July 19, 2017.

When I heard about Ed's death, the fear escalated within me. With fear comes a lot of emotional and psychological pain and suffering. There is no way to get through those times other than to be as strong as you can. I've just looked again at a video of Ed Hartley that Eileen and I saw being filmed by Jack Cadel at that London event, and you can sense that lovely way he had with people. We've tried to make sense of Ed's death through the authorities in Ho Chi Minh City, but they seem lost in red tape. He suffered, they say, a heart attack during a procedure to remove excess skin around his hip. He was fifty-three years old, and when I'd seen him a few months earlier he looked as fit as a fiddle, a tall, strong man able to carry himself without any problems. He left four daughters, all of whom said he didn't have that sort of vanity. And if there was a health problem he'd have had any procedure at home in America. On the last day of his life, he was also said by his office to be driving to Tan Son Nhat International Airport in Ho Chi Minh City for a flight home to Los Angeles. You don't stop for plastic surgery on the way, do you?

After his funeral on August 4, 2017, the family had not received any official explanation about his death. A colleague, concerned about what had happened to his friend, sent an American private detective to Su Van Hanh Street in District 10 in Ho Chi Minh City to investigate. He did a thorough job and asked lots of questions. Too many. He'd hardly been in Vietnam for forty-eight hours when he got a flight back to Los Angeles. He kept his travel expenses but returned his advance money after apologizing and saying it was too complex, too deadly for him to continue his inquiries.

Ed's friend told me the story about the private detective and said he felt Ed's "heart attack" was far more sinister than any of us had been led to believe. I remember the gut-wrenching, sick feeling at the pit of my stomach when I first heard that. It hurt. It seemed my life was being played out as a thriller movie. As shocking and real as it has always been, and still very much is, there are many times throughout when I say to myself, "How can all of this be real?" Eileen and I are from a small working-class Scottish town. Yet here we are, living every day the lives a mad fiction writer wouldn't make up.

Ruja's strongest weapon was and still is fear. OneCoin was such a cult that many investors were terrified of stepping out of line. After I went "rogue" in 2017, the French journalist Maxime Grimbert sought me out for an interview because he could find no victims in France who were willing to speak on the record. He had the same problem throughout Europe. He told me that most said the risk was too big. He expressed surprise that I was willing to speak with him and that he could use my name. He quoted one frightened victim to me: "A senior recruiter . . . advised me to take care of my health and that of my son."

I was seriously paranoid before Maxime contacted me, and his tales of intimidation only heightened that. He said that when he began his investigation into OneCoin and money laundering, the list of shell companies covered his desk and then one wall and then all the walls of his office. For every inquiry he made, there would be a threat in return. He asked to come to Scotland to talk to me, and we spent four days together, from seven in the morning into the evening. He was determined, and I liked him because of that. He brought a man named Clement with him; I wasn't sure about him. They wanted to come to my house, but I was too fearful when I was being bombarded with so many hateful threats. Eileen chipped in: "Bring them doon to my place—it's where it began." My nerves were at a screeching point, and whenever I went somewhere I'd lock the door behind me. I did that the instant we got to Eileen's, front and back door, the key turned and the bolt shot across. There were the four of us in Eileen's front room, where she and I did have our first serious talks about OneCoin. The French guys sat on one sofa next to the downstairs bedroom door, and Eileen and I sat on the sofa opposite. Maxime mentioned the mafia and death threats.

Clement was looking at us strangely. I was still taking in all the information about European gangs, and Eileen was looking like she'd sat on something sharp. It was tense. With that, a figure came through the bedroom door and screamed, "Boo!" I jumped in the air, Eileen was like a scalded cat with shock, Maxime gasped—and the Clement bloke didn't move a muscle. A suspicious, stoic character, I thought, for Eileen's youngest son, Logan, didn't scare him at all. The lad had been locked out, and we hadn't heard him knocking at the door so he'd climbed in the bedroom window. He'd heard my voice and thought it was me on a regular visit to his mother, and, typical Logan, he'd given us a fright. When he saw there were other people in the house, his face was a picture. When we settled, it was a moment of relief that had broken the ice, but the conversation carried on being chilling.

Maxime had much more to share. One victim had shown him a photograph he received of a hand with the index finger cut off and a picture of his partner. Maxime sent me a copy of his article, which included this comment about a victim he spoke to anonymously:

> The message to be silent is crystal clear in the world of OneCoiners; he even whispers the name of former executives of the organization who died in suspicious conditions. No solid evidence supports these legends, but they feed the *omertà*.

I had evidence closer to home—the death threats to me and those around me. Tim Curry in America was sent the photograph of a hand with a severed finger from a Twitter account called OneCoin Army. Another account put up images of his family and their home, with the caption: "Do you miss them?" Bjorn, who by 2021 had become the world's most consulted cryptocurrency expert by criminal investigators, was bullied by OneCoin with a 2017 defamation lawsuit in Norway. He finally won the case, but it disrupted his personal life and cost him all his savings in legal fees. So Bjorn had become a OneCoin victim too, but he fought and continues to fight. Maxime Grimbert was the first journalist to begin a full-time investigation of OneCoin—before we learned even more through the lawsuits and the disassembling of the scam.

I think he was as astonished by a dinner of Italian haggis (spaghetti and sauce are involved with our traditional dish) as my detailed OneCoin stories, although I think the supper was more pleasant and easier to digest. I was shaking with anger as I heard his disgusting OneCoin reports, which confirmed those I was receiving at high volume every day. With his team he had spoken to victims and recruiters worldwide, including a "fervent Nigerian Christian" who confessed to getting hundreds of his neighbors to invest in "this miracle currency." He showed me an Instagram message from this religious leader: I have never spent money myself in this currency, it is contrary to my reading of the Bible. But I was recruited to give lectures and convince others to invest. Maxime had done so much work and had scores of examples. There were the mundane, like Bree, an American housewife, who invested to prove to her successful husband that she too had business acumen. There were the scandalous: thousands of French families persuaded to give up their savings for a better future. Then there were the innocent aspirants like Viktor, a Ukrainian who thought OneCoin would give him membership in the "international financial elite" if his country didn't join the EU.

The long arm of the scam made me sad. Ruja's reach was boundless. I think of people like me who have had to struggle. I still remember hiding from the coal man and his bill, scraping together money to buy diapers and using boiled kitchen cloths when I couldn't: We were all in Ruja's bull's-eyes. We've lived on hope all our lives—the hope that tomorrow things would improve. And when the chance appears? It's attractive for a person or a family wanting to do better financially, to do more than put three meals a day on the table. And it's shameless for the con men to take away their last penny and their hope. For many, it was like the post–World War II days when "the pension man" came around every week to collect a few pence for working folks' future—although this was far more subversive. Ruja boasted of fifty thousand "distributors engaged in personal relationships of trust." In reality the OneCoin leaders were gathering cash as they always had and zigzagging it through a web of bank accounts, up, down, and through front companies and round and round again. The more paths and players—and there were hundreds of them—the more it became almost impossible to trace the funds as they washed up on faraway shores.

In America, one trick was to use Western Union to get victims to send cash payments to random people, usually immigrant workers, in the United Arab Emirates, who would be paid a small sum and led to OneCoin's Dubai office to deposit the money. No ID or other documents were required. The investor back in the United States, or any outlawed area, would then have their account credited electronically with the totally useless OneCoin. If an investor showed a glimmer of interest a way would be found for their money to travel to Dr. Ruja. There were four major OneCoin networks operating from France and Belgium with branches in French Polynesia and, to my surprise, the Antarctic. There is always someone willing to "distribute," and Maxime Grimbert encouraged me to look into Laurent Louis, a former Belgian politician who in 2016 became "a broker" for OneCoin. He, you may recall, was the promoter of the idea of OneCoin as the Devil's coin, "the pure product of Satan." In 2010 he was elected federal deputy of the People's Party but was expelled within six months. He controversially remained in politics within different political groups until signing up with Ruja as a commercial recruiter. He did a good job bringing in many investors and their tens of thousands of euros. The money was sent to foreign accounts. "Afterwards, people have the right not to be happy with OneCoin" was how Laurent Louis defended himself. He has never been charged with anything and said he was "only a small fish" despite a network of three thousand members in France and Belgium. He maintains he did nothing wrong and has not been charged with a crime, while the Belgian authorities say OneCoin was an illegal Ponzi scheme. Stalemate, a familiar frustration. Whenever we managed to place a hurdle or even a strong obstacle in the way of the forward march of the scam, they leaped over it or craftily around it. They relied on innocence, and I'd been seriously guilty of that. I didn't take account of the UK warning by the Financial Conduct Authority (FCA) that was put in place in September 2016, when I was one of Ruja's most ardent fans. What did I know? It's not as if people like me check the financial world warnings every morning like we do the weather. The big players may be aware, but they're not out there alerting us. When I did find out about it, I was told by the OneCoin leaders that it was the work of haters and meant nothing. It did appear to be troubling Ruja when I had her under pressure, for she instructed Frank Schneider to get it taken down. He was told to fix it—and me.

In the summer of 2017, when Ed Hartley died, Ruja was living the life, flying around the world and visiting her money. She'd also created a summer getaway at the Black Sea resort of Sozopol; in Bulgaria that's a seaside and a popular summer tourist spot. Ruja didn't want to mix with the hoi polloi. She boastfully announced that her $3 million "holiday home" featured a "private beach" and "private vineyard," a "huge pool," and an interior stuffed with "extremely expensive custom-made furniture imported from Germany." She bought the three-story hotel next door as a guest house, and between the properties was a vast area reserved as "a children's playground." I presume that whole playground was for her daughter, Davina, whom she presented to the world at the end of 2016. When Eileen and I watched Ruja in her shapely purple dress giving her performance on stage in Bangkok in October 2016, she did not look the least bit pregnant. So where had Davina come from? She's claimed financial miracles, but this? Ruja appeared the doting mum on a promotional video introducing the baby to her followers, saying she wanted to spend more time with her family. She had a crowded life. When she held her daughter's christening party at the Sozopol mansion, I was fascinated to see her shamelessly mingling around the pool with key OneCoin laundryman Gilbert Armenta, the lover with whom she was besotted. He saw his work for Ruja following him like "a big black shadow." She regarded him as the love of her life. And posing by the swimming pool, all appeared in harmony. In the photographs she is snuggling with her onetime lover and her German husband, the lawyer Bjorn Strehl (who has not been implicated in any crimes), on a visit from the home she bought him in Frankfurt and from whom she may or not be officially divorced. I have many photographs of the event showing Ruja flagrantly flashing her wealth. Her father, Plamen, is there but I can't see her mother, Veska, who rarely leaves her office in Sofia. Also there is her brother, Konstantin. She'd become upset and suddenly fired her personal assistant, Denitza Godeva (who has not been charged with any crimes), whom she was told and believed was having an affair with Sebastian. She wanted someone she could trust, and Konstantin was family. After five years working in Germany, Konstantin left his $3,000-a-month job to be paid a little over $200 a month more to work as his sister's personal assistant.

Ruja likes everything done just her way. Working out of the Sofia office, one of Konstantin's main assignments was to ensure everything Ruja bought was sent to the correct address. There were so many mansions! Apparently, furniture for one mansion had gone to another, and a Cayenne Turbo S Class went missing. If he made mistakes there was great fury. If the Diet Coke was too warm, the offending can—and any other missiles at hand—were thrown at him, along with a verbal lashing. The South African Duncan Arthur was working for Northern Trust, a venerated American financial institution, when he was recruited by Ruja, who, he says, charmed him against all his misgivings. Duncan told me:

> She was disgusting to Konstantin and she used to physically assault him. She can be a complete bitch. She is also so charismatic, she could convince me of anything. She's incredibly eloquent, which is amazing, because English is about her third or fourth language. When I first met her, she knew everything about me, which was impressive, flattering. She knew the answer to everything. She was absolutely professional. There is no doubt that she is bloody, bloody bright, incredibly clever. There hasn't been anybody since Google who could put together what she did. It's a cult, absolutely a cult; once you're encompassed, you're encompassed forever. She regretted hiring me from the start because I asked questions and I wouldn't toe the line. I don't know if it was that, but Konstantin and I became good mates right from the start. We both love martial arts, and Konstantin has a fantastic sense of humor.

I'll let Konstantin enlighten you about his big sister's attitude. He testified in court in New York: "I had to make sure that everything worked smoothly: like the hotel, that she has reservations for dinner and that she has always a car waiting for her. Also I carried her shopping bag—shopping bags and handbag. And from time to time I had to work for her as an extra security guard. Ruja was always traveling with two to four bodyguards."

But, he said, after Davina's christening on July 8, 2017, his sister took a trip on her own. She flew to Bishkek, the capital of Kyrgyzstan, in central Asia. On her return she told Konstantin she'd bought a fake passport. When he inquired why, "she said that everybody around her has one. Gilbert Armenta and Sebastian and she said [in court testimony] Frank Schneider told her it might be useful to have one."

Foreign travel, by private and commercial airlines, was always easy for Ruja. Marriage to Bjorn Strehl gave her another German passport, to add to her collection of international documents including Ukrainian and Russian passports and diplomatic credentials from the United Arab Emirates obtained in a spectacular 2014 financial facilities deal.

Ruja believed herself untouchable. Her connections and the billions she was making for people—and some countries—motivated her, and she had to keep showing how successful she was and hosting parties on her yacht, *Davina*, docked at Sozopol. They were very much look-at-me affairs, and that July of 2017, she enrolled the American Grammy winner Bebe Rexha to provide entertainment for her guests. The singer and songwriter (of Eminem's "The Monster") was a huge hit with the crowd and with Ruja, who in photographs looks in full-on party mood and alive to her star performer. While the Albanian American Bebe Rexha sang for her supper on a custom-built stage in the gardens of Ruja's mansion overlooking the sea, I was starring on an international to-do list created by Chelgate.

Meeting with [REDACTED]
18 July 2017-07-18
1. Investigation ongoing
2. [REDACTED]
3. They will reply on 21/22 July
4. Germany—applying for license
5. [REDACTED]
6. [REDACTED]
7. [REDACTED]
8. India—IMAs had blocked accounts—possible charges against R
9. [REDACTED]

10. McCadum—Scottish lawyers advising on COLP [City of London Police]
11. [REDACTED]
12. [REDACTED]
13. [REDACTED]

It's still quite scary to see my name, even if spelled incorrectly, on what I was told by a whistleblower was a list of international problems to be dealt with by Chelgate and Terence Fane-Saunders. I have never been able to verify the document 100 percent, but I believe it was given to me in good faith to help me and other victims find justice. Knowing the source, I have full confidence it is genuine. They were paid by the government of Malta to look after the island's reputation following the murder by car bomb of the Maltese journalist Daphne Caruana Galizia in 2017. The company—which specializes in "crisis management under the personal supervision of Chelgate's chairman, Terence Fane-Saunders"—also worked with Harley Facades, the British firm that supplied the cladding panels to Grenfell Tower in London, which caught fire in 2017 with seventy-two deaths. Harley Facades has maintained it was not responsible, and no one has been held accountable for the tragedy. The Chelgate company website quotes Fane-Saunders's philosophy to "not support any . . . enterprise which is engaged in deliberate wrongdoing and to never knowingly lie or mislead. Quite simply, this would be bad business."

I don't know if I was good or bad for business. The sensitive memo has redacted items as it was "leaked" to me—not by Simon Harris, but anonymously. You'll understand my imagination played all manner of fearful tricks on me when I heard about this.

For without me raising a noise, Ruja thought she could carry on regardless of the law and regulations. She apparently had been given such advice. An article in the *Times* in London on November 25, 2019, could only "allege" that Ruja instructed the City of London law firm Hogan Lovells to carry out compliance inquiries in 2016 into the family investment company RavenR Capital Ltd., as they would not confirm that. It reported that Hogan Lovells "were thought to have identified some problems during an eight-month review, but indicated that these could be resolved and said OneCoin was not a pyramid scheme."

Another online report by BehindMLM, in April 2020, said there were documents revealing detailed recommendations made to her. Ruja took from the advice she was getting that if her victims didn't lose too much money she might get away without too much scrutiny in the UK.

In privileged court testimony in the US Southern District of New York on November 6, 2019, Konstantin Ignatova said his sister told him "she got either a legal opinion or a license, I can't recall completely, by sleeping with [redacted]." The *Times* article also reported that a specialist in banking law who was hired to run the "family office" said Ruja told him to instruct Carter-Ruck and Chelgate when the FCA posted its alert about OneCoin in September 2016.

Interestingly, the *Times* also reported: "Carter-Ruck did not comment on claims that it acted for RavenR. Terence Fane-Saunders, the chairman of the PR agency, *denied any association with RavenR or Ms. Ignatova*" [my italics].

I knew who Carter-Ruck did act for: I have my letter. Simon Harris, who worked for Chelgate for only a few weeks, also had evidence through emails, texts, and WhatsApp messages that the company worked for Ruja, OneCoin, and Frank Schneider. He presented what he knew to us in 2020, and by then there was much public awareness of Dr. Ruja, the now infamous cryptoqueen. But three years earlier I was wandering in a wilderness. There seemed nowhere to go. The focus of Tim, Bjorn, Crypto Xpose, and myself was solely to raise awareness. It seemed that no one really cared, that no one was listening to us and helping us. It had been a distressing and exhausting battle at that stage to raise awareness that just seemed to continue to go nowhere. This included the FCA and City of London Police not taking action against anyone involved.

DEVIL'S COIN

If Simon Harris had only appeared on his white horse earlier, but there you have it. Chelgate, meanwhile, was working with the clients the boss said they didn't have. The big shove was to get the FCA to remove its warning about OneCoin, and to do that there was liaison between Chelgate and Carter-Ruck, with Frank Schneider dealing with both firms.

Harris, some time after the happenings that disturbed him, wrote in August 2020 to the Public Relations and Communications Association (PRCA) in London with a complaint about Chelgate's behavior. One section of that letter (unedited) is revealing, and it is shocking to me that such efforts were employed by established UK companies in an attempt to stabilize the shaky scaffolding around Dr. Ruja:

> I started with Chelgate on August 1, 2017, and left nine weeks later. My line manager was Associate Director Robert Winstanley. One of my first jobs was to update daily a word document looking at the legal and regulatory issues that OneCoin was facing worldwide. This document is on the internet—not placed by me, as I didn't keep a copy. If I remember correctly it listed 37 different countries where OneCoin was in trouble. I have taken a screen grab from the internet. It is dated August 11 and I was in charge of that document then, but I don't recall adding the comments about the police but I did add the comment about the FCA. This document had to be ready every time Chelgate met with Carter-Ruck or Frank. Frank very occasionally came to the Chelgate offices. I have no documented evidence from this period as I was very new. But I do have a WhatsApp message from December 2017 long after I left that is relevant. Screen grab attached.

In January 2022, he told me he received no reply to the Harris letter of complaint, and when he asked why, he got no response. (In August 2020, apparently contradicting Terence Fane-Saunders's quote to the *Times* on November 25, 2019, Chelgate admitted in a statement that OneCoin and Dr. Ruja were clients who were paying a generous fee.)

444

What I still find upsetting is the successful efforts to get the FCA to take down its alert, which it did on August 1, 2017, granting Ruja and OneCoin an opportunity to market themselves as "legitimate."

Ruja's paid PR men got a result. According to Simon Harris, Terence Fane-Saunders said publicly that he was delighted the FCA "had capitulated."

Harris told the PRCA that Fane-Saunders had turned to him in the Chelgate offices and said the FCA dropping its warning that cursed July in 2017 proved that OneCoin was a genuine enterprise—which Ruja and OneCoin immediately used in a revved-up marketing campaign, virtually shouting: "Hey, we're legitimate." That was enough to seduce more people around the globe to invest in One-Coin, especially in Asia and Africa. Chelgate had earned their lumps of silver. Harris said Chelgate, along with Carter-Ruck, wrote to the FCA and the City of London Police—both carried the same warning about OneCoin on their respective websites—at the same time. What they called "the take down" letters were from Robert Winstanley of Chelgate and Claire Gill of Carter-Ruck. The FCA has always denied being "leaned on" and issued a standard statement to anyone who inquires about them taking down the OneCoin warning: "We published the consumer notice in 2016 at the request of the City of London Police. The decision to take our alert down was made in conjunction with the City of London Police who were investigating the matter. Our alerts are primarily intended to warn consumers about firms carrying on regulated activities without the required FCA authorization. The FCA does not regulate crypto assets and therefore it could not take this matter further." Well, there *were* no OneCoin crypto assets—it was all worthless. But could they not have regulated what Ruja was doing here with all that money from her Ponzi scheme? I had no wish to be any more aware of Carter-Ruck, but I read Andrew Penman's report in the *Daily Mirror* on August 13, 2020, about the FCA's actions: "I contacted Carter-Ruck, which not only seems proud to have acted for OneCoin, it reckons that its action helped get that FCA warning taken down. 'On behalf of our client we made legal representations to the FCA about the publication of its consumer warning, following which the FCA informed us that the warning would be removed,' a spokesman for the law firm told me."

I felt like Alice in Wonderland with all this avalanche of material and contradictions crashing into my life, racing down rabbit hole after rabbit hole to discover more. Simon Harris had become friendly with Robert Winstanley and said he was there when Chelgate chief executive officer Liam Herbert congratulated the team on the removal of the website warnings. He said that "Sofia was pleased."

Harris wrote to the PRCA: "The real villain in the conversation was someone called Kieron Vaughan and I heard that Frank was 'looking into him.'" After Liam had left I asked who Frank was and I was told he was OneCoin's "enforcer." We joked about *The Godfather*, and I called him "The Capo." I asked my colleague if OneCoin was legitimate and he said "no," but the contract was particularly "lucrative" and added, "This deeply concerned me . . ."

Well, if he was concerned, how did the millions of people whose lives had been plundered by Ruja and her OneCoin army of scam artists feel?

Harris also showed me a series of WhatsApp messages with a colleague, which he had attached as evidence to his complaint. Of course, they are private messages so I can't show the correspondence here, but I found it very unsettling. They showed what was going on at Chelgate and Carter-Ruck. People I had felt had tried to intimidate me now seemed to be laughing about the situation. I was shocked.

This was overwhelming for me, information that so many people were fighting to save Ruja's empire while no one in authority appeared to be trying to help her victims. It was so them and us: the proceeds of fraud being used to pay for the protection of the fraudsters. Harris shared his "conversation" with Robert Winstanley to illustrate that the victims of Ruja and OneCoin counted for nothing and were as worthless as OneCoin tokens in their corporate world.

ELEVEN

Ruja Roulette

As those god-awful months of 2017 went on, it was tense at home, for I was so wrapped up with taking on Ruja and trying to comfort the victims and follow the trail of their money—in that Pollyanna hope that one day they might see some of it returned—that there was such little time to concern myself with other things and the people I love. I kept so much to myself and knowingly let Gordon allow the drama to go over his head. He was concerned about my activism but understood me well enough to not try and put a stop to it. The constant call on my time interrupted every moment of the day and night. So where was the time to talk to Gordon? He is always so caring, especially when I'm suffering relapses with ME, generous with *his* time and empathy. I'd get frights of guilt about not embracing him with what was consuming my life. Gordon had suffered health problems of his own and, in my way, I absolve myself by saying I was protecting him. He never said anything, but he must have resented me for constantly skipping away for my tactical meetings with Eileen. There we'd sit in her wee front room until the early hours, fingers bashing away at laptop keyboards.

Oh, I'd been tempted at times to ignore the calls and texts and emails, but I never had the courage to take that risk, live with the consequences, exist with myself if my neglect contributed to anyone harming themselves. I felt I was in a duel with Ruja, and I could never let my guard down. And if I ever had a moment of hesitation the shameless manipulators of OneCoin would immediately turn me back into an avenger. Ruja had kidnapped my life and I was a changed person, still caring and concerned for others, but I was much more cynical, acutely aware of life's dark side, and finding it almost impossible to trust others. The malice and threats against me were ongoing and rarely subtle. I wasn't surprised. These bastards made people lose their lives, get sick, become hopeless—and then took off with all they had, without regret or even a glance at their victims, who were nothing but a commodity.

I was fighting a global fraud involving billions. The banks from Dublin to Dubai didn't seem able to add up the cash that Ruja moved through their accounts. This was a world of international hoodlums, clever and vicious racketeers, making those billions by making dupes of millions who only wanted a better life. I'd sadly learned the awful consequences of going against Ruja's empire through my victim support groups and from OneCoin whistleblowers. Many suffered when threats were realized. Those close to me were constantly nipping at my ear, telling me to slow down in my quest to vanquish the dragon queen. They understood I needed to fight Ruja, but because of my health they wanted me to slow my pace.

Yet how could I? I'd learned how a kind word could save a life or a person's sanity. OneCoin had plundered 177 countries, and I don't think there is a victim from a country that OneCoin targeted that I have not in some way communicated with. This included spending endless amounts of time on Google Translate to attempt to communicate messages with victims in their own language. I understood the pain, this dreadful limbo they were in. What could they do? The fear kept on escalating. Unsettling thoughts began to overwhelm me after I had disrupted the OneCoin world. To go through darkness is terrifying, but I believe that where there is light, even a glimmer, there is hope. I do believe that. Helen Keller, who was born deaf and blind and became a teacher and author, has been an inspiration to me since I was young. She memorably said: "The most beautiful things in the world cannot be seen or even touched, they must be felt with the heart."

As Eileen and I sat wrapped up in blankets at three o'clock many a morning, it would have cheered us up enormously had we known what "distress" Ruja was suffering in New York. And that the Americans were racing to our rescue. Ruja and Sebastian had hired expert US financial advisers and lawyers to set up creative and elaborate schemes to get around the laws prohibiting money laundering. They were betting on spinning the wheel on their thieved billions so swiftly and cleverly that the world's financial cops would miss it. As Ruja did her laundry, the federal authorities in America were picking up the dirty linen.

Even after all my years of tangling with Ruja and OneCoin and feeding information to authorities like the FBI and the UK and European fraud detectives, and despite the details shared by them and revealed in the New York courts and in scores of official bank and government documents, I think there are still missing pieces. Yet what I did learn was enough to make me choke with outrage and spill so many cups of tea I needed a new carpet. Because of my ME, I listen to many books on audiotape, and I can't think of any fictional stories that have surprised me with so many twists and turns and shocks. The betrayals and sins are biblical.

In the beginning, Ruja and Sebastian created OneCoin. What is now regarded by authorities worldwide as a lucrative global fraud soared beyond their wildest dreams. On June 11, 2014, Ruja emailed her cofounder Sebastian Greenwood:

> It might not be really clean or that I normally work on or even can be proud of (except with you in private when we make the money)— but . . . I am especially good in these very borderline cases, where the things become gray—and you as the magic sales machine, and me as someone who can really work with numbers, legal and back you up in a good and professional way—we could really make it big—like MLM meets bitch of Wall Street;-).

She described how they would use OneCoin to draw in investors by offering us victims ever-escalating returns. All the palaver with back offices and diamond leaders and coins and splits, all the cleverly parceled nonsense, was part of the illusion, to make you look the other way while the daylight robbery was going on. In June 2014, Ruja had privately set out her working scheme to her recruits: "We can manipulate the exchange by simulating some volatility and intraday pricing and always close on a high price . . . build confidence—better manipulation so *they* are happy."

"They" were the mugs, the peasants like me, who believed One-Coin was *mining* more coins when they were just issuing more coins whenever they wanted. Ruja was using encrypted Proton Mail electronic mail and Russian phones as well as burner phones, as were most of her co-conspirators, but despite such precautions the FBI was picking up her trail, following the money as always. Oh, and did they make money. They seemed to go from zero to zillions in global currency in a flash. One moment in 2016 Sebastian—who'd become, after Ruja, the most important person to me in the OneCoin world— "lifted" for personal use more than $100 million in cash from the OneCoin office in Seoul, South Korea. Ruja helped herself to cash whenever the notion accosted her. It's clear she'd fallen madly in love with herself, becoming giddy and sometimes drunk on her own cleverness. It was potent.

On a 2017 visit to the OneCoin offices in Hong Kong, where she expected her minions to refer to her as "Her Royal Highness," Ruja took rooms at the five-star Ritz-Carlton in West Kowloon. There she summoned an employee, who arrived with a concerned smile, an assistant, two bodyguards, and a backpack containing more than a million Hong Kong dollars—$100,000 US—in cash. She wanted to "do a little shopping," so she took off, with her two regular Russian bodyguards, to the Elements Shopping Mall on the podium level of the International Shopping Centre. As ever, she bought expensive clothes from names you don't see on the High Street and "trinkets" to contrast with the sparkle of her more than $1 million timepieces of jewelry bought "on mad afternoons" in Dubai, where she had her eighth mansion, a spectacular $20 million number, custom built. She kept her Rolls-Royce there, the Bentley in Sofia, along with the armored Lexus and a couple of "gassed up" Porsches with custom license plates like 911 GT2 RS. The police often moonlighted and collected Ruja's guests from the airport, and Dubai became very much her gilded perch from where she swooped into Europe and America, usually by private plane.

Her mission during that late summer of 2017 was to make all the millions and millions she'd stolen from all of us victims vanish by turning the money into untraceable commodities, properties, foundations, and "clean" investments like Silicon Valley startups. She'd long worried at the staggering amounts of cash cascading in. On August 6, 2015, she'd emailed Sebastian: This is the implication from the big sales 4 weeks ago. 1.3 [billion] fake coins. We are fucked, this came unexpected and now needs serious, serious thinking. That 1.3 billion fake coins were valued at $1.9032 *trillion*. No wonder she said they were fucked. The math had caught up with her. She was getting ridiculously rich too quickly.

The real money, the piles of cash, needed a home. Many of the schemes to secure their stolen fortunes were premeditated, and I don't think Ruja and Sebastian were initially alarmed by the vast amount of cash pouring in. I see them dancing on the moon about it. It was the speed by which they were making it that surprised them and gave them distribution problems. Hitting the jackpot was dizzying for them, and if problems appeared Ruja's sworn philosophy was that of a thief. She'd put it in an email to Sebastian on August 9, 2014: Take the money and run and blame someone else for this . . .

The groundwork for that escape tactic began around the time of OneCoin's creation. Other than in Bulgaria, Ruja planned to work out of London and the UAE, which has limited extradition treaties and none with the United States. By the time of my initial contact with the City of London Police, I had ruined her RavenR Capital "family fund" scheme to spread the money out of her top-of-the-market offices overlooking Hyde Park in London. She gave up on that after being politely asked by DC Kieron Vaughan to appear at his headquarters for an interview. That was when Ruja totally blew her top about me. She was outraged. She didn't like interference, but she had a backup safe haven having done glorious ongoing deals in Dubai. During the coronavirus pandemic, Dubai was one place in the world that permitted scammers to host live marketing events.

Ruja had taken her own brand of plague to Dubai much earlier, along with $16 million in cash to purchase a UAE bank license. Prosperia FZE, a shell company, was set up in the UAE in May 2014, and OneCoin Limited, another shell company, was established in the UAE one month later. When accounts were opened, both were presented as "management consultancy" businesses to the Mashreq Bank.

Not much management consultancy seemed to be involved by OneCoin Limited, and bank officials were wary when cash—way more than they were told to expect—started arriving by wire transfer, beginning with a OneCoin shell company transfer of more than $200 million. As the victims, from Loch Lomond to London to Lahore to Los Angeles and round again, sent their Starter package or Tycoon package cash transfer payments, they were primarily routed from accounts in Hong Kong to the Mashreq Bank (which has not been implicated in any wrongdoing).

What seems to me to be spectacularly wrong is that when the American authorities first smelled a rat with OneCoin and Ruja in 2015—before I even had my dad's money to invest—Dubai's General Department of Criminal Investigations was red-flagging money laundering in the dodgy accounts. Mashreq Bank officials asked questions when they saw the account was funded by incoming remittances from people and small companies in Bulgaria, Kuala Lumpur, Estonia, Hong Kong, Vietnam, Cambodia, Mexico, the United States, Gibraltar, and Australia, all with the stated purpose appearing as "username," "marketing and educational packages," "payment for equipment," or "payment for education." When quizzed about the money transferring out—more laundering—OneCoin presented contract invoices showing they were bulk-buying "flash games," the once popular internet browser games like Bowman, The Impossible Quiz, and Max Dirt Bike. That these games—and that OneCoin was, on paper, paying ten times the market price for them—had nothing to do with management consultancy was, you'd think, suspicious.

According to US court papers, an administrative officer at Mashreq Bank had a OneCoin contact: Karl Sebastian Greenwood. He reportedly gave the employee a "wedding gift" of AED 500,000 (UAE Dirham) worth more than $100,000. He and Ruja were named in letters about serious fraud and money laundering through the UAE banks. Despite raised eyebrows by some banking staff, who thought colleagues were colluding in the money washing, and a formal alert, the authorities in Dubai took no action against OneCoin or Sebastian and the others. If they had, maybe so much misery would never have happened. To date, no one in the UAE has ever been held accountable.

Which is another astonishment, for what happened next was and remains beyond belief. While Ruja and her companies were merrily laundering millions through the Mashreq Bank, the country's chief of police, Dhahi Khalf Tamim, received information delivered by courier from Kuwait's Ministry of the Interior. The Kuwaiti government documents said Ruja and OneCoin Ltd. may have been funding global terrorism.

The warnings, from the country's head of security, Major General Abdul Hamid Abdul Rahim Al-Awadi, reported that Ruja was working for a "state sponsor of terrorism." They did not identify the culprit but disclosed that Ruja was sending cash to Afghanistan, Pakistan, and Yemen, and traveling with huge amounts of cash on a diplomatic passport and private planes. Even if the warnings were acted on in any way, there remains no trace of any action being taken against Ruja. Instead, she got and maintains a UAE residence through Prosperia FZE. She seems to have been very fondly adopted by oil-rich states and was comfortably elevated to Ruja of Arabia. There is another sensational twist in this tale, for Ruja, who created cryptocurrency that didn't accept cryptocurrency payments, became the second largest owner of Bitcoin after the legitimate digital currency's creator, Satoshi Nakamoto. My only repeatable response when I learned this was "Holy shit!" It was too incredible. I felt I was on a cliff edge in a *Mission: Impossible* film. And I was furious at the hypocrisy of it all. It's strange how, despite all the gross criminal actions by Ruja, it was her flaunting of the simple rules of human decency that most make me boil with rage. It's just indecent.

She and her goons warned me and all the victim-investors that if we purchased any other digital currency our accounts would be, in effect, forfeited. She argued that it would be like a Coca-Cola truck driver drinking Pepsi on the job.

The round-the-clock seeker of justice Lynndel Edgington, my much relied upon and trusted Eagle 1 in America, messaged me to say that through one of his contacts he believed the FBI was closing in on Ruja and Sebastian and was working with overseas governments. I was excited by that, but I didn't tell the victims' groups as I didn't want to alert Ruja, who had all our contact rooms bugged. Ruja boasted that, as a former international secret policeman, Frank Schneider "had contacts everywhere," and annoyingly, and unbeknownst to us at this time, he received a similar inside tip-off from US law enforcement that an investigative squad was looking at Ruja and OneCoin.

They had a treasure chest to find, although Ruja was still confident that it had been thoroughly washed by Gilbert Armenta and a well-fed Florida lawyer, Mark Scott, who was another one with a passion for yachts and Porsches. These fraudsters seem to make a few million and buy sports cars, then a few million more and buy a yacht. I was told that some call it the "menoporsche," or midlife crisis. Scott was paid $50 million by Ruja to help bankroll his hot flashes, and court documents also said: three multimillion-dollar seaside homes in Cape Cod, Massachusetts; a fifty-seven-foot Sunseeker yacht; a $250,000 Ferrari 599 GTB 2011; and *three* Porsches with a total value of almost $700,000. Some of Scott's "toys" were paid for with funds "originating" at an account in the Bank of Ireland, Fenero Tradenext.

Tradenext also funded the $1,310,000 innocently received by Nautikos Sunseeker Group, based at Bayshore in Miami, Florida, for his yacht. It all makes my brain want to explode when I think these gross indulgences were paid for by so much misery. Dr. Ruja was careful in how she chose the people around her, but underworld inclinations don't reflect loyalty and character.

It was with guidance from Frank Schneider that Ruja connected with Mark Scott through the US legal company Locke Lord, which had advised her on the London property investments I spoiled for her. Scott gave up his equity partnership with the company, and from his home in Coral Gables, Florida, Scott began commuting to Sofia via Frankfurt in late 2015. He was pampered by first-class treatment on his first visits to Bulgaria, and in early meetings the second floor of the OneCoin offices were cleared for him and Ruja to consult privately.

There was much to talk about and lots and lots of cash to deal with, for the acknowledged sales revenue generated when he began work was $3.859 billion. That's US dollars, but the amounts are so vast that even in sterling or euros the sums are impossible for me to add up. I can't imagine so much money. What would you do with it? Especially if you had stolen the majority of it from poor people in the most deprived parts of the world. I understand why you'd want to clean it up and cover up the polluted trail. Mark Scott was good at that. As was Gilbert Armenta, who was involved in making the earth move for Ruja as well as her money. These two American lawyers became her business partners and money launderers. For me, finding out what they did with the stolen funds was like sinking into quicksand. I had to take deep breaths fearing I'd drown in the depths of the remarkable schemes they created to bury Ruja's treasure. She had cash in bundles of currency stacked in offices and apartments in Bulgaria, Hong Kong, Dubai, South Korea, London, and New York. When I worked behind the bar in pubs there was always the problem of staff pilfering a few pounds or the missing bottle of whiskey. When I worked at a bank, if £5 was overdrawn we had to spend hours after work, searching unpaid through endless accounts until we had found that missing money. With OneCoin the "petty thieving" was often in the tens of millions of dollars.

Ruja had to maneuver our billions in investments back to herself and her co-conspirators, but they couldn't receive them in transparent transfers. She'd have been open season for bank alerts on suspicious transactions flagging herself and OneCoin to the anti-fraud police. Instead, there were Mark Scott schemes, like the Madagascar oil well. There were stables in Abu Dhabi for thoroughbred racehorses. And there was Gilbert Armenta flying down to make deals in Rio de Janeiro and Bogotá while Scott set up phony investment funds in the British Virgin Islands. Monies were brought into these despicable serial funds—the Fenero Funds—supposedly from wealthy and aristocratic European families. I suppose the idea was that if the people were posh their cash couldn't smell. Initially, banks and trusts all over the world were satisfied by Scott's lies that the people and monies involved were legitimate and therefore the enormous cash movements must be too.

The illicit cash was laundered through financial institutions in at least twenty-one countries, including Hong Kong, Singapore, the United States, the Cayman Islands, the Channel Islands, the Republic of Ireland, and Georgia (in Eastern Europe, not the American state). This was all on top of the "Happy Mondays" in the United Arab Emirates. The money was funneled back to Dr. Ruja, Sebastian, and others at the top of the alleged pyramid. Money in the funds was treated as another commodity, and huge fees were generated by financial institutions when a few taps on a keyboard moved the millions around.

I was intrigued how our money was being recycled, and what happened closest to home, only a forty-five-minute flight across the Irish Sea from Glasgow, offered me a clear picture of how this particular money-washing machine worked. I found much of it came back to these lively Fenero Funds and from there directly to Ruja.

On March 11, 2016, an Irish lawyer from Mason Hayes & Curran, a business law firm with offices in Dublin, New York, and London, unwittingly introduced Mark Scott by email to a Bank of Ireland official and copied other bank employees at the bank's office in Burlington Road, Dublin:

> By way of background, Mark Scott is establishing an investment business that will operate out of Ireland. Mark is hoping to establish a relationship with a bank in Ireland that can look after his needs. Perhaps you can start a conversation around this following this email and I would be happy to assist in any way that I can.

Quickly, on March 13, 2016, Scott replied. He sent the bank legal documents about the company based in the British Virgin Islands, which he claimed owned the investment company he worked for, the Fenero Funds. Fenero Equity Investments (Ireland) was set up in April 2016. The Fenero Tradenext Holding Limited (Ireland) was established at the same time, as was Fenero Pct Holdings Limited (Ireland). Bank forms that Scott completed said the new companies expected turnover in their accounts to be between £10 million and £25 million a year. He said Fenero was a nearly £90 million fund that managed the fortunes of four rich European families. Scott explained he'd worked with these families on deals worth more than £1.8 billion for several years, and they were amalgamating their liquid assets to invest. The bank designated Fenero as "high-risk" because it was based in the British Virgin Islands, but they explained at Scott's trial that this wasn't unusual.

At least £273 million was laundered by Scott through Ireland. Of that, my FBI contact, Special Agent Ron Shimko, said his investigators reckon about £185 million was washed between February 2017 and April 2017, through the "Ireland Fund" to a UAE investment fund. It was when Scott, through Fenero Equity Investments (Ireland) Dublin, tried to make a payment to Phoenix Fund Invest in Dubai that a banker sounded an internal bank alert. Who was the money for? What was the Phoenix Fund? She also wanted more details about Fenero. Scott called off that deal to stop the bank delving too much more into his dodgy business dealings. Which was understandable.

Headquartered in Dubai, Amer Abdulaziz Salman started Phoenix Thoroughbreds in 2017 as the "world's first regulated thoroughbred fund" and became a hugely important person in bloodstock deals and international racing. His ability to pay big money elevated him in the world of racehorse ownership. He could "buy" champions. Not long after the Fenero Funds were set up, Phoenix Thoroughbreds on March 1, 2017, bought its first horses at Fasig-Tipton, the renowned American auction house for great winners. Abdulaziz's business was a for-profit fund dedicated to equine assets. He said the fund had been set up in Frank Schneider's comfort zone, Luxembourg, and clients were queueing up to invest. He was the named account holder on the Phoenix Fund. Yes, the source of the funds was Abdulaziz. OneCoin had an office in the Phoenix Business Center in Dubai that he owned and was able to draw on this as payments for Starter packages and the other OneCoin offers began. In US court documents, Konstantin accused Abdulaziz of being another laundry for Ruja and said that he was a spendthrift, who bought a racehorse for more than $28 million and "stole" more than $115 million from Ruja. I don't know how you steal from a thief, but she says he did it. He has always denied the allegations. And no one could report such a theft. One man following all this—I'll call him Hector—works undercover for European banks as a specialist in anti-fraud methods. He tries to protect bank customers from being scammed and, if a scam does happen, shuts it down as fast as possible. But it's not that simple with twenty-first-century data protection and—get this—the complex rules put in place to stop money laundering.

Hector has been a friend and an unofficial adviser to me and the victims' groups, and he shares our frustrations at the lack of official action. He points out that "in the old days" if unusual transactions were spotted: "The bank manager would just have said to the customer: 'It's a fraud, don't do it.' You can't do that anymore—data protection rules." Throughout the European Union and in the UK, with open banking, he says there are systems that can detect at the moment of investment if you're sending money to a bad place. Clients can be asked to consider if what they're doing is a good idea. One-Coin was usually one count ahead of the warnings. And when the money was cleaned, it was gone.

The racing world is, like property and art, a rich environment for dodgy funds. Hector told me:

As long as there's a transaction and an invoice, it legitimizes the money.

I think a lot of the Ruja money is going to be found in the US banks and a huge part in the UAE, in a new tower block in Dubai or a shopping center in Denver or Dublin or wherever. And through many transactions. One company specializes in making saddles for racehorses. A Russian customer wants to have a new saddle for his horse, to fit exactly the horse, exactly the jockey. They put the horse on a plane and fly it to the saddle-maker. The saddle costs £70,000 and on top of that is the cost of travel for the horse and the jockey and all the other expenses and suddenly it's £200,000 to make a saddle for a horse. The potential for money laundering in such an operation is absolutely crazy. If you have ten horses, that's £2 million, and you can change jockeys as often as you want. Phoenix Thoroughbreds could easily have laundered money into the horse racing because you have very high transactions. For instance, if a syndicate buys a Grand National winner for twenty million and puts it out to stud and gets another twenty million, by the time this is done, all the money has vanished. The illegal money is now horse dung, in a sense, isn't it? It's all come out the other end.

At first, Phoenix Thoroughbreds only had horses with one trainer at Newmarket in Suffolk, England, but later claimed to have three hundred horses, including stallions and broodmares, with twenty-seven trainers working around the world with them. Phoenix Thoroughbreds was a registered owner in Ireland in 2021 and did have half a dozen horses training there. Phoenix and Abdulaziz (both have not been charged with any crime) prospered, with their white and orange silks becoming familiar in winning enclosures in America, Australia, and Royal Ascot (Signora Cabello in 2018) in the UK. This brought together high finance and racing, the money-sucking worlds loved by Ruja and her laundrymen. Mark Scott adored them, all the money, the garish lifestyle. Every day he'd choose a different style from his collection of sixteen watches: Rolex, Omega, and boutique-engraved Panerai.

In tandem, Gilbert Armenta was joining Ruja for "business meetings" all over Europe, a favorite location being the Art Hotel in Barcelona. It wasn't all business, as they had fun too, making time to visit her money at the JSC Capital Bank in Tblisi, the capital of Georgia, located on history's "Silk Road," at the crossroads of Europe and Asia. If you're going to move money, this is another established Yellow Brick Road to pots of gold. By that money-laundering super spree toward the end of summer in 2017, Ruja was planning on Armenta leaving his wife; they would move in together, marry, and have a family. They'd talked about what names they'd give their children. They would elope and fulfill her pledge to take the money and run. The tall, gently spoken FBI special agent Ron Shimko had other ideas about that. He didn't see their relationship being a future marriage made in heaven. Agent Shimko is based in Washington, DC, but his investigations into Ruja and OneCoin have taken him around the world in the past few years. In my conversations with him I've found him to be a man who listens. He doesn't give much away. His trade is information based, but he wants it going his way. He has a strong, confident personality, and that comes through in his manner. For the first time I truly felt I had contact with someone I could trust and who would do his utmost to get justice for all of Ruja's victims.

On the other side of that cursed coin was Frank Schneider, who heard on that inner-circle former intelligence officers' grapevine that the American authorities were moving in, but Scott and Armenta had focused on keeping their financial skulduggery outside US jurisdiction. It was too late for that. While I was getting nowhere with the City of London Police, the FBI had been gathering information throughout the rest of Europe. Scott had established a slew of companies as vehicles to put Ruja's billions on a carousel. There was such a maze of accounts within accounts worldwide, companies within companies registered at Cayman Island PO boxes and in the British Virgin Islands. It comprised an inspired financial jigsaw. How could anyone put all the pieces together? It seemed to me that if you stuck a credit card in any ATM anywhere in the world, out would pour OneCoin profits. Ruja was drowning in cash. And becoming more paranoid, nervous that Scott was a weak link in the conspiracy and getting herself in a lather. She'd heard that someone—"a highly-placed US informant"—was talking as part of a deal with American government agents. There was a "mole" in her organization. She allegedly instructed Frank Schneider to pull some strings.

TWELVE

Under the Bright Lights

With OneCoin's embarrassment of riches, everything, including Ruja, was going pear shaped. As the feverish rush was on to recycle billions of dollars, she appeared more concerned about her love life. Increasingly, she arranged European trysts with Gilbert Armenta and was irritated by his frequent need for laundry trips to South America and Mexico.

I've always said she's devious, and she proved that once again by paying a woman to befriend Armenta's wife in Fort Lauderdale, Florida, and to pry out the inside track on the state of her lover's marriage. As Ruja fretted about when Armenta would finally leave his wife, the authorities were still chasing the money. The FBI played its cards cleverly with Ruja, but with Frank Schneider she had an ace in the hole: He knew much of what the special agents were holding. He is alleged to have warned her of impending action just as he had kept her informed of my campaign and "dealt with" the UK authorities. (There has been no official acknowledgment that she had advance notice she was in the FBI's spotlight, but events challenge any denial that some sort of leak occurred.) Ruja set up a trip to Paris for herself and Armenta in September 2017, and invited Armenta's son to go with them. Her personal assistant, brother Konstantin, was to go along as a "babysitter" for the youngster. Suddenly, Armenta could not make the time to be in romantic Paris. Unbeknownst to Ruja, who was concerned with Mark Scott's loyalty, her lover was cooperating with Special Agent Ron Shimko. As I discovered such details, I found myself thinking differently. It was a struggle to not become deeply cynical about how people and the world turned. I tried to keep in sight my core values about thinking the best of people, trying to do the right thing, helping those in trouble. With these abhorrent characters in my life, I so often hid my head in my hands in horror.

The contrast with those who had invested with Ruja and "her team" makes me shudder when I dwell on it. As Ruja concerned herself with someone else's husband, I continued to receive appeals from OneCoin victims around the world. Often when I opened up my computer to see the appeals for help and cries for attention, at the same time I was pushed back in my chair by vile messages and the now ubiquitous death threats. It doesn't matter how many times your life is threatened, it still sends a chill up and down your spine. It's the fear you can't escape. The ring of the phone can set off terrifying thoughts. Who wants me? What do they want? How careful should I be? The knock on the door: Is that someone come to kill me or the Amazon delivery? Madness? Maybe, but that's how my mind began to work when I learned the details of how Ruja and her gangsters operated. There were no rules.

The FBI had to play by the rules, however, and elaborate precautions were taken to get the paperwork watertight; they didn't want to give a $10,000-an-hour lawyer in a sharkskin suit accessorized with loopholes any chance of getting their client off the hook. As it played out, they had Gilbert Armenta hook, line, and sinker. Ruja's lover and launderer was monitored electronically and kept under physical surveillance as he moved about the East Coast of America holding meetings. Without fuss, on Tuesday, September 12, 2017, a grand jury indicted him on three counts of extortion, including threats of serious physical violence to be carried out in London if a UK associate didn't pay over millions; conspiracy to commit extortion; attempted extortion; and travel act extortion. To me, that meant he was willing to kick anybody about, or worse, to get his cash. The charges, and there were more outrageous ones to follow, were enough to allow the FBI and Internal Revenue Service (IRS) agents to move in. The next day, in Connecticut, Ron Shimko and IRS agents Rich Reinhart and John Abram arrested Armenta. He rolled over—I'm told that is the official terminology—and began cooperating with the investigation as quickly as he once opened bank accounts: in a few minutes. For Ruja, who knew nothing of the arrest, no apology would be enough for what Armenta was about to do.

Many felt her marriage was more for show than anything else. Her baby daughter appeared out of thin air and all the OneCoin chatter centered on gossip that a surrogate had carried the child for her. Her real love truly was Gilbert Armenta. She really thought he was going to divorce his wife so they could marry. The emotional earthquake truly shook her. Despite Armenta calling off his Paris trip, the other three had gone to France, and for the first three days the mood was light and happy. It got much darker. Finally, Ruja sent her brother and Armenta's son home while she flew off to a secret destination, saying she had "things to do"; it surprised Konstantin because his sister never liked to travel alone, as she always wanted someone to carry her handbags. But these were extreme circumstances for Ruja: Her paid female informant who'd befriended Armenta's wife had reported that it didn't seem likely that he was going to dump his family and create a new life with Ruja. She said it seemed Mr. and Mrs. Armenta saw Ruja as a bit of a joke, someone to be laughed at. Frank Schneider's men had already been engaged in superspy work in Fort Lauderdale, and one of them had bought the apartment exactly below the Armenta home and pretended to live in it. It took no time to drill into the ceiling and wire the upstairs with microphones in the living areas and bedroom. Ruja hated what she heard. Her brother, Konstantin, said that when he first saw her after the Paris trip "she was having more or less a nervous breakdown." He'd wanted to surprise her with packages of her favorite food, but his sister was going crazy. She'd discovered through her wiretap that

Armenta wanted to do a deal with the FBI—and give her up in exchange for a favorable arrangement. Her mood got worse and worse as she and her brother talked in the living room of Ruja's house in Sofia. He indicated she seemed most pissed off with being betrayed by Armenta about their love and future life together. She went on and on, saying Armenta had stolen her money and—a bigger sin—he and his wife were making a very good life from it. He was financing his private jet with her money, and all of the expensive gifts for his wife were paid for by Ruja; almost every luxury that he had in his life was because of Ruja. All was paid for by the wonderful crypto-queen. What appears to have hurt most was that Armenta and his wife were "making a lot of fun" of her.

Konstantin said his sister was tired after their talk but she told him to not be afraid: "Everything will be okay, Gilbert's plan won't work out." He didn't hear the wiretap recordings but saw transcripts of them on a desk in Ruja's living room. But I was going to hear Ruja's voice splendidly revealing her own rotten character, her absolute hypocrisy.

This was during more than thirty secretly recorded phone calls between Gilbert and Ruja during the second two weeks of September and the first three weeks of October 2017, which were set up by the FBI, as revealed in US court documents. An early call on September 24, 2017, was made from a car park on East Broward Boulevard, near Gilbert Armenta's Fort Lauderdale office, and Ruja sounds as if she is not yet aware of how far the man whom she planned to elope with has turned on her:

> *Gilbert, we can get access to your emails between now and twenty-four hours if we want to. You cannot prevent this shit. You have to be fucking careful. What these Russian guys can do, you cannot imagine. I mean, if they can do it, everybody can do it. The only advice that you get from me, do not use emails. Do not—like, just face-to-face or encrypted phones. Nothing else is safe. Just believe me. Please.*

Armenta agreed, but Ruja emphasized her point:

I can get everything I want within twenty-four hours. And if I can, they can too. I'm really worried. You have to be careful with communication. Everybody has to be careful with communication. Like, extremely.

Other calls were instigated from the US Attorney's Office in Manhattan. Ron Shimko and IRS agent Rich Reinhart were with Armenta when he placed the calls to Ruja. It was all done by the book, with Armenta agreeing for the calls, which were played in court, to be recorded. Many of the conversations went on for more than one hour. It was cat and mouse, and Ruja's moods were like a pendulum, never making it clear to Armenta—and the listening-in US federal agents—if she knew he was working with the FBI. At that point they had another Paris trip planned. She did have her claws out on the calls, telling Armenta on September 28, 2017, when he asks her how she was:

I had an amazing day. I had again my fuckers coming, informing me what's going on. I love the tape of you and your wife where I tell you that you're not marrying me. I love this one; I want to keep it. Like whenever I want, I'll listen to it again. You know, this is the shit that I'm getting every day and I think, "What the fuck am I having? Who is this person on the other side?" So, this is actually the funny thing. Normally I said to them, I don't want to listen to shit like this anymore, but this one, actually, was good to hear. Gilbert, what the fuck is wrong with you? Like, really? You, I never thought that you were like a spineless asshole. Are you?

Armenta attempted to get a word in: "Well, the big issue right now is . . ."

I exploded with anger listening to the recording. This was the biggest witch and con woman in the world preaching about ethics and honesty and integrity. It was breathtaking. I nearly choked at the cheek of her when I first heard it. Ruja raged back at Armenta that same day:

> *No, no. No need. No need. I don't want to hear it because it's actually very clear. I was like, it's—like shit, like everywhere, just dirt. It's disgusting, actually. So, yeah, I think—well, you know what I think. So let's put Paris on hold and then do whatever needs to be done. There's no need for you to be in a situation like this, dear. Like you obviously are not, you know— there's no point for you, for me, for anyone, or for her. Like, poor woman. Like, poor me. Like, I don't like people to lie to me. I threw up. Do you understand? I threw up my dinner. I don't want this anymore. I know people are assholes. I know people can be weak. I know people can do a lot of things to get what they want over there, but I don't deserve this, and she does not deserve this. And whatever you think you are, that you're smarter than anyone, it's not. You understand? It's just not. It's not cool. There's one thing that's called personal integrity. Google it. It might be good. I don't want to be with a person who has no personal integrity and who is just like saying bad things behind my back. You understand? I'm sure you do. And good night to you.*

Her nerves must have been screaming too. Her spinning One-Coin world was tearing at them. Big on her agenda was a motivational weekend in Portugal for promoters, October 6–8, 2017. In truth, it was a scammers convention.

It was to be announced when the long-awaited opening of the private online exchange would happen and investors could convert their virtual OneCoin into pounds, dollars, euros, or whatever other currency paid their bills. Of course, this was fairy-tale nonsense. All the usual suspects were in Lisbon, including Sally Losa and John Munero, who were still selling the scam as hard as they could. As Eileen and I watched the video streams of the event, I felt great shame. There was Mitchell Thomson, whom I'd brought into OneCoin, still going at it with all he had, a fully fledged scammer. With him was another of his Scottish recruits, who delighted in a photograph of herself making the OneCoin hand signal and posing with Scotland's first minister, Nicola Sturgeon. I was beside myself. The hard-sell merchants were present: One even outdid himself by telling the audience that OneCoin was the foundation of a billion-dollar cryptocurrency industry. Tim in California emailed me as he watched the video stream: Mad and frustrated listening to the same brainwashing bullshit. Of Pierre Arens, OneCoin's nervous CEO, there was no sign. It was announced that he had a virus, a chest infection. He was a serious no-show. The calamity was the sudden realization by the OneCoin organizers that Ruja wasn't going to be appearing on the Lisbon stage any time soon. They pressed the panic button. The OneCoin leaders, the black diamonds, floundered for excuses. "Dr. Zafar" did a nervous dance on stage while others desperately tried to track down Ruja. There had been no advance word that she was not coming. This was heresy in her world. She was punctual to the point of pedantry. The conspiracy theories were wildly promoted for cover: She'd been kidnapped by the world banks who felt threatened by the success of OneCoin. It was the Americans, who didn't want OneCoin as the world's first digital money to replace flat currency. No one suggested Ruja was scared of, at best, being arrested.

Ludicrous excuses were made to the promoters in Lisbon, and the weekend events, despite little enthusiasm for the Friday-night gala dinner of stale-looking lasagna, continued. Shamelessly as ever, the big motivational—brainwashing—Sunday sessions were pitched as celebrations of the wonderful world of OneCoin. As the self-acclaim cavalcade waved the OneCoin flag in Lisbon, Ruja was trying to find a welcoming jurisdiction out of reach of the FBI. What we know for sure is that on October 23, 2017, Ruja called a crisis meeting with the OneCoin management group at her home offices in Sofia. Her brother was not involved, and he sat in the kitchen monitoring the internet on his phone. When the meeting ended, Ruja called him in and asked him to book her a flight to Vienna in forty-eight hours. He was not to worry, as she would soon be back home. Konstantin did as he was asked, but afterward his sister telephoned him and said she wanted to fly to Athens on the same day as the flight to Austria. Did she want him to cancel the Vienna flight? At that, she flew into a rage and started screaming at Konstantin that she needed "both fucking flights." She certainly needed an escape route. In a moment, between the different flight requests to her brother, Ruja had been told by Frank Schneider, via a leak from Bulgarian, German, or American prosecutors, that she had been indicted by a New York grand jury on October 12, 2017. The FBI's Ron Shimko and his agents had wanted to keep the indictment secret to prevent what was about to happen from happening. The charges (only the first): one count of conspiracy to commit wire fraud, one count of wire fraud; and one count of money-laundering conspiracy. If convicted, these would send her to jail. The US Department of Justice also said they would be knocking on her door to get our money from her. Schneider told her she faced being locked away for a very long time. They might—and I would have suggested that they please do this—throw away the key. Ruja did not have to hear that twice.

Early the next morning, October 25, 2017, Ruja, carrying only a purse and with one of her bodyguards, shunned her usual private jet and took an unsociable flight on the Dublin-based low-budget airline Ryanair to Greece. Her bodyguard returned from Athens that evening and told Konstantin his sister had been met at the airport by a group who spoke in Russian. Some weeks earlier she'd told him she'd had contact with "somebody who is very powerful and rich from Russia." Konstantin said Ruja never named the person, or whether it was a man or a woman. He's never seen her since—or heard from her, he says. And neither, publicly, has anyone else. That was the day Ruja became the "missing cryptoqueen," and my life and that of thousands and thousands of other victims was plunged into more turmoil. With Ruja gone and no one for the authorities to take to court, what chance would we have of any recompense or the simple satisfaction of justice, of seeing her behind bars? And, after the first flurry of media interest in her vanishing, who would care? Just as panicked and concerned were the other side of the OneCoin operation, the people who had been making a crooked fortune with Ruja and didn't like the idea of the money tap being turned off. There were other and even more ominous characters who had invested with her. They wanted their money—with interest. The internal anger was fierce, and on the victims' groups we were leaked lots of information about the threats and promises of evil being made by those left out in the cold. With all the ferocious talk it sounded like the last days of the Roman Empire. Was this Ruja deploying her planned "exit strategy," the one outlined in her email to Sebastian: Take the money and run and blame someone else for this. Standard approach. Frank Schneider, after a life of living conspiracy theories, had darker thoughts. He believed Ruja had been kidnapped. Yet Konstantin did not consult with Schneider until nearly the end of November 2017. He kept expecting his sister to reappear. Still, he was concerned enough to immediately hire a private detective to source out her whereabouts, but this Bulgarian detective got nowhere. When he did talk to Schneider, the former spymaster wanted to begin a worldwide hunt, but Konstantin asked him to hold off for another four weeks. He was convinced Ruja would surface—she'd told him she would return.

When she didn't, Schneider appeared at the OneCoin offices in Sofia with a former Special Forces kidnapping specialist and an agent with links to Gilbert Armenta. Through his contacts, Schneider had ways of tracking calls on various systems. They knew Ruja used crypto phones for "special calls" and a mobile phone for emails, as well as WhatsApp messaging, and from these devices they believed they might pinpoint her location. It's possible that Schneider was blowing smoke up everyone's backside because he knew—and still knows—where Ruja scarpered to, and so he was only playing out a rehearsed role at the start of 2018. If so, he's an Oscar winner and Ruja's disappearance was an award-winning act. There have been a lot of people looking for her for a very long time.

Ruja taking off didn't stop our OneCoin nightmare. It didn't even pause it. Instead, the pressure turned on her brother, as I found out from US court documents. What immediately happened to Konstantin frightened me—it was such a violent snapshot of the world I was fighting against. In 2018, he received phone calls saying that if anything went wrong with OneCoin, if Ruja's promises were not fulfilled, he'd be killed. The death threats continued, and one March evening he was walking back to his car from the OneCoin offices in Sofia when a gun was pushed into his back. He was shoved into a blue minivan and driven at speed to the Sofia suburbs, where he was beaten; a finger was broken as "a reminder," and he was viciously threatened with a high-powered pistol. The thugs told him that if Ruja had gone with the cash, they would return and kill him. If he went to the police—which seems a laugh-out-loud suggestion—they would return and cut out one of his internal organs; they didn't specify which.

I don't know if Konstantin is that bright, for he walked into all that sort of stuff all over again in September 2018. He says he was contacted by a high-ranking member of the Hells Angels and "invited" to Zurich to answer questions. If he didn't fly to Switzerland, he was told, things would "end badly for him." So there he was in a Zurich hotel room with a gun pointing at him, before it was pressed between his lips and into his mouth. He was told that the cash invested by the Hells Angels in the OneCoin laundry was worth more than his life.

This was a business incentive for him and, pumped up by his new man-in-charge role, Konstantin happily carried on. He found a supporter in his mother, Veska, who, with Ruja gone, was touted as "the matriarch of the family." And Konstantin Ignatova, the animal-loving factory worker of a few years earlier, became the successful head-to-toe tattooed front man for OneCoin. He moved from the $200,000 house Ruja had bought him and into one of her mansions on the outskirts of Sofia. Bolstered by Ruja's fraudster associates, and confiding in Sebastian and Mark Scott, Konstantin trumpeted that even with Ruja out of sight, OneCoin remained very much in business. He gloried in the lifestyle, and wanted to keep that and the gangsters around him happy. Governments throughout Asia were being bribed. He convinced the global networks and all those marketing OneCoin that he was in touch with Ruja and that she was advising him in his new role as the "face" of the company. He'd learned how to lie like she could, and although he wasn't so hot on the fake sincerity, he'd picked up enough bullshit-speak to be the figurehead. I think he really liked being in the spotlight. He began wearing the designer clothes his sister bought him ("She said she doesn't want to be embarrassed anymore when I'm around her friends and business partners"), but the tattoos snaking from his back and chest and around his neckline were more the Moscow gangster look than corporate. I've seen photographs of him lording it up on the steps of a jet emblazoned with the OneCoin logo parked at the Silvio Pettirossi International Airport at Luque in Paraguay, and posing in a pair of tight Brazilian briefs on the beach in Rio de Janeiro. That didn't turn my stomach as much as watching Konstantin move from stealing from the poor in South America to exploiting them in Africa, which had been prime plundering locations for his sister. It was the Ruja way: find a struggling community, sell them hope, and then milk them for every penny and cent they have. Stamp all over the lives of millions and millions of "the unbankable" and you end up stashing suitcases of cash in hotel rooms worldwide.

After all our battles to raise awareness, with all the people calling in with severe depression, the dozens talking suicide and the thousands upon thousands of lives being financially and emotionally ruined, OneCoin was like Dracula: It wouldn't die, and it was luring more victims than ever.

What makes me most upset is that OneCoin focused even more on targeting the poorest countries, especially those where English was not widely spoken and internet access was expensive. The One-Coin message was spread by church pastors, priests, holy men, witch doctors—anyone who had a congregation or a following and who had the status to influence many, many people. These were people who'd already proved they wanted to have faith in something. Religious groups were a natural target, but for Ruja the church collections were not to help pursue good works. Ruja and OneCoin targeted "communities," and the poor of the world comprise the largest of them all.

I was ill and bedbound when OneCoin began a live stream from Uganda in October 2018. Konstantin was there to promote OneCoin and host a huge marketing event. He was there with his friend and OneCoin associate from South Africa Duncan Arthur, as well as promoters from Southeast Asia and the UK. Duncan, who has never been accused or charged with wrongdoing, was the DealShaker keynote speaker at the East African OneLife Summit held in Kampala on October 19–20, 2018. I was watching the stream from bed along with the victims' groups around the world. I will never, ever forget that moment in time, because the tears were flowing down my face. I have never felt so helpless. It was like watching a car crash happening in front of you and you can't do anything about it. I was screaming at the screen, calling them every name under the sun. There was nothing we could do to stop that. What troubled me most is that the Ugandans treated him like a prince. He arrived at Entebbe International Airport on October 19, 2018, and was greeted by a huge gathering of what I can only call fans. They rushed at him as if he was a rock star, wanting selfies and presenting him with bouquets of flowers. He wore a weak grin and a red baseball cap and, at least for a moment, looked embarrassed. Outside the airport terminal there was another crowd in spotless white uniforms and caps making the OneCoin signal and waving flags. The greeting looked almost presidential. The late-evening motorcade, which escorted him the twenty-five miles to his luxury hotel in Kampala, most certainly was. Big, black, shiny vehicles with their hazard lights flashing went ahead of his customized limousine, which was followed by police cars and even more shiny cars making up the evil entourage. On his arrival at the hotel, there was a rally of supporters cheering and waving more flags. They saw him as their savior. They sang for him. They went to his hotel to give him flowers and allowed him into their schools, including one for deaf children, to preach the OneCoin sermon, while teachers and the more cynical officials pocketed the backhanders, the bribes.

An image of Konstantin holding shoeless Ugandan children in his arms and speaking of a wonderful future for them appeared on my screen, and I said, "You bastard." I kept repeating it and repeating it. "You bastard." I meant it.

It was horrific watching Konstantin smile and scam a country. I knew then, no matter what emotional and physical dangers there might be, that I would never give up the fight to bring them all to justice. It was such a brazenly evil act against innocent people like my friend Daniel, who joined the victims' group after he and his family lost everything. I am telling my story for them.

THIRTEEN

Collateral Damage

I have to contrast the pornographic wealth acquired by the bunch of bastards involved with OneCoin with the financial misery of so many of the victims I speak with every day.

With Ruja getting out before she was nabbed by the FBI, it was open season on the cash kept in OneCoin's offices and apartments. One Chinese networker was said to have walked off with nearly $40 million, and the horseman Amer Abdulaziz apparently had nearly $100 million of other people's investments. He's not been charged with wrongdoing. Sebastian had been cornered by Ruja into returning much of the cash he'd spirited away, but with her on the run, it is thought he may have moved millions of dollars from a Hong Kong apartment as well as some of the money neatly bundled in apartments in South Korea and dubious Dubai. Others were also on a plunder spree, while at the same time furiously hosting events and media-marketing OneCoin. They were making it as fast as they were stealing it from one another. And the authorities were telling me there was nothing they could do.

What I'm trying to highlight is this bestial lust for money against the plight of the victims like Daniel who believed it was the second coming when Konstantin and his OneCoin troops invaded Kampala to thieve every Ugandan shilling they could. Daniel now knows it was a scam, but he's had no one but me to complain to, and neither do the tens of thousands of his countrymen who were cheated. If he did, he might be roughed up, he might be jailed, he might "disappear." He was eighteen years old in 2016 when his father, Julius, was pulled into the OneCoin world by—like us all—supposedly his new best friend forever.

This friend took Julius to the OneCoin offices set up in Kampala, and the two of them talked about the "wonderful future for your family." Julius did not invest, telling his friend he wanted Daniel to be with him in order to advise him. For once, the family had a lump sum of money, $3,500, from many, many years of saving. That cash miracle had been achieved by Daniel's mother, Loyce, who, alongside Julius, had worked in the fields at their village two hundred miles from Kampala, with short breaks to give birth to five children. She'd ruined her health with the grueling hours, and the family plan was to set up a store for her to sell maize (corn). The dream was for Loyce to be able to sit down while she worked—no more than that. After many years, with the first $700 saved, they had invested in one and a half hectares of passion fruit, which they'd farmed before cashing in the harvest in 2016. Daniel was at school in Kampala, taking an early morning bakery class before lessons, and with his younger brother selling milk by the roadside every evening, from seven o'clock to midnight. On a good night he'd sell 80 liters and make $17. From that he had to meet his rent, school fees, and also send what money he could to his village, particularly for his parents to buy sugar, which is expensive. Anything left was saved for medical care and to pay for electricity and water; the expenses were usually greater than the income, and he had to juggle. But his mood matched the blue skies over Kampala. With his parents moving to the capital, his mother in business selling maize and his father fit to work, the future finally looked bright for the life and education for himself and his brothers.

With cryptocurrency, there are huge gaps in financial literacy, not only in emerging economies and places like Uganda but in the developed world, where even experienced investors pursue unrealistic gains. When language and communication are askew, the big edge is certainly with the scammers. It's best if Daniel tells you his story, in his words, to see how callously clever and invidious the marketing is. It all but compels victims to instantly buy, alerting them to not miss out! It breaks my heart, for Daniel is so smart, so wise beyond his years, so intent on doing the right thing, so innocent. He wanted the best for himself and his family and for his community, but, as one of the world's vulnerable "unbankable," he was perfect quarry to be victimized:

> My father trusted me because he believed I was more educated than him, that my head is more open minded. We went together three of us, my father, myself, and our sponsor, and studied about OneCoin. It was really very amazing and the best business idea I'd ever heard. The transactional technology was changing, and definitely the future would be cashless. For somebody to come with that kind of technology and say you can easily earn this money and within two years from now, or one year, we'll be exchanging them and getting billions of money. We never knew about Bitcoin so we couldn't compare it with OneCoin. What was made clear was that we had to invest quickly, and we did it without even asking anyone, telling anyone, because we were warned third parties might not understand and be negative. They advised us to tell people after our investment. It was a quick, quick, quick in this and get ready for the future. For us it was a lifeline. We were ready to set up the maize store when our sponsor approached my father about OneCoin. We were shown pictures of people around the world who were buying not just houses but land and buildings, buying lakes and boats. It was a sure deal and we invested everything so we really could get out of poverty forever. Our sponsor said the exchange of coins for cash was only eight months away. Soon we'd be tycoons. My mother, she is very weak, she is old now and cannot do much work; she should have surgery, could have a supermarket, not a roadside maize stall. She'd worked in pain alongside my father for years, and after all the energy and time we had this opportunity we'd never dreamed of. It was really very amazing. My father said it was the best business idea I've ever had. And he himself, my father, he screamed out: "Lord, my Lord, our

Lord and our Lord." He was in delight because we had the scene, a big, big, big opportunity more than the maize store. We decided to put that money into the cryptocurrency, OneCoin, the thing that would bring billions of money; the maize store, maybe it would be earning something like $14 a day, or let's say $30 or $40 a day, and you cannot compare even $40 a day with something that is going to bring you billions and billions of money. My father bought me a modest package costing about $290 and five other packages for himself, which used up our investment cash. We put our lives into OneCoin. All we had.

We were promised a visit, but Dr. Ruja never came here, and the dates of the exchanges when we could get cash from our investment kept changing. It was June 2017, and then there were always so many, many extensions, many postponements of the launch date. I prayed it was all okay, and my mother was always asking when we were getting our money. I'd almost given up any hope when Dr. Ruja's brother, Konstantin, came here. I was very happy because I knew that these were the guys in the system. I couldn't go to his hotel event. There was an entrance fee, one into the hotel and another into the meeting. I had no money—it was all in OneCoin. My sponsor was very, very motivated. She took selfies, showing me how many people were there, the excitement at the place. Apparently that was a great time, and there was a new hope because Konstantin announced a new date for the exchange. He was a very good actor—he acted like a father, like a missionary, here to help us; but in his mind and in his programs he definitely knew the plan was to take every shilling he could from the poor Africans. When the exchange didn't happen, I started investigating OneCoin online. It was on Facebook that I found Miss Jen McAdam. I was scrolling down, reading that it was a scam and saw the proof on all the screenshots she published and testimony from other people. I joined the WhatsApp victim support group, and that's when she began helping me, listening to my story. I began warning everyone I could here in Uganda, and I talked to my sponsor. I asked her about the exchange date and said I thought it was a scam, that I'd read all about it and talked to Miss Jen. She said Miss Jen was a OneCoin hater.

She told me: "Daniel, believe me, this is the real deal. People are haters.

They are paid by certain organizations, by America, to say this. The US government, the governments of all those developed countries, are very scared about OneCoin and they will do anything to stop us. OneCoin top leaders tell us all the time that the governments are fearful that OneCoin will take away the dollar, that OneCoin will take away the pounds and the euros. Banks and financial institutions are hiring people to put down Dr. Ruja's vision."

I would go on Miss Jen's groups and see that the real information being posted was true. The people on it were honest and had evidence of what they had invested and nothing had returned.

When I got back to my sponsor she was angry. "They are paid to say that. Please, don't listen to them. You don't want to waste your future with these whites, those already rich people. They don't care about Africans, they hate Africans—they want us to lose the opportunity to have money."

Many people listened to her and the other promoters because, like my mother, they could not believe they'd lost everything. They were waiting to buy land and lakes and boats to sail them on. It is a comfortable feeling when you invest and are expecting a lot in return. We stopped planning; we were thinking of big buildings, buying nice cars, buying a big farm, relocating from the village to the city. We were waiting two years for the money, which never came. It was tough on everyone. We had no business. I finished my semester at the end of 2017, but in 2018 I had to drop out of school. I lost my course. My parents lost everything they had. We were bankrupt, and there was no money for school for my younger brothers. We started again, my mother in the village growing local food to feed my small brothers. My father is here in Kampala trying to recover our lives. I am on YouTube trying to raise awareness, to help Miss Jen get justice. I think maybe one time, one day, justice will be granted. I couldn't do anything about OneCoin in Uganda, even report it to the police station, because for the governments of Africa being scammed is not a case. There are rape cases, murder cases, corruption case, accident cases that go unsolved. So telling them that I went to this OneCoin office and I gave them money but now I want it back is not a gift at all for a Ugandan policeman. And they are paid not to bother too much. One time we were at the OneCoin office to *find out about the exchange, and the police came and closed the office. Three hours later it was open again and taking investments. There is nothing to do in Africa but cry for yourself and look for other opportunities. Asking for justice in Africa is impossible. Very, very impossible. You can't even waste your time and waste the $30 it costs to file a complaint.*

I talk with Daniel all the time and I feel he is strong enough to pull himself and his family into a better future, but for every Daniel there are so many who won't survive. Or who may, but with their lives so abruptly and cruelly changed, as my friend Layla's was by an extremely successful OneCoin lowlife. This lowlife's sales patter is based on religious piety and false friendship. He would do anything for you (in order to take your money). His target area is his own Muslim community, from London to Bangladesh and all points in between. There's a OneCoin promotional video on YouTube that shows him "interviewing" Ruja, asking what advice she had for her diamond leaders and her plans for their charity work. It should go in some fraudster Hall of Fame for the cheek of it. How he stole more than £50,000 from Layla and big amounts from so many others, the misery he wrought, begs for action. I can't comprehend how someone can treat another human being with so much disdain for that person's hopes and dreams. Layla, like me, got nowhere with her complaints to the only place in the UK open for them, the City of London Police. The fraud policeman DC Kieron Vaughan was also her point of contact, but, again, it's best you hear it firsthand, as we did:

This man was a family friend and he was, in character, a trustworthy, practicing, and observant Muslim and quite known within my social circle. He asked me to go and support women's entrepreneurship at a OneCoin event at a hotel in London in the summer in 2016. There were lots of South Asian people from the Muslim community, British Bangladeshi Muslims, people wearing the hijab, men and women I felt comfortable with. It was like being with family and friends. There were about one thousand people, very well dressed, professional people and all very confident. I didn't have any cryptocurrency background knowledge, so I was there to find out what it was all about. What was I missing? There was a lot of motivational speaking. Two leaders, James and Harry Stone, gave a huge speech about their lives, their journey from dishwasher boys to where they were as black diamonds. They were very boastful about Ruja and how to make more than £400,000 a month. I felt I was missing out on something. I asked my friend for details, and he said cryptocurrency was the next big thing and OneCoin would be bigger than Bitcoin. But I had to invest quickly to make the most money.

I took notes and asked questions, and they said it was Sharia compliant: It was legally lawful within Islam to invest in OneCoin. They showed a certificate stating this, which made me feel less anxious. [The Centre of Islamic Banking and Economics, which supposedly issued the certificate, said it didn't certify OneCoin as Sharia compliant.] He knew my hopes and that I had money saved. I trusted him and I didn't do my due diligence. I didn't Google, I didn't do anything. I just read what my friend said. And he was very positive. At that time my father had passed away, so I was vulnerable. I was single, and I had £55,200 saved up for a down payment on a home. I had worked doing two jobs for twelve years to save so much money. The initial question I had for him was how much I needed to invest to get into cryptocurrency. He said £6,900. On the same day that I'd given him the £6,900, he called me back and said, "Layla, I have a big package for you. You're going to be super rich. We're gonna find the man of your dreams. You're gonna make over £400,000 if you invest £13,800 in this Premium package, and this is gonna blow up your life." He went on and on. He was going to give me the dream returns of cryptocurrency and I was going to be a millionaire. I didn't have to work this nine-to-five again and he said God willing, that God was a witness. He played with my faith, and from there on all these packages for me followed. The true minimum investment was something like £100, not £6,900, but the more money he got, the more commission the leaders made. That's what he was salivating about because he knew I had been sitting there waiting for my moment, with money saved. I'd talked to him about working so hard to save, to have something for married life and my own home deposit. He played on *that and I went along because I was getting brainwashed, I was getting nurtured by a big-time liar. I was too trusting. I'd met him at a youth center. I believed there was an ongoing, honest rapport, so I didn't doubt his information. He pledged that in a couple of months I would be able to draw cash because the cryptocurrency was so huge. The goal line was October 1, 2016. And if I didn't get in, I'd be missing out on an opportunity, on a dream. That got me even more excited, and I felt this was Islamic and I was not going to be alone. I said to him that this was so complex, could it be a fraud? He told me, "Layla, you're young, you're vulnerable, you're single. I would never hurt you and, God willing, God's word, everything will be happy for you."*

I really felt that he was looking after me as a brother. Over the next two months, I ended up buying lots of packages, because I got my mom, my brother, my sister, and my friends involved. I invested it all in OneCoin because of what he told me. But the exchange didn't open on October 1. I investigated online and things didn't add up, so I started asking my OneCoin leader how this worked. He wasn't able to answer. I started prompting him but he didn't give me clarity. He would shut me up and not be responsive. I was also asking lots of questions: Hi guys, can you break it down to me how it's Sharia compliant? Can you tell me how it matches Islamic values? Why is there no business account? Can you give me the account details? As a newbie, a new investor, I tried speaking to the leaders in WhatsApp groups but I was locked out. I was told to stop challenging and if I had any questions I should ask my upline. That was my OneCoin leader, who was very evasive. I didn't know the other leaders, they didn't know me. As soon as I realized it was a scam and the technology wasn't working, I tried to go into my account but it wasn't working. I told my friend over dinner I knew this was a Ponzi scheme. I was getting people to sign up to something that didn't exist. This was not what I'm about. This was network marketing. It was not within my character, not my value. I wanted him to give me my money back. At that moment, he immediately said, "Okay, Layla, I will try and resell my house and I'll pay you out. But give me some time." As soon as he said "give me some time" I thought one, two months, but that's when he started being evasive. He started not answering my calls, which was unusual. He was someone who was very efficient, always very reliable, friendly. Now he was being this different person because he was getting caught. I started getting quite depressed, quite sad, because I realized my mistake. I wouldn't do anything that's against my faith, my values, and I wasn't bringing in people for him to steal from. He wasn't very happy that I wasn't playing the game and being used, and that's when he started getting upset with me. This was a huge amount of money for me. I begged him for my money, I pleaded with him, I met up with him. I have WhatsApp messages, evidence begging him because I went through the whole depression, anxiety, feeling helpless. There was a lot of anger that was built up. I couldn't do anything. It was killing me inside.

Overall, it broke my heart because this was a family friend, not just anybody, not somebody I met at a seminar. I started finding ways to deal with this. I contacted Action Fraud and then DC Kieron Vaughan at the City of London Police. He started listening to my story and he said he'd had similar stories. I gave him all my details, bank statements, information. I felt he wasn't really taking any notice initially; he said he would meet with me, interview me, but then he got sidetracked and he kept pushing me back: "Honestly, I'm really sorry, I forgot, maybe next week." Then he started passing me around from one place to the next. He said he'd get back to me within a week, which then became one month, two months, six months, and then I was contacting him on email. The response was very slow. I really did feel gullible. I wasn't challenging Ruja, as she didn't have my money. My OneCoin leader had my money in his account, and DC Vaughan said, "By all means take him to court, but we don't know how long your case will take." I kept making noise but only the OneCoin people heard it and I got the hater abuse, vile messages like Jen had. That was in March 2017. I was heavily depressed, I just wanted an authority to help me. I needed legal support and they had failed me as a citizen, as well as others who asked for help. They kept giving us reference numbers, buying time, and at the end, I approached the Action Fraud top boss, who wrote me a letter saying there wasn't enough for them to take it any further. Another slap in the face. I contacted my local MP [Jim Fitzpatrick, Labour MP for Poplar and

Limehouse until his retirement in 2019], and he was definitely helpful but unable to do anything to retrieve my money. I contacted my local authority, and the financial ombudsman, but it was reference numbers and no action. Did anyone care? If someone robbed your house you expect the authorities to come along and at least try and catch the burglar. In this case, it felt as if nobody was trying to catch anybody. It seems like a shrug of the shoulders, and that's what's so frustrating: It felt like nobody was willing to help. They seemed almost to be obstructive, stopping you from getting anywhere with it. I was making myself ill because it was driving me mentally even more mad and depressed. I didn't want OneCoin to be the only thing that was happening in my life. I wanted to be happy again. The money I put into OneCoin was for my lifelong goal, to be married, to have a home.

What has happened by this betrayal by a man pretending to be so pious, by the loss of the money, has made me much more humble. I haven't lost my faith or my morality. I question that of my friend, who is all "God willing" and going to Saudi Arabia, to Mecca, to God's house. It's extremely hypocritical, for the whole point of it is to go and revive your soul and do good. Instead he was targeting the deaf community with OneCoin. He held events at London Heathrow Airport. He was after communities to find victims, to get one to prey on another, be it through religion or disability—he had no prejudice about color or creed. He will rob anyone. I support my brother who's got learning disabilities, and he knew that. I was deliberately targeted by him because he knew about my fantasies. I was the perfect lead for him because I had networks, I had friends, I had my family's savings. I don't have them now, and it's the most expensive lesson I've learned. I made a mistake, and it cost me a lot of headache. My hair is much more gray. I'm hated by the scammers for revealing the truth. I'm hated like Jen is hated. But I think I've learned to sleep quite peacefully knowing I've gone out there and attacked to try and stop them. I'm in a good place because I've accepted I've made a mistake. You are not liable. It's my mistake. And the only person I hold accountable is my friend who introduced me to OneCoin. I was very angry. When I was going to work my whole mental health was really draining me because I was sad, emotional on the train, at the bus stop. I couldn't talk to my family. It took me a long time to come out and tell people I made a mistake—"Oh, by the way, it's a family friend, you guys will know him"—because it was a lot of self-humiliation. There's a lot of self-hate and blame that I went through. It took me a good two years to overcome my depression, and during that time there were suicidal thoughts, thinking about shortening my misery. I had those thoughts that if I disappeared, if something happened to me, I'd be better off. Of course, I haven't done away with myself, but for a long time I felt life wasn't worth living. I've messed it up. I'm supposed to be married, I'm supposed to have a family life, but because of one mistake . . . I did have these thoughts. But now I have learned to accept my mistake and I'm one of the most expensively educated people in all of this. I'm looking at the positive from the negative. It's my way to survive.

I'm always in tears after talking to Layla. It's that way for me with most of the victims, but I so admire her and Daniel for being so brave to speak out early on when others held back because of fear of reprisal or the shame of being duped, of looking silly. I am one who can understand the pain of the abuse they suffered and continue to suffer because of speaking out. I have to keep telling Daniel to be careful, for his campaign makes him a high-profile target in Uganda. Ruja may have vanished but she haunts all of us. Each person has suffered in their own way from her enterprise. Many have taken their lives, while others have been able to shrug off the loss of a few grand as part of a life experience. Some, like Abid Wadood Mufti in Peshawar, Pakistan, are left bewildered by what happened to them. He opened up his own OneCoin victim support group in Pakistan, and he's led the way in protecting others in Pakistan while trying to work toward justice. A graduate in computer science, Mufti was head of telecommunications in Peshawar for the United Nations for thirteen years, but even such high-level connections haven't helped him nail the fraudsters. He invested cash from his UN pension lump sum he received in 2015. His friends sold their homes, their possessions, everything they had of value, to buy OneCoin. It was, he said, like the American West gold rush, with thousands and thousands of his countrymen racing to invest in this new miracle money being promoted by the hard-working "Dr. Zafar." It would lead, in time, to frontier justice. Mufti was wide open for the bad doctor: He had worked long hours in law firms before joining the UN and felt an alien in his own family. This was an opportunity to boost all the savings he had made to pay for his children's education. He is calm when he speaks about it, but I always sense the torment in his voice. It was there when we spoke in 2021:

> From the first day of marriage my aim was to educate my children and raise them in a very civilized manner. That was my focus. When the opportunity of the pension sum, $50,000, came, my wife said we should take it and have a small business, and I could have time to "meet" my children again, time for them to get their father back. I had refused people who came to me with Bitcoin—I told them it was a very stupid idea, $250 for a number that will appear only on your computer screen—and then watched it go up in value. I didn't want to lose such an opportunity again when Dr. Zafar came calling. He said to buy this package and I would double my money. He told thousands and thousands of people in Pakistan this. I know how supply and demand works, and this is a thing everybody in Pakistan is fully involved with. There are huge conferences going on in London, and Dr. Ruja is appearing before forums. She was in China. She was in Germany. She was in America, she was everywhere. OneCoin was covering the whole world. Dr. Ruja said she would be bigger than Bitcoin and that OneCoin was going to be on the public exchange. I decided I was going to spend some of my pension money, and I gave them $27,000 for myself and I got $1,000 packages for all my other brothers. I sent the money to an account in Sofia, in Bulgaria. The pension and the savings, all I could give: You see how they hypnotize? It provoked my eagerness to believe in the words of all this marketing. Then Dr. Ruja did not appear at Lisbon when we were all waiting for the date of the exchange to be announced. It was a shock, all of Pakistan was in shock. So many families had put their money with her. Three of my cousins are senior police officers, and they investigated. OneCoin leaders took our money, made a huge

commission, and they left Pakistan and went to Dubai, where they have a very comfortable life. I knew I would never get my money back, but I wanted these people to be prosecuted. I contacted the United Nations Office on Drugs and Crime, but they said that was not "their area." OneCoin, any sort of digital currency, is not a lawful business in Pakistan, so you can't do anything legally. The authorities will not help, so working together with Jen to help victims is all I can do. I had a friend, a retired senior government official, who put all his money into OneCoin. He was so stressed when he understood that he'd lost everything, it brought on a heart attack that killed him.

There is another friend, polite and with a good nature, who is in another province. He called me and said he'd sold all his wife's gold ornaments and their house to put the money into OneCoin. He was crying on the phone. Jen helps him. But here in Pakistan people cannot help themselves. I call myself an educated person, but I was scammed. I was duped in a fraud scheme. I have worked in thirty-one countries, yet I've been scammed. My whole country has been. Especially Pakistanis and South Asians from my travels through Nepal to India and elsewhere, everybody is looking for the shortcuts. And when they ask you to put in some cash and you will get back a thousand times that money, you will sell everything you have. The clothes on their back. These are the ones in poverty. The poverty factor is catnip to the fraudsters. People in their millions will give them whatever pennies or dollars they have—because they will get that returned in billions! The eagerness to get more money, to get out of poverty, is what drives it. Human need, human nature: If you are a billion-dollar man, even then you want to make more money. This is what happened with us. It has turned against many of the OneCoin promoters, many of whom came here from Punjab, who stole and stole away. I cannot say how many have been killed, but there has been vigilante justice. We have a very tough cultural law separate from what happens in the courts. We are civilized, but some things are done outside the authorities. The man who was my direct upline, who was selling to the group I was in, is in hiding. He has gone underground, for he knows if he appears he will be killed. He did not know it was a fraud, but that is not an excuse for the people who lost their money. Most of the *local promoters working with OneCoin—some were innocent, some were scammers—are dead or under a death sentence. If you are not able to pay back the money—and the chief scammers have most of the cash in Dubai— the elderly people sit as a jury over in a corner and decide the cases that are brought to them. And then the men are armed with guns and they go out and hunt for justice. I can't do that. What's happened is that innocent people who were selling OneCoin with all good intentions as a legitimate business have a price on their head from people who've lost their money.*

For me, I trust more in the help I've had from Scotland. Jen listens when we talk; she's a wonderful lady, and she came in for me at a very crucial time. The awareness really comes from Jen, as all other people in Pakistan agree. She helps me too with my mind, for it has been difficult for me with my family, losing all the money we had for our future lives. My eldest son has been accepted to a German university, which is linked with a UK university. I know I'm his father, but he is very intelligent; most of my money goes to books for him. I don't stop him because of his eagerness for learning. He needed $17,000 for university but then got a scholarship, so the initial money required was almost $7,000. He was delighted to tell me that—I hadn't told the family about the OneCoin money being all gone. I've got three kids, and my wife and I have to balance everything. How do I tell him I can't afford his education? It was painful to think about. I want to help him. I will support him, and I should support him, but we have to accept the reality. We had dinner together, me and my son, and I asked him if he could drop it, this idea of Germany, because I didn't have money to pay for his education. He was so discouraged. I could see in his eyes he was totally lost. He's a very determined, focused young chap, but there are things that trip up your life. I told him the heaviest luggage for a traveler is an empty pocket. This is what is happening here. I'm trying my level best to meet and to balance all my things in life. But by opening the doors to Dr. Ruja and her devils, in the blink of an eye they take all your money and disappear, and the scales don't balance anymore. The United States, the superpowers, they should declare war on those peoples. They are not human, they cannot see and understand the evil they do to get money from the innocent people.

There are so many innocent people. Like Ted, a laid-back fifty-something leading a quiet and gentle life in a small community near Spokane in Washington State. Ted likes to putter about with electronics in his "man cave" and he follows the world on the internet. In the pioneer country of the American Northwest, he was not immune to the temptations of Ruja. He and his cousin Brenda invested $6,300 to buy a Starter and a Tycoon package, very much in good faith. Ted said he and the thirty-eight investors he recruited were tempted by the OneCoin promotional material and convinced by its founder. Ted told us his story:

> We were watching all of Ruja's videos on YouTube that we could find. She was some impressive gal. Cryptocurrency was the thing to get into, right? I'd missed out on Bitcoin, and they were promoting OneCoin as better than Bitcoin, which was doing very much okay. I didn't want to make another mistake. I was pretty gung-ho about it, and I talked it up to friends in California and lots of the people we knew locally—it's a tight community where I am in Deer Park, about twenty miles north of Spokane. The clincher for us was a OneCoin event in Coeur d'Alene, over in Idaho, hosted by this dude. He was high up in OneCoin and he gave a very good speech, very persuasive. There were about fifty people there, very well-off retired folks with cash to invest. Many of them went for the big-buck packages, one hundred grand or more. Brenda and I invested more modestly, but it was a lot of money for us—sixty-three hundred dollars is a lot of money. They wanted us to invest using a virtual private network, but I wasn't into that and ignored it. I handed it over in cash, crisp bills, three hundreds and a fistful of twenties, to this dude. He was a friendly guy from across the country. I shook his hand and he gave a receipt for the cash. In return we got gift codes, an ID, and a run of digits and letters, which when I got home and entered into the computer came back with a OneCoin account. What weirded me out—but didn't stop me, as I'd watched so many Ruja videos—was that because trading in OneCoin wasn't legal in the United States I had to register in the Virgin Islands. That was balanced by seeing people investing $100,000 a pop. And cryptocurrency was the thing

to get into—it was the future. If I'd put ten bucks in Bitcoin ten years ago I'd have been sitting pretty. And the Ruja videos were fantastic: Who'd invest so much money making them if it wasn't legit?

Our upline was this guy from across the country, and I met him a few times, but when things went south he was Mr. Silent. You tell other people about OneCoin, as it seems such an opportunity you want to share it around, you're being nice, you're trying to help people make a few bucks. I hated how it turned out because I don't want anybody to lose money from knowing me.

The disenchantment began when I asked about getting cash out. They make it so easy to put in, but how do I get my money out? I couldn't get a solid answer on that. And about that time Ruja stopped producing her videos and I began to get suspicious. There were lots of conspiracy theories spinning around that the central banks didn't want competition from OneCoin. Maybe she was legit and the banks had shut her down, paid her off, or offed her. There's so much evil going on in the world.

That was nonsense. When I went on the Facebook page of the OneCoin sales dude, who'd claimed to be a Christian and a man I had a good impression of, I couldn't get any answers. In my messaging I wasn't mean to him; I was very respectful, I simply wanted to know the story, what was going on. He never responded, and I thought that was kind of shitty. He should have given me a heads-up, be a man. But my granny said that if it wasn't for lumps in the gravy you wouldn't appreciate the gravy.

Ted is more philosophical than most of the victims I talk to, but he was happy when I told him that his OneCoin "dude" had been named in the proposed class-action lawsuit against OneCoin that began in New York but in 2022 had been incorporated into a similar lawsuit that American victims were pursuing in Europe. He was one of fifty-nine people cited as primary recruiters for OneCoin in America. The introduction of the case against Ruja and her cohorts originally presented by the Manhattan US attorney general Geoffrey Berman puts it all in a nutshell: "They created a multibillion-dollar cryptocurrency company based completely on lies and deceit. They promised big returns and minimal risk, but . . . this business was a pyramid scheme based on smoke and mirrors more than zeroes and ones. Investors were victimized while the defendants got rich."

People like Ted and Layla and Daniel and me were exploited.

Mercilessly.

Everywhere I turned there were contemptible people who were taking advantage of some of the most vulnerable. Always, I return to the story told to me by a OneCoin leader of Ruja sitting behind her huge desk at the OneCoin offices in Sofia every Monday morning during the glory days of her fraud. She would openly burn the account books, the registers of the monies, in cash, which had been generated the previous week and brought to her offices at 10:00 A.M., not a moment later, without penalty. The money, millions of dollars in folded money, was packed and squeezed into suitcases. As the suitcase people left, the promoter said Ruja would smile and say, "See you next Monday."

FOURTEEN

Red Alert

As I hunted for Ruja, following every internet trail, avidly researching the daily tips like a gambler on the horses, helping the ever-increasing number of victims over their miserable weeks and months, there was suddenly a moment to lift the gloom: Sebastian was arrested. The tricky, pouting poster boy of fraud who, I believe, is one of the world's greatest ever con men, was behind bars. The FBI got him following an undercover mission with Thailand's Crime Suppression Division (CSD), which picked him up in Bangkok where he was living with the attention-inviting Michaella Alena (who has not been accused of any real wrongdoing).

Sebastian had been indicted, quietly, under his full name of Karl (after his Swedish grandfather) Greenwood by a New York grand jury on February 6, 2018, on enough conspiracy charges to see him facing ninety years in jail: wire fraud, money laundering, securities fraud, and more, much like Ruja, who had been indicted five months before. This time the FBI kept their investigation carefully on a need-to-know basis. Sebastian, who was born on Boxing Day in 1976 and attended the private Regent's University in London, had by then graduated to an Interpol "Red Notice" and a US international arrest warrant. That hadn't dismayed him, but he got the wind right up his trousers when China stamped all over him. Based in Hunan in southern China, Sebastian had established vast OneCoin networks fanning out over twenty provinces and laundering into Hong Kong and the casinos of Macau. The Chinese didn't like being taken and, unlike the people I was speaking with in the UK, took action. They arrested and jailed 119 OneCoin promoters with sentences of five years and more. More terrifying for someone like Sebastian, they went after his money, freezing $7,140,000 they found in *one* of his Chinese bank accounts.

It was all so different from the UK, which offered only advice to investors to be careful and scammers to not be too naughty. Sebastian went into the shade and was last seen publicly, with Michaella Alena and smoking a hookah, at a OneCoin event in Kuala Lumpur in December 2017. He moved on from Malaysia to Thailand and his familiar environment of Bangkok, where he enjoyed the nightlife. Thai police intelligence detectives had their informants around the cafes and bars of Bangkok. When all was agreed with the FBI, the CSD watched him for forty-eight hours before moving in; it was all done under wraps, as was the extradition of "Karl Greenwood" to New York, where he was parked in Manhattan's Metropolitan Correctional Center under that name. I can't be particular on the date because, much to the dismay of the authorities, the arrest and extradition were only revealed, in error, in a lone paragraph in a fawning article about Thailand's CSD in the *Bangkok Post* on November 5, 2018. It was a global scoop. Greed, the desperation to sell OneCoin in the lucrative US market, had snagged Sebastian and, in absentia, Ruja. Because they'd hosted sales webinars and sold OneCoin packages to Americans, the Department of Justice was able to throw a library of books at Sebastian, CC-1 (co-conspirator 1) Ruja, and an unnamed American, CC-2; there's a good list of candidates for that role. William Sweeney Jr., a boss at the FBI, was asked about all the various charges and activity and said:

> Unlike authentic cryptocurrencies, which maintain records of their
> investors' transaction history, OneCoin had no real value. In fact, the
> only ones who stood to benefit from its existence were its founders and

*co-conspirators. It offered investors no method of tracing their money, and
it could not be used to purchase anything.*

I recall these remarks because they weren't totally accurate: One-
Coin did create a great deal of misery. Ellen in New Zealand was one
of the first people I talked with after news of Sebastian's arrest and
extradition came out. Like many investors, so many in Africa and
Asia who still believe "one day" they will be rich, Ellen clings to every straw she can. There's not much else for her to do. She now lives
in a damp one room—a garage—in New Plymouth, her savings and
cash from the sale of her home having enthusiastically gone to Ruja
to purchase a new future that never arrived.

She wasn't alone, for that whole hemisphere was a prime target.
Tens of thousands of New Zealanders, Australians, and Pacific Islanders, Filipinos at home in their western Pacific islands or chasing
a living throughout the region, were taunted by the promise of great
riches. For so many, it was, again, the offer of a chance to make good,
to make a little better life than they had. Ellen's husband had died,
and she sold the family home in Auckland but shared the proceeds
with her two stepsons. With cash gifts, she helped her financially
struggling daughter and son-in-law move to New Plymouth, and finally she was left with 50,000 New Zealand dollars (about $35,000
US) to invest in a home for herself. One Sunday, she went to church
and a friend whom she regularly sat next to told her about OneCoin.
There was a promoter who invited Ellen to a OneCoin launch at the
SkyCity Auckland Convention Centre. She got the brainwashing
treatment and was then invited to a "seminar," where she was hooked.
Her upline contact was Tina, but the leader of the group with a Fili-
pino lady in Wellington who dangled a fortune in front of Ellen:

*I was used to a nice home but all I could buy with that money I had left was
a one-bedroom unit, a condominium, so this OneCoin offer was insane.
They told me if I put in my 50,000 New Zealand dollars I'd be getting
back 800,000. The value of OneCoin kept going up. I moved to New*

Plymouth and got into renting until I could cash in when the exchange took place. I'd be able to buy a bigger property, I'd pay for driving lessons, buy a car and be independent, for here in New Plymouth public transport is not good. I bought packages worth 15,000 first and then invested the rest in more. My friend from church who introduced me to OneCoin used the Co-Operative Bank like me, so in June 2017 I got my money out in cash and put it in her account and she sent it to Bulgaria. Well, we belong to the same church, we trust each other. She only had a little put in, unlike me who had that much money, and I wanted it to grow. We were friends. This was a few months before Dr. Ruja disappeared. Being so far away, we heard so many stories but, mostly, that she was on "extended maternity leave." That seemed plausible. The weeks and months began to drag on and then the penny dropped. Well, it didn't—nothing dropped, but you understand.

There were people who were exploited so much more than me. All across New Zealand they sold out people but my network involved island people.

Filipinos and Asians too, but mostly Pacific Islanders who knew nothing about Bitcoin or digital currency. The promoters trapped people here and then went through the islands, from Guam to all points. The Seventh Day Adventist churches were used for "events," and wherever there was a Holiday Inn, there appeared to be a OneCoin gathering. That was all raging on and there had been no exchange, no hope of seeing anything back. It was good I found and joined Jen's victims' group because I had someone to talk to and someone who would listen and understand. There was no support here from the church, and the police said to contact the International Criminal Court [ICC] in the Hague. I sent an email to the Netherlands in 2018 relating my story. I am still waiting for a reply, and there's not much of 2021 left. What clues and information we gather here about the scammers, I send on to the victim support group. To have a voice we have to be together. It still hurts. When I found out it was a scam, I was absolutely devastated, and it takes a long time dealing with all the emotions. I have a small pension but it's only enough to rent one room. It's an old garage and it's damp, not very nice. When I first invested, I had a couple of driving lessons, but I stopped that. I don't think I'll be buying a car.

Of course, you don't need transport to be scammed, as OneCoin has a perfectly adequate at-home service. Location is also never a problem, as my friend Harry in Australia testifies. Sitting in Bundaberg, on the coast of Queensland, four hours in a car north of Brisbane, he bellows his view about Ruja and Sebastian over the phone: "BASTARDS!" Harry, who was retired at age seventy-three in 2021, is how I think of Australians. He speaks his mind but, after buying a selection of packages and losing many thousands of Australian dollars from his retirement fund, he was hesitant to go public about being taken for the money he'd wired to accounts in Singapore and Bulgaria:

A friend who lives in Perth, where I was for more than forty years before I retired, told me in 2016 she'd joined up with OneCoin and it was a good thing and I should join. Look at Bitcoin, look at where it went. And apparently OneCoin was taking off like a rocket, really going places. I went down to Brisbane for a OneCoin event and got the full treatment: sparkling lights, video presentations, rags-to-riches to stories, arse-licking jobs on the great Dr. Ruja and what a hardworking bunch Sebastian Greenwood and his mates were. I'd never have to go to Monte Carlo to break the bank, this was like striking oil. It appeared perfect, and I invested a couple of thousand. I followed up at another event in Brisbane, which was even more cultish; the great god Dr. Ruja was invoked time and time again. Still, I was reassured, for I presumed that if they could spend money on these big events they were a legitimate digital currency. That was all part of a big con and I was in for a little more than $16,000. Everybody seemed to be getting on OneCoin throughout the northern territories; the bastards stole millions and millions. There's a lot of people like me around, sitting on their cash, for few want to put it in the banks. That's a waste of time. We were perfect targets. I was shame-faced about being taken for a ride, but I got madder and madder, and when I joined the victims' group I read that Jen had asked if anyone wanted to speak up and go public with their OneCoin complaints. She was arguing that the more people who came forward, the stronger we'd all be. Many victims were apprehensive and scared of reprisals, but I got in touch with Jen. I mean, what the hell,

what has happened has happened. I'm not ashamed. I made a mistake. If
I'm putting my two cents toward bringing these bastards down, why not? I
got nasty trolling as a hater and was called everything from a kangaroo's
ding-dong to things I won't say, but if they came round me I'd be delighted.
I'd punch them in the face.

I understand Harry's feelings. If he is angry but accepting of how
he was duped by OneCoin, Shelley in South Africa is more strident in
her efforts to achieve justice and retribution. She watched the poorest
of the poor in the townships being bamboozled out of even the children's lunch money. Whole communities were left with the promises
of riches in return. She herself, comfortably off and with cash to invest (her husband's retirement annuity of half a million South African
rand, $37,000), joined a frenetic farce of a rush to break South Africa's
financial laws to lose their money to OneCoin. I'm sure Shelley—
who for reasons you will quickly understand wants to keep her ex-
act location private—wouldn't mind me calling her a tough lady, but
even she was aghast at the outrageously greedy methods deployed
by her local OneCoin promoters. They evangelized their targets to
the point of hysteria, inflated the OneCoin investment prices—for
instance, a $115 Starter package was priced at $1,150 or more—and
watched their wee cash hills move into mountains. The South African
surge was cleverly orchestrated by an American named Jane Ennis.
She was named, along with Sebastian and Ruja, in a class-action lawsuit brought in New York in May 2019 by Christine Grablis on behalf
of disgruntled US victims, but that case was dropped in October 2021
for jurisdictional reasons. In early 2022, Grablis, who lost $130,000
in OneCoin, and other American victims were pursuing a similar
lawsuit in Europe. Duncan Arthur was named as one of the victims
in this suit. But that was after Ennis had helped plunder South Africa.
Shelley told us the inside story:

The reason I played such a prominent role in South Africa was because I
was a team leader and a OneCoin champion. I thought it was marvelous

and I played it fair and square and in good faith with my downline investors. I was earning money on the internet with different MLM programs. In June 2015, a guy that I was involved with in that business contacted me and told me about Ruja and this product, OneCoin, which was going up and up and up. Jane Ennis had introduced OneCoin through a church in Lesotho, and they brought it into South Africa [as Lesotho is encircled by South Africa, this move was like night following day] and it spun out of control. The promoters were cheating and stealing from the outset. What should have cost 1,500 rand was costing 5,000 rand, and people were so desperate to be part of OneCoin they were paying way over the odds. It was incredible, unbelievable what they were charging them.

I was a believer and I was trying to educate people how to use OneCoin honestly—you can laugh—but they were mystified. They were not taught anything correctly by the promoters, they just gave them their money. I blame Jane Ennis for that 101 percent. She became a multimillionaire and boasted about it all over our OneCoin networks. OneCoin was booming, investors were arriving like bees to honey, but it became harder and harder for South Africans to get money into the system. We didn't want to miss out. People sent cash in envelopes to Ruja because we couldn't get the money out of South Africa. It was ludicrous. The banks created a very big problem for us. There's a limit to how much money you can take out of South Africa, a million rand [$65,000] per year. Now, the Premium package alone was half a million, with a bigger package that was more than one million. We got into such a complicated situation because my husband told the banks one story and I told them another story. We were going to send our money to England and then through to Germany. The banks turned us down. This annoyed us because, I mean, this is our money and we should be able to do as we want with our money. Government elements said no, the bank said no. The route we found was a trading company here in South Africa that bought euros, so it was very easy. I just transferred the half million straight into their bank account. They bought the euros and then they sent the euros to Germany and on to Dr. Ruja. It was all done in less than twenty-four hours with no bank charges! I sure thought we were winners. I got hold of the leaders of the other OneCoin teams and told *them the solution to getting the money out of the country, but even with a smoother system they went on charging exorbitant prices. I can't imagine saying this today, but I didn't want them tainting the name of OneCoin. I started making a nuisance, and I really stood up for OneCoin and for the people who were getting robbed. I went to a meeting. One of the big bosses in Johannesburg was there. I told people they were being scammed by some promoters—cheated twice over, as it turned out. When I got home there was a message on my house phone that I was going to be taken out: "It will look like a home invasion. Nobody will even ask a question. You take OneCoin warnings off your Facebook, or you disappear."*

I said to myself, "Shelley, you've overstepped the mark." They were ferocious about it. I was terrified, but I thought I could not let them do this. OneCoin is a good product and a lifeline for the people of South Africa, but they were destroying it. The African people were ruining it, exploiting everybody, scamming the people. My mission became to rectify this wrongdoing, and Jane Ennis sent people out from America and London to calm me down. No sooner had they gone than the bad practice was back again. When I think about how badly we victims got scammed: Those people from the townships and all over South Africa got triple, quadruple scammed. People who didn't want to be in those bad groups came to me to invest. I had more than six hundred sign-ups in my downline. I had a white leg and a black leg of investors. Mixing them was not an option. I had one white lady and she had about forty people under her. On the black leg there were more than five hundred, and each one had scores and scores of people under them. They were making massive money.

When we toured South Africa in 2016 to present OneCoin in the major cities where it hadn't been seen, I saw that the girl who was fourth in line under Jane Ennis had made one million rand in pure commission that trip. It was absolutely mind boggling. The money to be stolen made the promoters more and more outrageous. I went on warning people they were being overcharged but they believed they were going to be rich and they didn't care. When some folk learned the truth, they burned down the Johannesburg boss's house. In South Africa they torch houses by taking a brick, wrapping it in fabric, soaking it with petrol, and then throwing it through your window. In the photographs of the house engulfed in flames, you can clearly see the window with a perfect round hole where the brick went in. She was burned out but she was not at the top; she was only another Ruja recruit, another Ruja casualty. It didn't deter Ruja's warriors. They still wanted to sell OneCoin and get rich. I can't be too harsh on them. I pushed OneCoin so hard. I lived, breathed, slept OneCoin. It was on my own Facebook page, it was on my business page, I had OneCoin everywhere. I've got videos of one promoter in America with the MLM program that gave him high standing in cryptocurrency. Like him, I thought it was a true product. I would hear nothing bad against it. I'm not going to lie about it, I got sucked in hook, line, and sinker by something that spread like a wildfire.

I took OneCoin to my family, and my son turned his back on me completely. He made public announcements in my Facebook groups about me, that I was scamming people who were not only my friends but my family. He really hated me. He hated the product. He increased the public announcements so badly that I had to have him blocked. And then he came in under a different name and continued to hound me. It reached the point where he told me he was so disgusted with me that he wanted nothing more to do with me—he couldn't believe I would sink that low, to take money from people when it's a scam. He's told me over and over and over, and that was scary. He kept sending me internet links he said proved it was a scam—and those links were Tim Curry's.

What waved a big red flag in my face—as it did with Jen—occurred at the Bangkok event on October 1, 2016, when Ruja activated a "new" blockchain to the public and increased the number of coins. That was the day I realized it was all wrong because you can't meddle with a blockchain: There's no way in hell if you quadruple or whatever the number of coins that the value can remain the same. On stage Ruja, dolled up in all her finery, switched on the second blockchain to illustrate the fabulous and increased OneCoin "mining" going on. In California, Tim Curry realized it was archived footage, a Shutterstock green screen video. Before this he'd been constantly bombarding all the OneCoin networks, shouting it was a fraud. We were told he was another jealous hater, but now I began listening *to Tim. He convinced me it was a fraud and introduced me to Jen, who was a lifeline. I took all the scamming information from her victims' group and fed it to all my people, but they weren't interested. I was bad news for everyone, telling them OneCoin was a scam and if they couldn't resist to stop paying exorbitant prices. It was like telling Jim Jones's cult followers not to drink the Kool-Aid. I have a friend in China who invested way more than me, tens of thousands of dollars. She is so deep in depression. She's in a very bad way.*

I've been a lot stronger about it. I do try always, every day, to keep a strong face and be strong minded about it. I want to rectify this any way I can. I say we've got to take it easy on ourselves and give ourselves more time, because this can completely devour us. Especially women, because we can be more emotional about trying to make this right, to help others escape from the clutches of a horror like Ruja. It's in our nature to do these things.

Sometimes, I keep telling myself, "Shelley, just take a big step and accept it, walk away." It's an emotional turmoil for me, but if it's going to help anybody, I'm willing to come forward and I'm not going to be anonymous anymore. I want people to know the truth. I'm not here in the hope of getting my money back. It was my fault, I didn't do enough work on this. I believed human beings, and I should have looked much deeper at the science behind it. It was the desperation to make money, to have something when you go on a pension. There's a lot of different reasons why you shut off reality, and you just go along with this dream and you don't think. Ruja and her sales force used that and the ignorance of the people.

I understand what Shelley means about women being protective and, my goodness, I was trying to get preventive action from the authorities in the UK throughout 2018 but smashing again and again into that irritating, nonspeaking bureaucratic brick wall. There were moments when I, like Shelley, wanted to walk away, but then there would be another victim's story or someone suicidal to be comforted. What was almost as frustrating as the police doing nothing was the seeming lack of interest from mainstream media. Billions had been stolen—but from ordinary people. Was that the problem? Was it that no celebrities were involved? Tim and the guys and I talked a lot about the media disinterest, and we think cryptocurrency was too complicated for a couple of minutes on the evening news or a few paragraphs in the newspapers. The press seemed to regard it as some sort of insurance fraud; it was a money thing, and no real people were being hurt. With the stories you've read, you'll know that for every investor with cash simply chasing profit, there were desperate millions around the world risking the day's food for the family on a paper moon. Thankfully, for all of us seeking justice and retribution, behind the scenes US investigators were pursuing justice and my FBI man, the capable Ron Shimko, was moving in.

FIFTEEN

Lost and Found

With an arrogance elevated to absurd heights by ego, Konstantin Ignatova left the safety of his sister's bodyguarded Bulgarian mansion and took a long-haul flight to California toward the end of February 2019. He arrived at passport control listening to rock music through his earphones and with his passport in hand. When he was waved forward by the US Homeland Security officer, a Border Patrol agent intercepted him. A carefully orchestrated "sting" had begun.

Konstantin was quizzed about his visit to America. Was he there for business? He happily lied. He said he was a tourist and flying on to Las Vegas, where he planned "to have fun." Agents had checked his mobile phone and laptop during his interview; they confiscated his phone but returned his computer before allowing him to enter America. He made his forty-minute connecting flight to Las Vegas, where he did "have fun" for three days, but he also had meetings with US promoters keen on building the future of OneCoin. He was nervous enough about being stopped at the San Francisco airport that he claimed he discarded his computer in a rubbish bin on the Las Vegas Strip across from the MGM Grand Hotel. He thought that was that. It never is. With him in Las Vegas were his "good mate" Duncan Arthur, and he met several other "friends" who were undercover American agents. He'd been persuaded he was safe to visit America after having been fed a legal opinion that said the

United States didn't recognize cryptocurrency and had no jurisdiction. Konstantin was oblivious to possible consequences; Duncan said that although Konstantin was bright up to a point, his massive ego blotted out threats and he thought he was bulletproof. I asked Duncan if he thought he got his ego from his sister. "Sure, but no one has an ego as big as Ruja. Konstantin is an idiot, but Ruja is pure evil, Satan in a female form."

Although he was told by OneCoin officers in Sofia that visiting America was a risk he didn't need to take, Konstantin bulldozed in without any bodyguards, as they could not get American entry visas. He said he'd been told there would be no problem. Taking a random person from Vietnam at his word knocks quite a few more points off Konstantin's IQ score. It's believed this person played a part in the sting that coaxed Konstantin into a trap. As Ruja's replacement, he had been encouraged by this person to expand business in America. This person gloried in being one of OneCoin's biggest earners, having recruited tens of thousands of investors from his home and neighboring countries like Cambodia, Thailand, and Vietnam. He was a small, tough man with an American passport. During their early morning meetings in bugged Las Vegas hotel suites, Duncan said he had to kick his friend under the breakfast table to warn him to be careful not to implicate himself in scams. The undercover agents constantly offered Konstantin opportunities to agree to schemes that were clearly against American law. Konstantin grinned a lot and asked for more room-service waffles with extra Canadian maple syrup. "Tourist" Konstantin posted on Facebook pictures of himself grinning as he promoted OneCoin.

Seemingly unperturbed by the initial interest of American authorities, he flew from Las Vegas to Los Angles, where he did indulge in tourism. On March 4, 2019, the man all but controlling one of the biggest frauds in history posed at the corner of Hollywood and Vine in Los Angeles, on the Hollywood Walk of Fame, wearing a garish Hawaiian shirt. Snaking around his arms like his tattoos is a cream boa constrictor. Not being shy, Konstantin posted a snapshot of that moment on Instagram. The FBI also had their surveillance photographs, as did the Organized Crime Intelligence Division (OCID) of the Los Angeles Police Department. When Konstantin and Duncan took a limousine to Los Angeles Airport (LAX), Konstantin to fly to Sofia and Duncan to London, the following undercover entourage befitted royalty or an esteemed diplomat.

I'm so thrilled to be telling you that Konstantin was going to need his "fantastic sense of humor." Duncan, who created DealShaker to establish OneCoin as coupons that could be exchanged (plus cash) for goods, got in touch with me to explore whether his enterprise might help the victims. I was—and still am—wary of such things because they put us victims back in the firing line, but it did give me the perfect opportunity to talk to Duncan, who had the title DealShaker Project Manager, about his drama at LAX on March 6, 2019, and he was open:

Konstantin was arrested in front of me. Three big guys took him down, and it took less than a fraction of a second. Konstantin was there, the next he was handcuffed and he was gone. He looked absolutely confused, like he had no idea what just happened. I was escorted by two guys to a little room and they started firing off questions. They did the typical thing: One was aggressive, then one was nice, then vice versa. Where's Ruja? What do you know? Who's this person? Who's that person? It was the third degree, it was a very thorough interrogation. One of them looked at my Irish passport and said I didn't sound Irish. Quite right, I'm South African. I need a visa to get to the United States on my South African passport, not on my Irish. I asked them if I was getting on my flight, and they subtly implied that depended on my answers. They did say there was no fucking way Konstantin was flying anywhere. I really, really thought it was a bad dream. Everything flew out of my mind when I realized I was being questioned by not just by an FBI agent but a US IRS agent. It suddenly hit me in terms of the gravity of what I had just gone through. At the end of it they gave me a summons to appear before a grand jury in New York on March 7, 2019—the next day; given I was taking a night flight out of

LAX, that was six hours away. I told them that was physically impossible, and, essentially, they told me to fuck off and not come back to America. And I did fuck off. As fast as I could. I flew on to Sofia from London and asked the OneCoin people there to shut down because by carrying on they were jeopardizing Konstantin, who, to me, seemed like a constitutional monarch. The criminals there wouldn't even consider it, and that's when I absolutely lost faith. It's one thing to scam, but to betray your own . . .

Listening to Duncan describe that world gave me the shivers. He talks about bodyguards, and the closest I've been to one was that film with Kevin Costner and Whitney Houston. From that, you can imagine that what he told me next was confirmation of all my fears: I wasn't paranoid—Ruja *was* out to get me. She regarded me as her biggest critic in the UK and the person directly responsible for screwing up her plans to operate out of the London offices in Knightsbridge where Duncan worked with her at RavenR Capital. I'm so happy I fucked that up for her. And I take pride in knowing how much she hates me for doing that. It's a badge of honor. Duncan said that when the penthouse was repossessed, he sent all of Ruja's expensive designer gowns and dresses, her Jimmy Choo shoes and Prada outfits and her personal "trinkets," to Oxfam, near the Cromwell Road in London. I'd certainly spiked her Cinderella plans. He told me:

The attacks against you were well coordinated. . . . Early on you were identified to be made an example of. It was all a bit cloak-and-dagger. Because you spoke out, Pitt Arens [OneCoin's short-lived CEO] and Ruja both got letters for interviews under caution from the City of London Police, and that was never going to go down well. You, Jen, were different from everybody else in that you went after Ruja personally, and that's why you bore the brunt of what you did—the worse anyone got. They really wanted to bring you down. In terms of the people she sent after you, it indicates how personally Ruja took it. It was also at a time that she was trying to move to the UK, and she'd just bought her penthouse through

a company that was controlled by a trust through another trust. It was
taken very seriously. When Ruja got the police letter, she never returned to
England again. Wherever Ruja is, she'll still be angry with you.

Not half as angry as I am with her and her bunch of scammers.
Or the people who are protecting her for what is truly blood money.
But with her brother arrested and becoming a cooperating witness
for the US government—it was either that or a ninety-year sentence
and straight to the slammer—and revealing the inside story of the
OneCoin fraud, I felt we were closer to justice. It was a desperate attempt to prevent spending the rest of his life in jail, but when we do
see Ruja caught, all the evidence will be there as well as a prison cell
prepared for her.

Frustratingly, the FBI missed arresting Ruja in Ireland by about
eighteen months, but they did catch up with some of her dirty laundry. A couple of weeks before she vanished like a puff of smoke, Ruja
was in Dublin. As we understand, she'd flown there from Burgas Airport in Bulgaria on Ryanair using a false ID. It was said an assistant
traveled with her to, as usual, be someone to carry the bags. It was
suggested Ruja was retrieving items of significant value that only she
could personally sign for with a thumbprint passport or some sort of
high-tech "key." By then she knew she needed as much self-protection
insurance cash as possible.

It sounds like a pension fund run, for it was indicated she met
men mistaken for Russians who were, in fact, Icelandic and Austrian
moneymen. She's probably the only one who can tell me the ins and
outs of that adventure, but I don't think we are on speaking terms.
However, I did chat to the FBI. It was at 2:40 P.M. on March 28, 2019,
that Ron Shimko and two other United States special agents visited
the wide-window-fronted Bank of Ireland headquarters at Burlington
Plaza, in Dublin. With him, with a giveaway Brooks Brothers look,
were John Abram and Leo Rovensky, both of the Internal Revenue
Service Criminal Investigation team. The topic of the day was Mark
Scott's Fenero Funds. The bankers who had dealt directly with Scott

spoke freely, and there was "powerful evidence" about the money laundering from Derek Collins, who in 2016 was the executive vice president and relationship manager with the Bank of Ireland and not implicated in any wrongdoing. He had met Scott and been told by him that he planned to invest Fenero's funds in financial services and telecoms, disguising the fact, said Ron Shimko, "that the Fenero accounts were being used to move OneCoin proceeds."

As I've been learning about financial fraud and the way money is cleaned up here, there, and everywhere, and studying how the FBI built their legal case against Ruja and arrested Konstantin, Sebastian, Gilbert Armenta, and Mark Scott, I have also been shaken and often exasperated at how much of a side issue the victims have become. We can't be itemized on a balance sheet, so are not highlighted and that cost is never noted. I understand why many, many victims don't want to put themselves forward as witnesses, but this seems to bewilder the authorities. They don't get it that people are ashamed, or, as with OneCoin, often afraid to speak out. I've found only the most experienced of government investigators and fraud detectives have some understanding of how being scammed truly feels from the victims' perspective. When you've given all you have, the last thing you want to face is the fact that you've been scammed; you will keep your head buried because it's too painful. What's interesting to watch—no, terrifying to watch—is how OneCoin and Ruja can still rob new people, hundreds of thousands of them, because there remain locations where people are too scared to raise the alert.

I was determined to speak out and fight, and that finally attracted some media attention. Along with my daily hate mail and abuse, I received a private Twitter message from a lady named Georgia Catt: Hey, Jen, I'm a producer for the BBC—I'm working with Jamie Bartlett on a podcast that we're keen to speak to you about . . . This arrived on April 9, 2019, twelve days after the FBI made their visit to the Bank of Ireland. At last, some action. The BBC was casting around, seeking a OneCoin victim who would talk publicly about how they'd been scammed, and at that time I was the only volunteer. And a willing one. When myself, Tim, Bjorn, and Crypto Xpose agreed to collaborate on *The Missing Cryptoqueen*, we were all so thankful that a mainstream media platform was finally hearing our voices and plight. We weren't paid any money, not a penny: Our focus was to solely raise awareness; that was our mission. We thought no more than that, grateful they had come along and seemed to care, for until then it felt as if no one was listening and no one was helping us. This included the FCA and City of London Police.

It had been an extremely distressing, lonesome, tough, exhausting, heart- and soul-destroying three-year battle to raise awareness. But as my frustrations increased, so did the distressing stories from victims. We found ourselves alone to face never-ending daily abuse and threats. OneCoin was emphasizing to investors that we were haters; they were told to stand up, to defend their OneCoin and "take out" any critics. Georgia and Jamie were like the cavalry arriving. I told them my own story and I poured out the detailed information we'd been gathering. For the following months I worked with Jamie and Georgia closely—we all did, Tim, Bjorn, and Crypto Xpose too. They wanted to go to Africa, and Daniel in Uganda paved the way for them. I connected them to promoters, but it took me two months to convince one to take part in the podcast. He was hugely conscious about security, and for good reason, as it proved. When he left Ruja's by then toxic OneCoin in 2019 and set up a rival scheme again—I knew that wasn't wise. Not many months later he suffered an intrusion at his home.

With my contacts, the BBC was then able to go out and "hunt" for Ruja and at the same time get interesting interviews. It was the beginning of another stage of my battle against Ruja: what became *The Missing Cryptoqueen* podcast. It was a deserved hit, with millions of people around the world hearing my story and those of other victims. I was happy but so nervous, as I'd never done this sort of broadcasting. I worried about saying the wrong thing or making a "live" mistake. Of course, as they assured me, it was all recorded. If I stumbled my words, we could do it again. The first episode was scheduled for release on September 19, 2019, and I was invited to London to do some promotional work that day on Victoria Derbyshire's BBC TV show and also speak on some radio stations. It wasn't yet confirmed, however, and by noon on September 18 I hadn't heard; I thought it wasn't going to happen, and I was actually pleased about that. I'd had to go to the doctor, as I was feeling really horrible. I'd only put the antibiotics from the drugstore in my handbag when I got the call that I was "on." I didn't feel very "on," but I made the six o'clock train from Glasgow Central to London's Euston Station.

I also had news for Jamie and Georgia. The previous week I'd talked to DC Kieron Vaughan of the City of London fraud squad for updates on their inquiries. Any information we received we'd scrupulously sent around the world to police departments and financial product authorities. Tim Curry and Eagle 1 kept the American authorities aware, and I did the same in the UK. DC Vaughan knew I was frustrated that the 2016 FCA OneCoin warning removed in 2017 had not been put back after all the evidence of fraud we'd supplied. Why was the FCA not protecting UK citizens from those scammers? He came back with an encouraging reply. That weekend, he was going over to speak to his American counterparts, and with that information he would come back and speak to the FCA. They would work on the wording, and he was focusing on getting the warning put back up. I was happy about that. It was also good material for *The Missing Cryptoqueen*, which I was on my way to promote. I wasn't feeling that great on the train, but I was relaxed and taking positive news with me. It wasn't long after the stop at Newcastle that my phone pinged with an email from DC Vaughan. It was an official letter—I've got it framed—saying: Sorry, Jen, the investigation is being closed in the UK. No evidence.

I was on the train with all these commuters, and I went out into corridor and started messaging all the avenger groups, with disgruntled passengers jostling past me with drinks and snacks from the buffet car. What a mess! Crypto Xpose said it for all of us: "What the fuck!"

I was shaking. I thought I was going to have a panic attack. The next day I was going on television to promote a BBC podcast exposing Ruja and OneCoin, and this had dropped a few hours before: There was NO fraud inquiry in the UK. The podcast had been advertised, so they knew it was going out the next day. It was my turn to message Jamie and Georgia: They don't give a fuck. I became more coherent: More than £100 million had been stolen in the UK by that point, many millions more than that now, all from innocent people, and they closed the investigation? A multibillion-dollar money-laundering bonanza, and they couldn't find a paper trail? What had happened from the week before, when they'd gone off to talk to their US partners and came back and closed the investigation? I was devastated and I was angry. I felt the wind had been taken out of my sails—we all did.

I knew as soon as OneCoin heard this they'd be marketing even harder and having a party. This was devastating for the victims. I couldn't make a call and confront DC Vaughan then and there, as my train was getting close to Euston Station. I'd never met him, but I thought we'd built up a good enough relationship on the phone to at least talk things through. I messaged him back, saying I was astounded and dismayed at his news. I said I was on my way to London, but I asked if we could have a call when I got back. He agreed immediately and arranged the time. I couldn't comprehend what had gone on, as it was such a switch in attitude in a week or so. My mind was spinning with what had happened. I had to concentrate on going "live" on television, as the first episode of *The Missing Cryptoqueen* podcast went out on that Thursday, September 19, 2019. Jamie and Georgia met me at Euston; it was late, but I was starving. We went to a pizza place before they dropped me at a hotel; in the morning, Jamie met me there and together we went by tube to BBC Broadcasting House north of Oxford Street.

I was utterly sick and feeling shitty with my infection, but I think that took my mind off my nerves, for this was really a big thing for getting attention for the victims. My worry was that, with this being live TV, my infection could bring on ME symptoms like a brain fog. I didn't want to forget things during the questioning. I said to Jamie, who was appearing with me, that if I had "a moment" I'd look at him and he could step in. That did happen, and I can see it when Victoria Derbyshire asked me a particular question, but thankfully no one else noticed. It was over before I knew it. And the podcast still hadn't been broadcast! Georgia was waiting for the go-ahead to press the button, as it were, but the BBC lawyers were going back and forth, for OneCoin had campaigned against it. They knew of the show, and throughout all the networks and through the groups they put out a newsletter with a step-by-step guide in how to complain to the BBC. The BBC had never had anything like this before a program was even aired. OneCoin complained and complained, and that's why it was delayed for so many hours as the BBC compliance teams and lawyers dealt with it. We were having something to eat, and I'd hardly had my fork in my food when Jamie and I were asked to go on the popular show *talkRADIO* with Eamonn Holmes at 6:00 P.M.

A BBC official said they weren't sure about that, but I pointed out that I wasn't under contract to anyone; it was all about raising awareness, and I was free to speak to whomever I wanted. Jamie eventually got the go-ahead to do it—I think the BBC has a committee meeting before doing anything. Jamie and Georgia knew I was wiped out and, with the radio appearance, said I needed to stay another night in London; that was another committee meeting before they okayed the expense for that. I'd been working for free for them for six months and more. Eamonn Holmes was empathetic, and he had an understanding that anyone can be fooled. He said he suffered from chronic pain, as I did, and asked how I coped with it. His small talk took the pressure off me and made it easier, after what had been a long day. Which was just as well, as that was the start of mainstream media interest in me as *The Missing Cryptoqueen* began being broadcast week by week and gaining more listeners all the time, including some dangerous ones. The attention was from around the world, for it started rolling out on the BBC World Service, and I could see the traction moving into Europe and America.

I spoke to journalists from the UK, Greece, France, Italy, and Germany, as well as people from blockchain and crypto and digital media. It was overwhelming, and by the end of November, I was mentally exhausted. But it had been made clear to me very quickly that we'd delivered the anti-Ruja message out there.

The leave-us-alone-or-die message arrived in a video forwarded to me following the first episode of *The Missing Cryptoqueen*. The video was by the OneCoin "Captain" Cordel King Jayms, who is from Trinidad and Tobago, and it was filmed on a shooting range in Vietnam. He wore a red T-shirt with LEARN AND EARN on the front and JOIN ONE ACADEMY: BE AN AGENT FOR CHANGE on the back. On the video he is seen pumping bullets out of a machine gun at the range targets. He's also carrying an evil grin, and you get the full flash of it as he turns to the camera and stares. He admonishes OneCoin haters, highlighting Bjorn as one of them. Then, holding the machine gun, he says slowly, "It only takes one squeeze." I can still feel his eyes on me, frisking me. In 2022, King Jayms was a member of OneCoin's Global Leaders Group and part of their so-called Inner Circle. On the video sent to me he continued warning about haters before authoritatively intoning: "Leave the network alone. Be very aware."

He made it very clear what he meant in the final moments of his threat, which in 2022 could still be found on YouTube: "Leave the network alone or you die." He then laughs and says, "Nah, nah, nah, you know we're not about the violence," but it still felt like a chilling message.

It was an abrupt turnaround from the amiability of Eamonn Holmes when I returned from London. As I said, no matter how many times you get a death threat, it puts you in a dark place. And I had DC Vaughan to quiz about what had really gone on. I was waiting for my arranged call from him, and I decided to go down to Eileen's to hear it so that she could be a witness. He didn't call at two o'clock, and I knew he finished work at five, so when that time came and went I gave up for the day. It was a disappointment, and it had been an especially hurtful day because Eileen had made the final payment on her £2,000 loan—£6,800 with the outrageous interest.

Eileen made some coffee for me, and about six o'clock an unknown number called, and it was DC Vaughan. Eileen was there to hear it all, but it was like speaking to a different person. It was like speaking to a robot: He was cold, and he stuck to the same statement—that the investigation was closed. Do you know what it's like when you're trying to speak and you can't get it out? I was like that. The words were glued in my mouth.

My tears were flowing, and I was talking about all the victims and he was closing the investigation. I didn't understand it, and the fact that he kept repeating the same statement was upsetting me more. I said to myself, "Where's this guy I've been sending information to, the guy I've been speaking to for two years? Who is this person?" Eileen's eyes were getting bigger and bigger, and she was mouthing to me: "They don't give a fuck."

I asked him again, "What am I going to tell the victims?"

He came back in that robot voice: "What I am telling you is to contact the USA Department of Justice with any evidence you have and to tell others to do the same."

I went on: "But . . . but . . . they're still continuing, they're still scamming as we speak, more victims are created as we talk . . . I've been doing this for nearly three years. I am shattered. There's no help. There's no support. I'm speaking to people every day that are totally devastated. Some are suicidal. And you expect me to tell them this?"

He hesitated. He clearly had no choice, and replied: "Yes, exactly. Tell them to contact the USA Department of Justice." It didn't matter what angle I came in from, the answer was always the same: "Tell them to contact the USA Department of Justice."

That was when I couldn't take it anymore, and I said, "I can't speak, I have to go. I'll email you more questions." That was that.

I felt that his voice sounded unhappy with his words, but he clicked back into official-speak. I can never forgive the official attitude, which was summed up by a statement from the City of London Police that made me physically sick. After all the information we'd given them, the £100 million stolen from the UK, the massive money-laundering schemes, the official line was:

> The City of London Police has concluded its investigation into suspects linked to OneCoin. It was the decision of the City of London Police that there was insufficient evidence to support criminal proceedings against individuals based in the UK. The companies and individuals behind OneCoin are based outside UK jurisdiction. We've been unable to identify UK-based assets, which could be used to compensate UK investors.

Well, that was a huge disappointment for the victims, especially as they were expecting action with all the attention we were getting from the podcast, which had run for two months exposing OneCoin— which prospered so successfully in the UK because the FCA warning was removed. It was months before I finally got an acknowledgment of the complaint sent to DC Kieron Vaughan and the UK commissioner of economic fraud, Karen Baxter, in September 2019, after my robot call about the investigation ending. On January 2, 2020, Acting DI Paul Curtis from the City of London Police fraud squad telephoned me and verified he was the chap who made the decision to close the UK investigation. It was the usual stuff about resources and not having evidence against suspects. I mentioned the Stone cousins, "Dr. Zafar," and all the other vultures. He seemed unaware of the names. I asked if they had been apprehended and questioned, and he said they hadn't. Some of the biggest scammers, and they hadn't even been questioned? I asked then who *had* they questioned, and he said he couldn't tell me but he said they'd found no evidence.

I pointed out, as politely as I was able to, that along with Ruja they'd introduced OneCoin to the UK and allegedly stolen at least

£100 million. Which seemed rather a lot of money. He said it was really sad and frustrating, and they advised people who were telephoned with an offer to put the phone down. He appeared to me to have no idea of the cultish aspects of OneCoin, how it operated through family and friends. You don't put the phone down on your mum! Or your best friend. After that late-afternoon call, it was an unsettling time. My mind was taken in all sorts of directions. On December 21, 2019, our avenger groups were told by a Japanese One-Coin promoter turned whistleblower, Mark Nishiyama, that there were plans to sell the OneCoin network.

The sellers wanted £10 million, calculated at £15 per head for each person in the network; this included all their personal data. I decided to divide the £10 million by £15 to give me the claimed number of OneCoin members. On the little screen on my calculator, up came the numbers 666,666.66666666. I'd always said Ruja was doing the devil's work, but this! By now my mind was as vulnerable as my body. It all seemed to be raining down on me. I could feel myself getting unwell again with all the round-the-clock demands. But this is what I'd been trying to do: get people to listen to us, to hear our stories. And now I was getting overwhelmed by the very thing I and everyone else had worked so hard to achieve. Who said life's fair?

Suddenly, I felt I was a commodity to be exploited.

SIXTEEN

Stormy Weather

I've heard some flannel in my time, especially around closing time when I was working behind the bar in pubs, and I didn't believe I could ever be as popular as that until I met people wanting to tell this story for me. With the success of the BBC podcast and after appearing on TV current affairs programs, I was invited to contribute to similar shows around the world. I did this readily, always emphasizing that the purpose is to promote justice for the victims. Some of the journalists in Europe, especially in Germany, France, and Belgium, were anxious to expose OneCoin but couldn't find a "voice" for the victims. As their countrymen were frightened to go public, I, hidden away in a corner of Scotland, became the OneCoin rebel to ask.

When filmmakers, for both documentaries and dramatizations, approached me, they came on heavily with their "vision" of what happened to me. I'd explain my story but, no, they saw it this way or that. They listened to my stories of death threats and fears for my family, but they still wanted me to open up my home for them to film, to introduce them to people they could interview. I'd spent the past years in uncharted territory dealing with scammers and the Bulgarian mafia and goodness knows how many other horrors. Now I was being besieged in a completely different way. A friend who'd supported me from Australia, was back living in Scotland, and she came to some pitch meetings with me. She doesn't hold back, and she was a good mediator for me, as I was often discussed in the third person: "Jen believes this," "Jen believes that," "Jen won't do that," "Jen may do this." It was strange. At one meeting at a Glasgow hotel there was mention of money—I thought it was a huge amount—and my friend responded, "I don't think that's an appropriate figure." I didn't know where to look—this was high anxiety—and I sat up quickly, nearly scattering a serving tray. "Anybody for another coffee?"

I wasn't comfortable with any of it, and my friend said it was lucky I'd not signed away my life rights for a pittance. If it hadn't been for taking so much care after OneCoin, I probably would have. As the podcast became more and more successful and went out on the BBC World Service, with millions of people listening to it, the BBC kept asking me to do interviews with BBC journalists, shows like Radio 4's flagship *Woman's Hour*, BBC news for their website, and various BBC radio stations throughout the UK. Everyone wanted to talk to me, and I understood that I was a real victim, the human face of a high-tech story. The journalists wanted me to talk about the death threats, and I was continuously telling the story and reliving it. It was mentally and emotionally draining. I was dealing with all this on my own, as there was no middle person. I hadn't anticipated this, but I was committed to getting Ruja in a courtroom and I would never say no. We'd had barren publicity years, and this was a welcome if exhausting bonanza. In the middle of this I got two letters from the BBC. One was an invoice for £50 sent directly to my bank account, an "attendance fee" for the *Victoria Derbyshire Show*. The other letter was a receipt for the payment, but it had other contractual pages attached to it in the smallest of smallest print; and because of OneCoin I now read everything. It said, as I understood it, that if I did not return the £50 within so many days then the BBC owned me and the rights to my story, which I'd happily shared to help all victims, and I was to be available to the BBC. I was thinking then of writing this book, for the podcast had only scratched the surface of the story and I had so much more to say about my fight with Ruja and the victims. My book,

I believed, would get rid of all the anxiety I had and I'd feel better. And I truly wanted to feel better. I didn't know anything about life-story rights, but I was learning. I was concerned that my story would become distorted the more the media reported it; the details were already becoming mangled. The only way to get the truth out was to tell it myself, which I was praying would bring self-healing along the way. Yet, was this the BBC wanting my story for £50? I had done absolutely everything for them: the meetings I'd set up, the people I got for them. Because of my experience with OneCoin, I was sus-picious of everything. I talked to Jamie Bartlett the next day, and he said it was a standard contract, like "a mobile phone contract." I said, "I don't want a mobile phone contract. I haven't asked for it, I don't want it, I'm not signing it, and that money's getting returned."

I was confused by it all. It was a new world to me and after being kicked about by Ruja, I never wanted to go into anything without knowing—and checking—every detail. The show was getting mil-lions of listeners; it got into the top ten of podcasts and then all the way to number one.

It was all crashing in on me, and I didn't know what to do. I talked to Jamie Bartlett, and he could tell from my voice that I was strug-gling. My head was spinning as though I was on the other side of the bar at closing. I wanted to tell the story of my journey, as it was becoming a heavy load to carry. He said I needed to take professional advice, and I knew I did. He introduced me to an agent who abruptly asked me what I wanted to do. I replied, "Tell my story exactly as it happened. I want to write a book." He seemed to think that was preposterous, which, for me, was a red rag to a bull. What an incen-tive. He told me on the telephone that he and various BBC execu-tives were at that time meeting with people whom I was proudly told were "A-list" drama and documentary producers, negotiating to sell the rights of *The Missing Cryptoqueen*. The BBC sold the rights but never gave anyone who appeared on that hugely successful program a dime—not one penny toward a victims' fund, which I thought was the very least they could do. I didn't want money for participating—none of us did—but I felt they could have shown their appreciation and helped the victims in some way.

I was Cinderella in that scenario, but I did get to go to the ball. I'm not sure that even now I believe any of it. I do pinch myself, for it seems as crazy as the outrageous antics and frauds of Dr. Ruja. It began with the literary agent I decided to work with, Rachel Mills, a wee angel. She asked me straightaway, "Jen, what do you want to do?"

I told her, "Rachel, I'm carrying such heavy baggage and I need to tell the story, to offload it as an alert to others and as a self-healing approach for myself. The only way I feel I can really do that is to write a book."

Immediately, she said, "Well, let's get that organized." And she did. For once, I felt someone really cared and was willing to help me tell my own and the victims' story fully.

Only the outline was written when she arranged a Zoom meeting about a Hollywood film being adapted from this book. The writer-director was to be the hugely talented Scott Z. Burns, who wrote *The Bourne Ultimatum* (2007) and *Contagion* (2011), which had an extraordinary revival in 2020 with its prescient focus on a pandemic, as well as *The Report* and *Laundromat* (both 2019). The producer was to be the champion film producer Jennifer Todd, whose incredible films—including the Austin Powers franchise, *Jason Bourne*, and *Memento*—have generated nearly $3 billion at the box office. I was to be an executive producer on the film. Who'd have thought? After that I was in constant touch with Scott Burns and Jen Todd, who understood all the reasons for the book and what I was trying to say. They wanted to invite justice by showing the extent of the scam and the damage it had done to so many lives. What to me had seemed the impossible dream was coming true.

After that first Zoom call I couldn't even talk to Gordon about it. I had to get out of the house. I *had* to get some fresh air, for I could hardly breathe. Outside, the street was quiet, for it was the first lockdown in Scotland because of the COVID pandemic. We were all being careful, especially me and Eileen with our health complications.

I was walking along with my head and my memories way up there in the clouds, and then I bumped into Lilly, Callum's older sister. Lilly asked me how I was and what was going on; I said if I told her she'd never believe it. Lilly knows as well as anybody our family history, and when I did tell her this latest Hollywood episode she burst into tears. My instinct was to rush in and hug her, but I knew with COVID surging in our area I couldn't do that. We stood our distance and gazed at each other, Lilly still in tears. I looked at Lilly, thinking of how kind her dad, Eddie, had been to me about Callum and the birth of Lee and what a long journey it had been since those days. It was bewildering for me: I was living at a time when I couldn't physically comfort someone I'd known most of my life, a life that was now being planned as a Hollywood film. None of it seemed remotely real. Was this life on Mars? It was certainly a new life chapter for me.

I've felt comfortable and confident about getting the story of myself and all the victims of that evil witch Ruja out in public since that Hollywood endorsement. Sadly, I'm also acutely aware that the film and this book are not the end of OneCoin or any of its variations, for the scammers go on, with all the awful consequences that go with them. Hollywood's attention couldn't dispel that reality even as the film deal was completed. Ruja might have vanished off the face of the earth, but she still had her poisoned grip on my life that eventful summer.

By July 2020, the files of courts in New York and Los Angeles were bulging with prison-invitation criminal charge sheets against my nemesis (in absentia) and her top tier of associates. I will never forget the evening I read the court documents revealing Konstantin's early testimony in New York. A whole lot of emotions began to flood over me and over many other OneCoin victims within the support groups as we learned the extent of their infamy.

As for OneCoin, they decided to inform investors within their cult groups that the United States was lying and it was a conspiracy against them. OneCoin said the United States was a nation of haters who did not wish OneCoin to take over as the world's first digital money. They told their followers that was why Ruja had gone into hiding and why Satoshi Nakamoto remains anonymous—otherwise the banking and financial elites and governments, most especially the United States, would take them out any way they could. I don't know about Satoshi Nakamoto's wish for anonymity, but Ruja had gone into hiding because she found out her money-laundering lover, Gilbert Armenta, had turned FBI informant against her and she was aware US authorities were coming for her with a probable hundred-year jail sentence. OneCoin leaders are remarkable for taking a truth and turning it into a lie, an everyday habit for them. Other than the UK, governments and authorities throughout Europe, Asia, Central and South America, Australia, New Zealand, and the Pacific Islands were building fraud cases against Ruja and the OneCoin marketeers. It was a complex job, but OneCoin fraudsters around the world were being arrested. Their heartless followers were not intimidated.

That July up popped an image of Dr. Ruja smiling graciously from a giant poster in Ho Chi Minh City. It was advertising a pro-motional event in Vietnam's capital for OneCoin fraud spin-offs like Duncan Arthur's DealShaker. I turned to social media to check it out (I feel I've not only virtually visited but actually been there, walking the streets of Ho Chi Minh City through the power of the inter-net), and there was a reminder of why I was going to go on fighting. First, Ruja on the poster, like a cheeky lassie teasing me. And now here on Facebook was machine-gun-waving Cordel King Jayms, who laughed about how easy it would be to silence us, urging: This event need be shared every hour that passes.

On his page were photographs of the preparations for the event, empty chairs in the meeting rooms waiting to be filled by people who were going to lose their money and their pride and probably even more. Included was a live link for this OneCoin jamboree, and it was dreadful to think of people at that moment still being scammed and then being left feeling helpless. For me, it was so frustrating after long months of exposing OneCoin, and still victims were being created in large numbers. The hapless authorities still seemed to be doing nothing to stop it, letting the enterprise carry on regardless. It's morally repulsive. I get so angry, and I can't wait for the day I see Ruja in court. But even in those moments of praying for revenge and retribution, the OneCoin story will rear up and question what you are wishing for. Yes, I want to see the cryptoqueen and her enablers pay for their crimes, but my thoughts of fire and brimstone only go so far. That was horribly brought home to me that same July in 2020 when two South American OneCoin promoters turned up dead in Mexico. They had died for their "crime" of upsetting members of the Sinaloa clan, known as the world's most powerful and deadly drug cartel. (They like to cut off the heads of those who "irritate" them and roll them like bowling balls into cafes and restaurants as warnings.)

The news came through on our victim support network, and I gasped at the photograph of one of the victims, Oscar Brito Ibarra. He was from Chile, a nice-looking lad with a warm smile. He appeared as if butter wouldn't melt in his mouth, but it seems he wasn't as nice as he looked. On social media he had broadcast that The size of your risk will determine the size of your REWARD. He and Ignacio Ibarra, who was no relation and from Argentina, had been suffocated, mutilated, and stuffed into suitcases, which were abandoned in a vacant car park. One version I received said some body parts were found in plastic bags in a rubbish bin; apparently, they couldn't fit all the parts into the suitcase.

The story of how the two young men had been entrapped into the world of OneCoin was all too familiar to me and highlighted our belief that OneCoin was as much a global money-laundering operation, on a corporate scale, as a take-my-money-and-drive-off-in-a-Lamborghini fraud. The Sinaloa cartel is a trillion-dollar drug-trafficking business, worth that many running zeroes for being the bridge to get the Colombian drug shipments over the border and into the hungry American market. All that cash has to be legalized somehow, but the cartel moneymen are constantly inventive. When we looked into laundering, it became quickly clear that it's not just magical mathematics. There has to be a buy-and-sell equation, and cryptocurrencies—real or fantasy like OneCoin—are the cutest twenty-first-century gimmick. You don't have to parcel up OneCoin and send it in the post; it zings through the air as fast as the cash it generates is washed through deposit accounts worldwide.

The Mexican cartels—Los Zetas, Jalisco Nueva Generación, as well as the Sinaloa—are experienced at using virtual currencies to transfer and clean up amounts of money that I find hard to imagine. I never knew there could be that much money in the world. Yet, with what they're doing for their profits, I also can't imagine how they could be enjoying their quite staggering wealth. Oscar Brito Ibarra and his partner Ignacio Ibarra were small-time players in this world, a world in which it is the little guys and women who always get squashed. The two of them got involved in 2017 after Ruja had vanished and OneCoin was branded as a scam. But, along with Chilean groups, they peddled OneCoin and then the DealShaker platform throughout Argentina, Brazil, and Colombia.

By early 2020 they were in trouble and had joined up with an auto company that accepted cryptocurrency as payment for cars. They offered discounts for buying cars with OneCoin tokens. And, of course, cash. Victims lost hundreds of thousands of dollars when the promised cars were never delivered throughout South America; some victims were offered their worthless OneCoins back but not the cash they'd paid up front. Initially, it was thought the two men lost their lives when they introduced the same scheme to the wrong people in Mexico.

So many people around the cryptoqueen have vanished or died or been financially and emotionally ruined. It's been argued that Ruja began her cryptocurrency business with good intentions, but I don't believe it for a moment. Duncan Arthur swore to me that Ruja was all angel until she met Sebastian, and then her husband and all good intentions went out the window. He forgets that this couple of scammers met for the first time setting up the BigCoin fraud, which then developed into the more sophisticated and hyper-successful OneCoin. They were joined early on by the alleged career fraudster Frank Ricketts, born on the Isle of Wight. If you recall, I sent the £5,000 to buy my first OneCoin package to International Marketing Strategies (IMS), which, with its beaches of shell companies, is part of Frank Ricketts's alleged money-laundering empire. The empire was crumbling in 2021 when its partners were indicted in Münster, in western Germany, on a string of fraud charges involving the laundering of more than $345 million. The crucial charge was that IMS accepted payments from OneCoin investors like me and forwarded them to accounts all over the world, which then filtered them to Ruja. The accused were being represented by the German law firm SBS Legal.

Stephan Schulenberg of SBS Legal represented OneCoin in Germany and was or is Ruja's personal lawyer. He's in for a busy time. He was also looking after the interests of another IMS partner, the Munich lawyer Martin Rudolf Alexander Breidenbach, who went on trial in Germany in 2021 along with Ricketts.

Their Mr. Fixit was the ever-resourceful former spy Frank Schneider, who was listed as a member of the Executive Committee of ACHAM Luxembourg (the American Chamber of Commerce Luxembourg). As the OneCoin house of cards folded in July 2021, it was also revealed that Schneider's Sandstone company worked for the European Investment Bank (EIB) from 2015 until the summer of 2020—after the whistle had been blown on his dealings with Dr. Ruja.

By 2021, the OneCoin mob were sheltering from the storm created by the FBI operating in partnership with an international squad of cops. They sought refuge around the world. The victim support groups were buzzing almost every day, and there was much celebrating over the internet if the bad guys were taken down. Never more so than when a French SWAT team arrested Schneider on April 29, 2021, on an international warrant issued by the New York courts. That arrest was a cat-and-mouse operation that was suddenly sprung at Joudreville, which is thirty minutes by car from the Luxembourg-France border. The agents knew Schneider had solid contacts throughout European law enforcement, and insisted every move was need-to-know in the joint operation, planned over three years by the Americans working with German, Belgian, and French authorities. The police took no chances, using the specialist unit from the Brigade de Recherché et d'Intervention—real tough guys—to apprehend Schneider before he crossed the border.

Frank Schneider was dumbfounded. A onetime boss in Luxembourg's intelligence agency, the Service de Renseignement de l'État Luxembourgeois (SREL), was surprised to find himself surrounded, taken from his car, and handcuffed. He believed his network of informants would protect him from capture. He'd shamelessly been running around on his little legs, he thought with impunity, between his homes in Dubai, Luxembourg, and Meurthe-et-Moselle in France, but the FBI had their eyes on him, hoping he'd lead them to Ruja. The police believe he remains one of the best bets for finding her. The spy—who'd hired the London image company Chelgate for £40,000 a month to deal with the problems I was causing with the London law firm Carter-Ruck—was locked up in the French town of Nancy in June 2021, waiting for the paperwork for a US extradition request to be completed. That month two FBI agents, one the liaison officer at the French Embassy in Paris, the other from Washington, went there to thank their European counterparts for their remarkable coup. They exchanged gifts and posed for PR photographs. I can't help feeling embarrassment and disgust with the City of London Police. They walked away and closed the investigation. They should have been framed in the "Gotcha!" photos too instead of having their heads up their own arses. Happily for me, the Americans were granted their extradition request for Schneider by the court of appeal in Nancy on January 19, 2022, but his lawyer, Emmanuel Marsigny, said they would appeal. Prosecutor Jean-Jacques Bosc explained that although all the appeal options had been used, getting Schneider to New York would still be a long job.

I was skeptical when I heard, after three very long and turbulent years, from the Stone cousins. James Stone texted on WhatsApp:

I know you don't like us for not supporting you on this journey . . .

Well, that was accurate. He went on to ask if the cousins could speak to me, and I said I would. I wanted answers to so many things. I said we could do a Zoom call or something similar. Within minutes I got this:

I've spoken to Harry and he suggests we meet in person. Are you OK to travel? We can book a flight to Dubai.

I had to smile at the outrageousness of it, the cheek of them. Fly free to the United Arab Emirates, to be hosted by this band of crooks? This was where the OneCoin billions were laundered, prime Ruja outlaw country.

First class from Glasgow to Dubai. Very nice.

But absolutely fucking not.

SEVENTEEN

Retribution

A friend told me the other day that I'd turned into Braveheart and meant it as a compliment, sizing me up with Scotland's freedom fighter William Wallace. He hadn't thought it through, and it gave me pause, for the kilted movie myth portrayed by Mel Gibson was hung, drawn, and quartered by the end of the film's closing credits. It was true to historical fact, but, although I have my fearful moments, I hope for happier endings.

Of course, I have as much idea as Mel Gibson how that torture must truly have felt, but I think I can sympathize. I've been torn apart emotionally and physically for the past few years. Everything has a price. For many it's losing dignity or pride; it may be self-worth or love; it may be money. But in the dreamworld of Dr. Ruja it's proved to be all of that *and* people's lives. On this journey I've been wounded, scarred by doing battle with adversaries I am still incapable of fully comprehending. I suppose if you can't think evil, you can't properly understand it. What I have learned is the machinery of it, how innocent people—and some not so innocent—can be so easily trapped by crooks.

They may have flashy cars and expensive suits, designer gowns and diamond jewelry, all the accoutrements of financial success, but what a price they've paid. Of course, they're shameless in their exploitation, people who would kick a dying dog out of their way. It's hard for me to even be shocked by the gratuitous indulgences that have been displayed. One disturbing moment was a social media posting by Sebastian's girlfriend Michaella Alena. She was in New York to be near him, but while he waited in prison for his day in court, she found it all quite nerve-racking. She took her customized and mind-bogglingly curvaceous body out to the smart stores of Manhattan and wrote on her Facebook page:

> I was going through a rough time and took all my stress into shopping. May sound superficial but it made me happy for a few minutes. I had to rent another hotel room to store some more. It was a crazy time . . . and this was only a week of shopping.

Beneath her words is a photograph of just half of her second hotel room packed with shopping bags from Louis Vuitton and Chanel, and the room's furniture is covered in designer handbags and bouquets of flowers.

I do want to see them punished.

At the same time, as we've been hunting for Ruja and her gangs of accomplices, helping the police and governments as much as possible, the victims' groups have been working with asset-recovery groups. The victims and I are going after the billions Ruja stole, the asset empire she built on the back of fraud, with two legal and asset-recovery companies that are among the world's most proficient in their field. I've been able to supply them with information gathered over our years of investigation. They instantly got tips on where the money had gone. They may be calling on an office block or housing development near you at any moment. There will certainly be banks and other financial institutions with questions to answer about the multibillions taking a fairground ride through their accounts. It will be another long haul, but there is hope that enough money will be recovered to reward all victims with at least a percentage of their losses. Tragically, it will be those looted of their lives in Africa, Asia, China, and South America who will never see anything.

Many still do not understand what has happened to them. In Uganda, Daniel's mother, Loyce, continues to believe. When she saw a stranger arrive in her village, she said, "It is the man come with all our money, the man has arrived to make us rich."

Some things will never change.

I was still waiting for a reply from Karen Baxter, the UK commissioner of economic fraud, in 2021 when, in a long-awaited letter, DC Vaughan informed me she had left that job. He stated once again that while COLP was supporting actions in other countries, the UK case had been closed and they did not have sufficient evidence to reopen the investigation, and went on to say that any victims of fraud should report their concerns to Action Fraud.

After all the action by the FBI, the co-operation with the European police forces, President Biden flying into the UK and announcing an onslaught on cryptocurrency fraud, this was it: Call Action Fraud and you'll be given a number. I have to calm down when I think of it, for I feel my blood pressure shoot through the roof, and that's not good. I have no words. For me, for what all the victims and I have gone through, the system is as believable as a three-legged haggis. I was angry and upset, dealing with the same emotions and feelings all over again, just as I had to the first time I received their email letter on September 18, 2019, when they notified me that they'd decided to close the UK investigation. It never made any sense then and makes no sense now.

But there are moments of hope and, I admit, glee. Dear Daniel Leinhardt in Uganda is a constant inspiration. In May 2020, I helped him file a formal complaint in Kampala about the OneCoin scammers. Daniel never believed the Ugandan authorities would act, but they did. In early February 2022, arrests were made and fraud charges were brought involving 3 billion Ugandan shillings, which is a little more than $1 million US—money thieved from folks who have trouble putting food on the table. When they eventually get in court, I trust justice will be served and any punishment will be appropriate.

Apparently in the UK, the OneCoin fraudsters will continue to be ignored despite all evidence; there will be no arrests and no justice for the victims. It is clearly evident that the City of London Police and the FCA pass the buck between them and divert what they can. This is unacceptable for the victims left in this OneCoin hell and it's unacceptable that these fraudsters are free to continue their criminal activity within the UK. Victims need justice. Only then can they begin to heal. Thankfully, Sebastian and the others are facing the consequences in the American courts. When Ruja joins them, it will be cream cake with tea for me round at Eileen's.

The Pledge

I'm sitting in the back garden of my wee council house. I love it here, and I imagine my dad pottering about the shed and tidying the bedding plants. I went to the garden center the other day and bought some roses and two smart pots to plant them in. I had some of my mother's ashes left but not a lot. As they were placed in the ground I couldn't let her go, so I've grabbed a handful back, which I've kept since 2003. They went into the pot with one rose. It stands on one side of my little bit of decking. On the other side, in its pot, is "Dad's rose." Finally, with a OneCoin asset-recovery action plan in place and the bad guys being caught or hunted, I was able to unpack his ashes. The crematorium presented them in a nice box, and inside they were neatly wrapped in a package with WILLIAM MCADAM written on it.

My breathing nearly caught in my throat when I saw that, but it was time to unwrap him and all the hurt that had gone on since he died. I'd never properly grieved and said goodbye because of the distractions. Now Adele had given them to me. As I poured his ashes into the pot and put his rose in place, I was engulfed with emotions, overcome. It seemed a lifetime since the bagpipes saluted his farewell and Ruja entered my life. I'd fought back with all my heart and soul, and Dad would have been pleased with that.

By celebrating him in this little personal ceremony, I believe I was finally able to let him go, lose the burden of grief and retain the good memories.

I did my planting with one hand. In the other hand was my phone. As Eileen says, I'm glued to it. As I am to my mission of finding Ruja and seeing her go to prison for a very long time.

That's one thing I'll never let go of.

Every night I dream of Ruja wearing that American jailhouse couture, baggy, orange polyester, and being served bread and water in a bare cell.

By me.

Author's Note

Thank you for joining me on my journey. One day you're living your normal life and the next day it's as though you walked through a sliding door and entered a nightmare that's relentless and has no mercy. What happened to me was alien to my world, so fantastic and terrifying that I feel I must remind readers that this is not a work of fiction but my true story. And not one involving cooking the books or insider trading but one of history's deadliest conspiracies, which connects to the Eastern European mafia, money launderers, and the worst type of fraudster criminals you'd witness in a brutal Hollywood movie. And that's not even the kind of film I like to watch. As such, I've been too wary to tell you exactly where I live—western Scotland, where I was born, will have to do. But I'll never be too fearful to tell my story. I'm aware of the ongoing risks, but I badly want justice for victims.

Due to the criminal connections, I've suffered intimidation and fear for several years. I've not stopped looking over my shoulder. When the threats and the abuse began, I was concerned for my family, but they told me to fight on. Unless I'm six feet under, the perpetrators who brought ruin, distress, and death to families around the world won't be free of me. Dr. Ruja Ignatova seemed to target me as OneCoin's public enemy number one. It wasn't her best idea. I was working out the arithmetic of a OneCoin dirty deal and my calculator hit the jackpot with the numbers 666,666.66666666, which made me wonder. Many times I'd said that Ruja, my nemesis, was doing the devil's work. Now I had her number, and the title of this book: *Devil's Coin*.

As I write this, that menace to the world, Dr. Ruja Ignatova, still remains at large and in hiding. The US Department of Justice charged her in absentia. In April 2022, she was added to Interpol's Red Notice List and Europol's most-wanted-fugitives list. Europol also added a danger warning: "Ignatova and her companions could potentially be armed and that anyone willing to collaborate with the authorities should be careful." A reward of up to €5,000 was offered for any crucial information leading to her arrest. The Bulgarian Ministry of Interior also announced in April that she was internationally wanted at the request of German authorities. She was reported to the Schengen Information System (SIS) and, if found, is set to be arrested and extradited on the basis of a European arrest warrant issued by the Bielefeld Court in Germany. Her Bulgarian citizenship has also been revoked. When she's caught—and she will be—she faces a string of US indictment charges, which are: conspiracy to commit wire fraud, wire fraud, conspiracy to commit money laundering, conspiracy to commit securities fraud, and securities fraud. When caught, and if found guilty, Ruja Ignatova is facing up to ninety years in jail.

Sebastian Greenwood, since his extradition from Thailand to the United States, has been remanded and held in the Metropolitan Detention Center (MDC) in Brooklyn, New York, awaiting his trial, scheduled for May 15, 2023. He has pleaded not guilty to his indictment charges, which comprise: conspiracy to commit wire fraud, wire fraud, conspiracy to commit money laundering, conspiracy to commit securities fraud, and securities fraud. If found guilty, he also faces up to ninety years in prison. Konstantin Ignatova who pleaded guilty to all his charges, accepted a US "5K" plea deal, which involved him becoming a government witness in consideration for a lesser sentence than the charges merited.

However, he was accused of perjury (which he hasn't admitted or denied) in his testimony at Mark Scott's trial, which may influence that deal. The New York indictment charges he pleaded guilty to are conspiracy to commit wire fraud, wire fraud, conspiracy to commit money laundering, and conspiracy to commit bank fraud. He appointed a new lawyer in 2022 and his sentencing control date was scheduled for August 10, 2022. He also can be sentenced to up to ninety years in jail.

Scott was found guilty at his New York trial for conspiracy to commit money laundering in connection to laundering $400 million of OneCoin's cash. His sentence was pending in October 2022, awaiting a judicial decision after his lawyers argued for a retrial due to Konstantin's alleged perjury.

Gilbert Armenta pleaded guilty to his five US criminal indictment charges, which are conspiracy to commit wire fraud, three counts of conspiracy to commit money laundering, and conspiracy to commit extortion. He was to be sentenced on the July 27, 2022. He too is facing a long prison term.

Frank Ricketts; his wife, Manon Hubenthal; and his Munich attorney, Martin Breidenbach, are accused in Germany of money-laundering offenses. They have pleaded innocent to all charges. The prosecution's case against the defendants is fifteen thousand pages long. Ricketts and his wife are accused of taking €320 million from around sixty thousand German OneCoin customers through their now-dissolved company International Marketing Services (IMS) empire from the end of 2015 to the end of 2016. Funds allegedly laundered through IMS were transferred through the Cayman Islands to Sofia, Bulgaria; London; and Dubai. Martin Breidenbach, who worked as Ruja's personal lawyer, is alleged in a Münster case to have negotiated a number of her contracts, and to have received €20 million on behalf of Ruja and forwarded the money at the beginning of 2016 to a London law firm that then bought two London apartments for Ruja. It is also alleged in the Münster case that Breidenbach laundered around €75 million to the Cayman Islands from the end of June 2016 and concealed the origin of the money. The district court in the

Münster case has set the trial for Frank Ricketts, Manon Hubenthal, and Martin Breidenbach for August 23, 2023.

Frank Schneider was in limbo after a French court agreed to his extradition to the United States. His American indictment charges are conspiracy to commit electronic fraud and conspiracy to commit money laundering. The court in Nancy, France, agreed to extradition after hearing allegations that Schneider provided "industrial espionage and money laundering services" to OneCoin and its principals; provided confidential police information to OneCoin's principals, leading to Ruja Ignatova's evading arrest; and assisting OneCoin's operations through a UAE shell company incorporated in Schneider's name. He is facing twenty years' imprisonment on each count of fraud. On January 19, 2022, the court of appeal in Nancy, France, endorsed his extradition. His lawyers are appealing that decision. Schneider, then fifty-three, said in an interview with Luxembourg public radio in June 2022 that he was Ruja's "crisis manager" and that she trusted him. Schneider, who was subject to 24/7 monitoring and home confinement with an electronic bracelet, said in the interview that only now had he realized his activities could be ruled as criminal. He said he wasn't aware that he'd been involved in "illegalities" but said of working with OneCoin and Ruja, "Yes, there were always indications where one could have said, this is going too far." Schneider said his company, Sandstone, made a profit of €4 to €5 million through working for Ruja—and that this could not be ruled out now as "money laundering." He said he had received money from the Fenero Funds set up by Mark Scott. He explained, "Many years have passed, and large sums of money have probably disappeared." He also said he believed that "a billon" euros remained in funds in Dubai, Australia, and South Korea. He said his job was "to solve problems" for Ruja, whom he last spoke with in October 2017. He stated that he had not and would not have helped "to make people disappear." He said he wanted to talk about the OneCoin business in court—but not in America. He wanted to go on trial in Luxembourg, where he could face five years rather than more than forty in the United States. A conviction in America would be, he said, like "a death sentence." He had not entered a formal plea to the charges brought against him by American authorities.

OneCoin continued in the summer of 2022 to operate its head office in Sofia, Bulgaria. It remains very much open for business and no charges have been brought directly against the company, which has issued no public denial of wrongdoing.

In Italy, criminal proceedings began in the summer of 2022 against twelve OneCoin promoters. Trials in Argentina were beginning against fourteen OneCoin promoters, and the US attorney general's office announced it was to begin providing information on its website for worldwide OneCoin victims. This is a joy for us victims and, I guess, better late than never—and a crucial public service, which is important for victims to be aware of. And at the same time, the OneCoin world rolls on for me: Larry Butler from Massachusetts contacted me to join one of the OneCoin victim support groups—he lost $200,000 to the OneCoin fraud. As happenstance would have it, as Larry's request arrived, a bunch of OneCoin cheerleaders were all over Instagram bragging about their luxurious super-jet life. That angered me—but not as much as the video that month of a lavish OneCoin-style event in South America. And others, here, there, and everywhere around the globe. The South American conference hall was packed with people wanting to establish a financial future in these ever more perilous days—exactly as I once had. It's heartbreaking. The fight for justice—the David-versus-Goliath struggle—goes on, but I believe in a more powerful and positive way than before, even against monstrous people and odds. I will never forget June 30, 2022, when the FBI placed Ruja on their Ten Most Wanted Fugitives list. On this list, she joined a history of monsters, serial killers, kidnappers, and terrorists, who have been on that infamous roll call. What we finally achieved with this result proved to me that together we truly can all make a difference and make the world a better place.

Jennifer McAdam
July 2022

Acknowledgments

This book was made possible with the help of incredibly caring and supportive people worldwide. I would like to share a very special thank-you to them.

Douglas Thompson, thank you from the very bottom of my heart. Three years ago, we first met to discuss writing this book together. I was searching for an author to help me write the book and we connected instantly. Your Chic Murray jokes certainly helped break the ice. I really do feel that it was meant to be that we would cross each other's paths. I needed to open my heart, and revisit raw and painful memories and emotions. With your kindness, empathy, patience, care, and support, I felt much more at ease and was able to revisit and discuss with you emotionally painful trips. I never once felt alone. You are the very best writing partner and an outstanding author, and you have become a very dear friend to me. I have learned so much from you. It has been an immense pleasure, privilege, and honor to work with you on the book, Douglas. I'm so grateful you said "yes."

Rachel Mills, my literary agent, I am so very thankful to you. You realized the importance I put on being able to tell my story, and if it were not for your care and support, this book would not have happened. You understood the story, the message, and, most of all, me and my journey. From the moment we first spoke, and you asked "Jen, what do you want to do?" and I replied "Write my story in a book," your reply was "Right, then, let's make this happen." The next day you set the wheels in motion, and ever since, you and your colleagues at Rachel Mills Literary have been so focused and have worked so hard to make this happen. You're an incredible literary agent and an amazing person, Rachel. Thank you for believing in me.

To my book publishers and editors, thank you so much for your enthusiasm and faith in my story. A "thank you" just does not seem enough. I am so very grateful to all the book publishing teams who have worked so hard and provided such excellent support and advice along the way. It's been an unforgettable and cherished experience.

To the victims, media, journalists, producers, and others who have helped expose this heinous and cruel fraud worldwide, thank you. You helped immensely in raising awareness, which helps protect innocent and vulnerable people further. People like you are what is good in this world. Thank you so much for caring and allowing the victims to have a voice and be heard. Thank you for sharing, caring, and bringing hope for justice to the victims.

Finally, my appreciation to the US Department of Justice for being the leading global authority in taking action to arrest and indict the OneCoin criminals. You have encouraged hope and faith that justice may soon be delivered, and victims can begin to heal. Where other international law agencies were hesitant, the US DoJ was and is strong and relentless.

Photo Credits

ABOUT THE AUTHORS

JENNIFER McADAM had a long career in the marketing industry before launching her own consultancy, working with IT companies throughout Scotland and abroad. Illness forced her to cut back on work, but she remains active in the industry. Since 2016 she has worked full time, even from her sickbed, through her online victim support groups to fight for retribution for the OneCoin fraud and to see the perpetrators brought to justice.

DOUGLAS THOMPSON is the author of many nonfiction books covering an eclectic mix of subjects from major Hollywood biographies to revelatory bestsellers about remarkable people and events. The author, broadcaster, and international journalist is a director of one of Britain's best-loved literary festivals. He divides his time between a medieval Suffolk village and California, where he was based as a Fleet Street correspondent and columnist for more than twenty years.